THE ESCAPE OF JACK *the* RIPPER

The Full Truth about the Cover-Up and His Flight from Justice

Jonathan Hainsworth & Christine Ward-Agius

AMBERLEY

...ah, with sincere thanks
...l support.
Christine Ward-Agius

...friend and
...itic
Jonathan Hainsworth

In loving memory of Jenni Lans (Larizza)
1963–2018

This edition published 2021

Amberley Publishing
The Hill, Stroud
Gloucestershire, GL5 4EP

www.amberley-books.com

ISBN 978 1 3981 0962 9 (paperback)
ISBN 978 1 4456 9815 1 (ebook)

Typesetting by Aura Technology and Software Services, India.
Printed in the UK.

OF

JACK

the

RIPPER

Montague John Druitt, 18, as a member of the 1875 Winchester College XV team. (Courtesy of the Warden and Scholars of Winchester College)

Contents

Acknowledgements

To write this book from the distance of Adelaide, South Australia, has only been possible with the kindness and assistance of a multitude of people and institutions.

Firstly, without the support and encouragement of our wonderful agent in London, Andrew Lownie, this book could not have existed. We wish to thank: Shaun Barrington and the staff at Amberley Publishing, for your helpful advice and effort involved in putting this book together; Roger J. Palmer (USA), a brilliant writer and experienced researcher, and who found the critical newspaper article about an English patient in a French asylum, one who is reportedly the Whitechapel murderer; Mark Kent, writer (PA, USA), you provided to us a valuable sounding board and also showed great generosity in sharing some of your own leads which have often guided the threads of our research and the Warden and Scholars of Winchester College, and particularly Suzanne Foster the college archivist for her polite and patient help.

We have utilised *The Druitt Papers* in the West Sussex Record Office for many years and have appreciated the help and advice we have received from the wonderful staff there. Our visits to Chichester in 2018 and 2019 to scour the contents of this fascinating repository could not have been so productive without the patience and professionalism of the many staff at the Record Office who have helped us along the way. The letters from this archive and the photographs in the plate section have, we believe, really brought this interesting story to life. To Pat Arculus, a volunteer at the Record Office, thank you for your generous offer of help and the help you then gave us when we were back in London and then Adelaide.

To the staff at the British Library, thank you for helping us to access manuscripts and archives, books and microfiche and being very patient and professional in the process. Thank you also for the indispensable British Newspaper Archive, which we have utilised now for many years; it is a wonderful resource.

For the help of The British Library via Bridgeman Images, thank you to Giovanni Forti and Rob Lloyd for your assistance in procuring the Canning Club photograph for publication.

To the staff at the National Archives in Kew: your help and promptness in arranging access for us to the archive material was very much appreciated. May we also thank the extremely helpful security staff who tried valiantly to find a taxi for a very tired couple with a flat battery in their phone who had that day arrived from Paris!

To the Wellcome Collection in London, thank you for the wealth of knowledge your repository offers free of charge. It has proved to be invaluable to our research.

To Ancestry UK, we have relied on the contents of this collection for many years to confirm or discount many of the threads of our research. It is has proved to be invaluable.

To Jeremy Clinch, our resourceful London cabbie who 'saved' us in Kew in 2018 and then helped us in 2019 to visit the many interesting locations pertinent to this story, to allow Sarah to photograph them for this book. Jeremy, you're a legend!

To Sarah Agius, thank you for your help in London by taking many of the photographs for this book and also by assisting us with compiling and preparing the other photographs we have needed.

To Matthew Agius, many thanks again for your invaluable help and insight with our website and social media.

To Tony Agius, your on-the-spot IT assistance is again, very much appreciated.

To Irene Newbery (formerly Ward) thank you Mum for all of your encouragement and practical help to 'keep our home fires burning'.

To Dr D. R. Hainsworth, thank you Dad for your insightful feedback about this topic and period of British history.

We have often needed hastily arranged travel plans and have relied very much on Jackie Pool and her staff at Phil Hoffman Modbury for their reliable assistance over many years.

A big thank you to the following people who have generously assisted us with advice or practical help in the creation or production of this book. Jonathan Jackson, Tim Tate, Stewart P. Evans, Richard Ward (Blackheath Cricket Club) and Barnaby Bryan (Middle Temple).

Dramatis Personae

Smith, Emma (1843–1888) Attacked on Osborne Street, Whitechapel, by an unidentified gang on April 3, 1888, and died four days later in the London Hospital. Retrospectively she was believed by some to have been a victim of 'Jack the Ripper'.

Tabram, Martha (1849–1888) Murdered at George Yard Buildings, Spitalfields, by an unknown assailant on August 7, 1888. Retrospectively she was believed by some to have been a victim of 'Jack the Ripper'.

*Nichols, Mary Ann 'Polly' (1845–1888) Murdered in the street, Bucks Row, Whitechapel, on August 31, 1888. Her throat was slit and her body had been horrifically mutilated post mortem.

*Chapman, Annie (1841–1888) Murdered in the backyard of 29 Hanbury Street, Whitechapel, on September 8, 1888. Her throat was slit and her body had been horrifically mutilated post mortem.

*Stride, Elizabeth (1843–1888) Murdered in Berner Street, Whitechapel, on September 30, 1888. Her throat was slit, no other mutilations.

*Eddowes, Catherine (1842–1888) Murdered in Mitre Square, Whitechapel, on September 30, 1888. Her throat was slit and her body had been horrifically mutilated post mortem.

*Kelly, Mary Jane (1863–1888) Murdered in her lodgings at 13 Miller's Court, Dorset Street, Spitalfields, on November 9, 1888. Her body was horrifically mutilated post mortem.

Mylett, Rose (1859–1888) Found deceased at Clarke's Yard, Poplar High Street, on December 20, 1888. She may have been murdered by an unknown assailant by way of strangulation (there were no mutilation wounds), or possibly it was a death from a natural cause such as malnutrition. Some in the press ascribed the death to 'Jack the Ripper'.

Hart, Lydia (dates unknown) The dismembered remains of a woman were found in Pinchin Street on September 10, 1889. It was never satisfactorily established that it was the missing Hart's remains. It was believed by some to be a murder by 'Jack the Ripper'.

McKenzie, Alice (1849–1889) Murdered by stabbing in Flower and Dean Street, Whitechapel, on July 17, 1889, by an unknown assailant, believed by many to be 'Jack the Ripper'.

Coles, Frances (1865–1891) Murdered by stabbing, throat cut in Swallow Gardens, Whitechapel, on February 13, 1891, by an unknown assailant who was believed by many in the press, the public, and the police to be 'Jack the Ripper'.

Graham, Alice (dates unknown) severely assaulted on February 15, 1895, with a knife by William Grant in Butler Street, Spitalfields. Grant was believed by some, including his own lawyer, to be 'Jack the Ripper'.

*Murders believed to be committed by Montague John Druitt.

THE DRUITT CLAN

The Immediate family of Montague John Druitt

Druitt, Ann, née Harvey (1830–1890) Montague's mother. With her husband, Dr. William Druitt, she had four sons and three daughters. Suffering from depression, delusions, and clinical paranoia from midlife, she died in the Manor House Asylum at Chiswick, which was operated by the Tuke brothers.

Druitt, Dr. William (1820–1885) Montague's father; he was a local doctor and surgeon in Wimborne, Dorset. He was a staunch member of the Conservative Party and the Church of England, and he was diligently involved in local philanthropy.

Hough, Georgiana, née Druitt (1855–1933) Montague's oldest sister. She worked tirelessly as a mother, wife, and supporter of her husband's clerical career. She fell from a window and died in her late seventies in a suspected suicide.

Hough, Reverend William (1859–1934) Montague's brother-in-law. He ran the Corpus Christi Mission, Old Kent Road, with his wife, Georgiana, and rose to the position of Second Bishop of Woolwich.

Druitt, William Harvey (1856–1909) Montague's oldest brother. A solicitor, he ran a legal practice with a cousin, James Druitt Jr., in Bournemouth. He was the only family member to appear at the coroner's inquest into Montague's suicide and appears to have orchestrated a cover-up.

Druitt, Montague John (1857–1888) Born in Wimborne, Dorset, and educated at Winchester College and Oxford. Committed suicide in the River Thames at Chiswick on December 4, 1888. A talented barrister of the Middle Temple, part-time teacher, and talented sportsman, he was believed to be 'Jack the Ripper' by certain members of his clan and by a handful of reputable outsiders.

Druitt, Lt. Col. Edward (1859–1922) Montague's younger brother, who married a Catholic aristocrat and relocated to Australia and then Scotland.

Druitt, Arthur (1863–1943) Montague's youngest brother, who became a schoolmaster in Scotland.

Druitt, Edith (1867–1935) Montague's second sister.

Druitt, Ethel (1871–1950) Montague's youngest sister.

Dr. Robert Druitt's family

Druitt, Dr. Robert (1814–1883) Montague's uncle and a famous physician, public health expert, and promoter of the health benefits of lighter wine. He presented numerous papers concerning public sanitation, alcoholism, and prostitution. He was the patriarch of the Druitt clan until his death. Montague was close to this wing of the family and was a regular visitor to their home in Strathmore Gardens, Kensington.

Druitt, Isabella, née Hopkinson (1823–1899) Montague's aunt, married to Dr. Robert Druitt. After her husband's death she was looked upon as the matriarch of the clan. A strong and intelligent woman, she was dedicated to her immediate and wider family, as recorded in an archive of her family letters. We believe she knew the secret truth about her nephew Montague.

Druitt, Robert, Jr. (1847–1917) Montague's cousin, who operated a legal practice with his uncle, James Druitt Sr., in Christchurch.

Druitt, Reverend Charles (1848–1900) Cousin to Montague; it is believed he took the latter's confession as Jack the Ripper. In 1888 he married Isabel Majendie Hill, the daughter of a step-cousin of Colonel Sir Vivian Majendie's.

Druitt, Isabel Majendie, née Hill (1856–1925) Her marriage to Montague's cousin, Charles, linked the Druitts with the du Boulay, Hill, and Majendie clans.

Druitt, Emily (1856–1928) Cousin to Montague, confidante to her mother, Isabella Druitt, and her brother, the Reverend Charles.

Druitt, Gertrude (1862–1901) Cousin to Montague, confidante to her mother, Isabella Druitt, and also the family's genealogist.

Mayor James Druitt's family

Druitt, James, Sr. (1816–1904) Montague's uncle. Mayor of Christchurch 1850, 1859, 1867, 1888, 1896. Solicitor, coroner, justice of the peace, and town clerk. James personally knew Col. Sir Vivian Majendie and enjoyed a wide circle of influence. He commenced a family history book in early 1888 which he abruptly halted after Montague's suicide (he was one of the few to attend Montague's funeral). His son, James Druitt Jr., likely told him the rumours of Montague's deeds. He operated a legal practice in Christchurch with another nephew, Robert Druitt Jr. (brother of Rev. Charles).

Druitt, James, Jr. (1845–1929) Cousin to Montague and ran his father's legal practice (Druitt's Solicitors) in Bournemouth with his cousin (Montague's brother), William H. Druitt. From this legal practice Montague undertook cases in London, including an important civil case shortly before his death. James Druitt Jr. was one of the few to attend Montague's funeral and it is probable he would have learned of the events leading up to his cousin's suicide. He became mayor of Bournemouth in 1914.

THE MAJENDIE / *du BOULAY* / HILL CLAN

Hill, Maria, née du Boulay (1829–1905) Mother of Isabel Majendie Druitt and Arthur du Boulay Hill. The marriages of her mother, Susannah (née Ward), first into the du Boulay family and then, as a widow, into the Majendie family, united these clans.

du Boulay Hill, Arthur (1850–1937) Brother of Isabel Majendie Druitt and closest friend of Reverend Charles Druitt. He was an assistant master at Winchester College during Montague Druitt's senior years and knew him well. He was a vicar at Downton, Wiltshire, and then East Bridgford, Nottinghamshire. We believe him to be the 'north Country vicar' who revealed to the public some of the truth about 'Jack the Ripper' in 1899.

du Boulay, Reverend J. T. H. (1832–1915) Brother of Maria Hill and deputy head of Winchester College during Montague's years there. Henry Grylls Majendie, the son of his cousin Sir Vivian Majendie, lived with J. T. H. du Boulay and his family at Winchester.

Majendie, Colonel Sir Vivian Dering (1836–1898) Cousin of Maria Hill and J. T. H. du Boulay. A national hero as a bomb disposal expert and chief inspector of explosives at the Home Office. The colonel was very close friends with the police chief, Melville Leslie Macnaghten, and the popular writer, George Robert Sims.

Majendie, Henry Grylls (1865–1900) Only son of Col. Sir Vivian Majendie. Attended Winchester College and lived with J. T. H. du Boulay and his family while attending school at Winchester.

Majendie, Lady Margaret, née Lindsay (1850–1912) Sister of the Twenty-Sixth Earl of Crawford. She married Lewis Ashurst Majendie, a Conservative member of Parliament and a cousin of the Majendie/du Boulay clan. She was an author and known to George Robert Sims.

Lindsay, James Ludovic, Lord Crawford, Twenty-Sixth Earl of Crawford (1847–1913) Conservative politician, member of Parliament for Wigan (1874–1880), brother of Lady Margaret Majendie, astronomer, bibliophile, philatelist, and ornithologist; we believe he acted as a go-between for Mrs. Isabella Druitt and the police. 'The Crawford Letter' to police chief Dr. Robert Anderson about Jack the Ripper was written by him.

NON-RELATIVES WHO BELIEVED M. J. DRUITT WAS THE RIPPER

Macnaghten, Sir Melville Leslie (1853–1921) A senior police chief who rose to become assistant commissioner of the Criminal Investigation Department (1903–1913). Knighted in 1907 and retired prematurely due to ill health. A close friend of Col. Sir Vivian Majendie and George Robert Sims, he learned the Druitt family secret about Montague in 1891. We believe he orchestrated the second phase of the family's cover-up that required the public to be told something of the truth but also to be misdirected away from the exact identity of the young barrister (who for public consumption became a middle-aged surgeon). He ensured that no-one was wrongly charged and convicted for any of the Ripper murders.

Sims, George Robert (1847–1922) Bestselling playwright, poet, novelist, and a famous newspaper columnist; a very close friend of Melville Macnaghten and Col. Sir Vivian Majendie. He diligently wrote a column, 'Mustard and Cress,' on topics of public interest for The Referee. Sims was privy to the secret of Montague Druitt from 1891. His columns and short stories propagated a semi-fictionalized account of Montague Druitt as the Ripper. Edwardians were nevertheless privy to the basics: the case was not a mystery, as the killer had been an English gentleman and professional who drowned himself in the Thames River in 1888.

Farquharson, Henry Richard (1857–1895) Conservative member of Parliament for West Dorset, a neighbour of the Druitt family of Wimborne, and the 'West of England' MP who first told people in 1891 that the deceased (unnamed) Montague was the killer.

Nisbet, John Ferguson (1851–1899) Scottish-born journalist, writer, and dramatic critic for The Times. A colleague and friend of George Robert Sims in the theatre world, he also wrote a regular column for The Referee, by then partly owned by Sims. Nisbet was the first to reveal to the public that the Ripper's family had tried (and failed) to hush up the homicidal truth about their Montague.

Richardson, Frank (1870–1917) Educated at Marlborough and Oxford, he was a barrister of the Middle Temple in the chambers of Sir Charles Mathews, who had previously conducted court cases with Montague Druitt. Richardson was also a friend of George Robert Sims and a member with Sims, Macnaghten, and Mathews of the Garrick Club. Proof that Richardson knew about Montie's double life is contained, albeit cryptically, in two of his long forgotten novels from 1908, The Worst Man in the World and The Other Man's Wife.

McLaren, Christabel, née Macnaghten, Lady Aberconway (1890– 1974) Charming, liberal-minded, and iconoclastic, she was the third child and favourite daughter of Sir Melville Macnaghten. Lady Aberconway secretly preserved and eventually disseminated a copy of her father's 1894 memorandum, which named Druitt as the leading suspect, in order to protect her late father's legacy as the sleuth who had solved the case.

What Mystery?

The true identity of 'Jack the Ripper' is not one of the world's great unsolved true crime mysteries, as so many scores of books and documentaries claim. The Victorian-era cases of poor women of the East End driven into prostitution by poverty and then murdered – some horrifically mutilated post mortem – by an unknown killer were solved by a police sleuth. To be specific, the killer of five of about a dozen such Whitechapel murders between 1888 and 1891 was indeed identified, albeit posthumously. The police chief's solution was then shared with the general public in the last years of Queen Victoria's reign by means of his literary associates. Although it was a quasi-official announcement, in some quarters – even among ex-police detectives – it was greeted with open scepticism. And with good reason: the upper-class police chief had misled his middle-class colleagues with red herrings and dead ends, sharing his authentic inside information only with other upper-class men whom he personally trusted. With so much conflicting information floating around, the distance afforded to later generations interested in the case confused, rather than clarified, the mystery.

By the Edwardian era (1901–1914), the broad identity of 'Jack the Ripper' was quite familiar to the public. According to those writer friends of the police chief, the murderer had been an English gentleman who had taken his own life in the Thames River at the very end of 1888. It was not considered appropriate to reveal the man's name because he could never defend himself at a trial. Nonetheless, to Edwardians, 'Jack the Ripper' was not a mystery; he had been identified and was long deceased. It was only after the First World

War that the case was resurrected by a new generation of writers and researchers who were unable to find this unnamed suicide in major newspapers or official records and consequently assumed, wrongly, that the entire story was nothing more than a myth.[1]

This basic misunderstanding has obfuscated the truth about 'Jack the Ripper' for nearly a century.

In the 1900s, the snobbish and sectarian among the so-called 'better classes' sniffed at the 'Jack the Gentleman' solution as almost an affront to decency. Instead of the 'fiend's' being satisfyingly revealed to have been some wretched foreigner, a Hebrew, an immigrant, or indigent person – or a combination of all of the above – he was, supposedly, a middle-aged, affluent (though reclusive), semi-retired surgeon from a very prominent London-based family.[2] Before he committed his atrocities, the surgeon had twice been a voluntary patient in insane asylums, where he confessed his maniacal desire to savage the East End's poor women (Why on earth was he ever discharged? people wondered).[3]

Once the murders began in 1888, the ex-surgeon's friends were desperately worried that he was the culprit. After his most grotesque homicide, they decided he must be recommitted to an asylum – but they found that the 'mad doctor' had disappeared from where he lived. His frantic pals tried to find him. Failing in this endeavour, they made contact with Scotland Yard police chiefs – who, it turned out, had already ordered a fast-closing dragnet to arrest the insane medical man. Within a month it was learned that 'Jack the Ripper' had cheated earthly justice by drowning himself at the river's embankment in the centre of the metropolis, his rotting corpse having resurfaced a month later.[4]

We now know that this was a careful mix of fact and fiction, and this book will try and untangle which was which.

It is to the credit of the upper-class men who broadcast this solution that they were prepared to be so candid – up to a point. To them, the 'Ripper' had been 'one of us,' not 'one of them.' This is the origin of the iconic image of the murderer as an English gentleman sporting a top hat, carrying a medical bag, and vanishing into the London fog like a malevolent, unstoppable grim reaper. The murderer's actual name only became publicly known when Britain and the world were in the thrall of Beatlemania, nearly a century after the murders had taken place.[5] Only glimpses, footprints, and shadows survive about why contemporaries were so convinced this man was definitely the killer. These include members of his own family, who surely would have resisted such an appalling notion if they could, as it threatened their standing in a class-stratified society in which reputation was all.

The story of 'Jack the Ripper' isn't missing a resolution; what is actually missing, oddly enough, is the middle of the tale. In the Whitechapel crimes, we have Act One: the murders of destitute, vulnerable women in the East End. We have Act Three: credible people of the time believed the killer was this Thames suicide who had outwardly appeared to be a gentleman above suspicion. We know the identities of those people and of the man who they believed was the murderer. It is Act Two that survives only in fragments and which we have done our best to recover. Inevitably, we have had to use conjecture and speculation to make sense of this incomplete jigsaw puzzle. Some pieces have survived, while others are lost and must be guessed at – though we argue we have made informed guesses based on sound research. Either these Victorians who believed the killer was this drowned gentleman were right, or they were wrong. Yet consider what an extraordinary thing it would be to be wrong about – after all, for different reasons, none of them wanted it to be him, least of all his own relations. Subsequently, the murderer's exact identity was rendered unrecoverable to the press and public by being semi-fictionalized just enough to safeguard his respectable family (who in the altered account became 'friends' that responsibly alerted the police in 1888, when in reality their terrible secret was withheld from the authorities and only leaked in 1891).

In this book we have tried to reverse-engineer the missing Second Act's shape and substance from the too-slick propaganda offensive of the later Edwardian years.

Several authors have written exceptional works on this subject adding to our overall knowledge and understanding of the late Victorian era. Recently, Hallie Rubenhold's award-winning *The Five* (Doubleday, 2019) provided meticulous insight into the lives lived by the five victims (the specific victims, we contend, of the young English gentleman). A few authors have even grasped that it is a story with far more than an opening act, among them Stewart P. Evans (in collaboration with Paul Gainey, *Jack the Ripper: First American Serial Killer*, 1995);[5] the late Tom Cullen, with his masterly *Autumn of Terror: Jack the Ripper, His Crimes and Times* (The Bodley Head, 1965);[6] and Martin Fido, with his *Crimes, Detection and Death of Jack the Ripper* (Weidenfeld & Nicholson, 1987); though they all argued the likely guilt of different contemporaneous police suspects.

By contrast, most other authors on this subject are unaware that a Second and Third Act even exist. Repeating the mistaken paradigmatic shift that emerged in the late 1920s, many authors, commentators, and filmmakers concentrate almost exclusively on Act One, usually winding it up with a dismissive addendum about how some Victorian police in their dotage unconvincingly proposed their own pet suspect (and with each of their 'solutions' being different, they ipso facto cancel each other out). Some tabloid-driven books detail dozens upon dozens of supposed suspects, including the most outlandish candidates – Oscar Wilde, Lewis Carroll, Walter Sickert, the Duke of Clarence, even poor Vincent van Gogh – completely oblivious that the case was solved in 1891 by a police chief and the solution, albeit obscured, was semi-officially shared with the public within less than a decade.

A few years ago we published a well-received biography of that upper class police chief; it tried to rehabilitate this once highly regarded, hands on charmer from the clutches of so-called Ripperology, so much of which has denigrated his memory by portraying him as a know-nothing cipher.[7] It was also the first book ever to consider the reaction of the deceased murderer's family to seeing their drowned relative portrayed in the press, albeit unnamed, as 'Jack the Ripper'. Ergo that profile would have to be semi-fictitious to avoid a scandal or a lawsuit – and it is.

Our previous discoveries include that the police chief had a close friend at the Home Office who was connected by marriage to a relative of the murderer's family, providing the former with a personal motive to hide the exact identity of the 'Ripper' from his colleagues and the public. The murderer, brought up a Tory, was very likely a rogue convert to an extremist agenda that expressed itself in socialistically inspired, terroristic violence – an extraordinary notion first raised in 1888. We also argued that a tormented 'Jack' had confessed his crimes to a clergyman, who convinced another clergyman to reveal the truth within ten years – and that second vicar is provisionally identified here for the first time. This clergyman's intervention forced the discreet police chief's hand; he had to deploy his own semi-fictionalized version of the truth ahead of this 'turbulent priest.'

In this book – for the first time – we reveal the textual proof that the gentlemen who later partially disguised the murderer's identity originally knew his authentic particulars: that he was young, not a qualified doctor, and had expressed remorse for his crimes and killed himself in the middle of a series of about twelve homicides of poor women, known as the Whitechapel murders (and not conveniently at their conclusion).

Our other new discoveries include letters written by the murderer's family from a valuable archive, surprisingly neglected by researchers on this subject. This was a family of prolific letter-writers, yet for the period in question – from the second half of 1888 to mid-1889 – the archive is almost non-existent. This gap is a disruption of their regular pattern of writing to one another, so one could reasonably surmise that the letters from this crucial period were destroyed. And letters by members of the same family composed a year later show – quite unlike their earlier correspondence – a use of cryptic phrasing regarding something that is causing strain.

We make the case that the barrister and part-time teacher who was the probable murderer briefly dabbled in medicine as a career before switching to law. We argue that it was very likely that the bloodstained gentleman maniac had been detained by the constabulary in Whitechapel but had managed to bluff his way to freedom. We make a circumstantial case that his family placed him in an asylum in France under an alias – an elaborate and expensive manoeuvre that floundered almost immediately. Perhaps most intriguingly, we found that before these infamous murders, the barrister had defended a murderer in court by trying to shift the blame onto his client's wife – a woman who worked as a prostitute.

One of our most conclusive discoveries is a source from 1894 by a writer who learned the truth almost certainly from that same police chief. It perfectly encapsulates our thesis of a family cover-up which partially fell apart as, obviously, it has reached the public domain:

... the relatives of Jack the Ripper did at last know, or suspect the truth about their charge though, for reasons that can be well understood, they preferred to hush up the affair.

I

In Defence of Murder

A little more than a year before the so-called 'Jack the Ripper' murders, which would later transfix millions, a heinous crime was committed. It is hard to conceive of anything more despicable than a lethal assault upon a defenceless baby. Yet this monstrous act had been committed by a previously law-abiding citizen, which left his community dumbfounded. The perpetrator had seemed incapable of such a horrific act – until the night he asphyxiated his unwanted stepson. On 12 February 1887 in the picturesque coastal town of Poole in the county of Dorset, the shoemaker Henry William Young said goodbye to Elizabeth Young, née Juggs, his young and heavily pregnant wife of only a few months. She was departing from their modest two-storey abode on Dear Hay Lane to go 'shopping'. Her regular, nocturnal grocery expeditions could take up to several hours.[1]

For decades Poole had been experiencing hard times because the larger ships could no longer berth in its shallow port to unload their colonial goods. Fortunately, tourists were flocking in ever greater numbers to enjoy Poole's sunny beaches.[2] As with thousands of other struggling women across an England that was devoid of even a rudimentary welfare system,[3] Elizabeth Young made ends meet by selling her body. Her 27-year-old husband would have been expected to have confronted his wife and begged her to desist from such shameful and scandalous behaviour. In Victorian society reputation was all – and Henry was known by the local townsfolk to be industrious and honest, a Sunday school teacher and a member of the Blue Ribbon Army: 'a most quiet and inoffensive young man' as one newspaper would later praise him. Further evidence of his usually placid nature is that the new couple had agreed to bring up as their own Elizabeth's illegitimate baby from a previous liaison. The child was named Percival John Ings. Henry expressed no misgivings. However, behind the respectable husband's facade of a quietly spoken, church-going 'good chap' a cancerous rage must have metastasised inside him and finally exploded against a vulnerable innocent. Did Henry Young daily limp down the streets of Poole – he had a wooden leg – feeling humiliated by the whispered derision of his fellow townspeople; poor cripple, poor cuckold, does he not know where his wife really goes at night?[4] He did know; the problem was they needed the money. What he could no longer cope with was her attention to a child not his own, with another child on the way. He hoped to save Elizabeth from her sinful life, but his income remained stubbornly meagre, just a few coins ahead of eviction.

Night after night, Henry Young sat at home, alone, staring at a ten-month-old baby who was not his. Was the child the living, intolerably irritating, reminder of his wife's double life and of his own impotence to halt her continuing to live it? Like many Victorian domestic would-be murderers, Henry Young initially tried his hand at poison – and failed.[5] He was presumably trying to discreetly eliminate little Percy by making it appear to be a death due to natural causes. Children died like flies in Queen Victoria's England; from cholera, typhoid fever and consumption, a veritable legion of diseases due to foully polluted water and overcrowded homes. Too often people of all ages collapsed as a result of inhaling the black, noxious gunk exhaled daily into the air by Britain's industrial lungs.[6]

What difference, Henry must have calculated, would one more pitiful tyke's passing really make? For the cost of some soda from the local chemist (a Mr Williams) mixed with milk and water Henry could, with one stroke, remove this blemish from their lives while denying Elizabeth her economic motive for being 'on the game' – too many mouths to feed.[7] On the night of 8 February 1887 a sick Percy was alarmingly spewing up blood and phlegm. The local doctor, Lawton, was summoned when the crisis was most acute and, though he was perplexed by the baby's symptoms, since they subsided after a few days he did not suspect foul play and nor, unfortunately, did the baby's mother. After all, Elizabeth would later lament, she and her husband had not once quarrelled about the step-child, and Henry had never so much as hinted at intending violence against anybody.[8]

Four days later Elizabeth returned from 'shopping' much earlier than usual; in a little less than an hour. She found her husband in a strange pose; he was standing perfectly still in the downstairs room staring into blank space. Upstairs not a sound could be heard from little Percy. Was he asleep, Elizabeth asked? No reply came from her zombie-like spouse, nor did her query break the spell of his fascination with the opposite wall.[9] Reaching the upstairs bedroom, Elizabeth was shocked to find the fire was out; the dark interior as cold as a cemetery. As her gaze accustomed to the gloom and swung to the bed Elizabeth let out a blood-curdling scream. The blanket she had left securely up to her baby's chin had been drawn back, exposing his tiny chest to the frigid air. Examining Percy she found he was gasping for breath, his contorted face a distinct shade of blue. Henry did not respond to the sound of his wife's distress. Bolting back downstairs she saw that her husband was now slumped in a chair still stupefied.[10] Frantic, Elizabeth raced next door and aroused a neighbour, Susan King, who came at once. The neighbour immediately took in Henry's disturbing apathy and that the ill baby seemed to be lying in what looked like bloodstained sheets. Susan confronted Henry, snapping him out of his spell, and, without a word he dutifully hobbled out of the door to fetch help.

Dr Lawton arrived a few minutes later and solemnly pronounced what the mother and her neighbour already tearfully knew – Percy had died, seemingly of suffocation. Despite Henry's decidedly suspicious behaviour, nobody seemed any the wiser as to what had caused Percy's premature demise. Had it not been for a guilty conscience, Henry might have got away with murder. With his rage over, Henry began to relive what he had done – and the memory proved intolerably hellish. As the coroner would discern from a belated post-mortem examination, Henry had punched Percy's forehead, struck his left groin, and pummelled his chest. These blows fractured the baby's third, fourth, fifth, six and seventh ribs, his tiny liver rendered irreparably damaged. The *coup de grace* was the stepfather using his thumb to break the baby's windpipe. From that final, fateful act nothing could have stopped Percy from drowning in his own blood.[11]

A grief-stricken Elizabeth interrogated Henry as to whether he had contributed to Percy's painful demise. The tormented step-father did not admit the whole truth – the neighbour remained overnight to comfort the mother – conceding only the earlier attempt at injuring the baby: 'I have a guilty conscience; I attempted to get rid of him once.' Elizabeth Young wasted no time. She immediately informed Dr Lawton of her husband's quasi-confession and incriminating behaviour, and the physician conferred with the coroner, Mr G. B. Aldridge, who promptly ordered a post-mortem (conducted by Dr Lawton with the assistance of a Dr Turner).

Knowing his arrest would be imminent once the authorities discovered from a more thorough examination little Percy's extensive internal wounds, a repentant Henry decided to end it all. He tried making a pyre of his own house and to throw himself upon it. But the neighbours, suspicious and alert after Percy's death, quickly spotted the smoke, put out the blaze that he had started in the cellar and among the upstairs bedclothes, and hauled him to safety.[12] Taken into custody and charged with the murder of his stepson (a charge of arson was later dropped) Henry found out a few days later that a traumatised Elizabeth, now consigned to the dreaded workhouse, had gone into premature labour and given birth to a stillborn child.[13] A week later, brooding in his cell as the shadow of the hangman's scaffold loomed as high as Big Ben, Henry Young's death spiral was suddenly broken, or at least momentarily arrested.

Into his cell stepped a man of 29 with a hawkish profile who, by his grooming and bearing, was obviously an educated and prosperous gentleman. A puzzled Henry Young would have further observed that the man was about 5 feet 7 inches in height and, though wiry in build, moved with the confidence and grace of an athlete. Beneath a high forehead were a pair of closely set intense blue eyes. His prominent nose was large yet noble. This aquiline visage was framed by dark hair, parted in the centre and sleek against his skull. He was clean-shaven, save for a neat fair moustache that was cut off square at the ends. The stranger had the reddest of 'apple cheeks' – due to perpetual sunburn from playing gentlemen's sports, such as cricket and tennis.[14] The handsome stranger extended his hand to the demoralised prisoner and, no doubt with a professional's well-practised smile, clarified his identity and the purpose of his visit. He was the barrister appointed to defend the prisoner and his name was Montague Druitt.

Mr Druitt would have explained to Mr Young that while he had made no effort to obtain counsel (he certainly could not afford to) because of the extremely serious nature of the offence, a lawyer had been appointed on his behalf by the presiding judge, the Honourable George Denman, who had previously observed the talented young barrister at work in court.[15] The latter had selected a relatively new yet effective advocate from the local court circuit; a silver-tongued graduate of both the exclusive boys' college Winchester and Oxford University (a card-carrying member of the Victorian establishment; both an Old Wykehamist and an Oxonian), an advocate who would be effusively praised two years hence in a local newspaper as 'well known and much respected in the neighbourhood ... a barrister of bright talent ... a promising future before him...'[16]

It is possible that Henry might have asked his lawyer, upon learning his surname, if he was related to the famous Dr Robert Druitt, whose research and credentials were often used in advertisements promoting light wine. To which the reply would have been, yes – this Montague was none other than a nephew of the late celebrity physician. Henry Young could have only been dazzled by another of his young barrister's V.I.P. connections, if he was so told: Mr Druitt had played cricket alongside none other than the legendary batsman W. G. Grace.[17] But what could Mr Montague Druitt actually do to prevent his imminent and inevitable execution for an atrocity for which he was guilty of committing? Judge Denham would have advised Montague Druitt that the accused child killer must enjoy a vigorous defence because in British law an accused person is presumed innocent until proven guilty. So this was exactly the sort of trial in which a young barrister could prove his mettle and enhance his reputation. After conferring with Henry – and no doubt dismissing the latter's semi-confession to his wife as easily disposable – Druitt decided he would shift the blame for the murder of Percy onto somebody else and, in effect, put them on trial for their unreliable and notorious character.

This barrister did have experience in winning over a jury, as can be seen by a civil case he had fought the previous year on behalf of the young and attractive Miss Marion Mildon. This case of a woman scorned had generated enormous press attention, both regional and national. As jovially reported in *The Whitby Gazette* of 29 May 1886 (An Amusing Breach of Promise Case) Miss Mildon's ex-fiancé, a Mr Binstead – a draper's assistant who, fortunately for him, did not show up in court to be mercilessly mocked – had for three years professed his undying love to this chief maid of a titled lady near Selborne. Marion had been introduced to Mr Binstead's family as his betrothed and had even received an engagement ring. The reason for the sudden cooling of Mr Binstead's affections was that his recently deceased mother had left him a tidy sum and he had decided to keep the lot for himself. The damning evidence was the defendant's own words as recorded in a series of letters to Marion assuring her 'that her darling image and lovely form occupied his waking hours and sleeping dreams'. In court Druitt read into the record from this embarrassingly effusive and self-incriminating correspondence, to the enjoyment of all in attendance:

> My dearest Marion, – You can hardly imagine how your lovely letter of this morning relieved my poor dull brain of all the weary thoughts that generally occur in bachelor solitude. (A laugh.) But thanks,

darling, your sweet, loving, little epistle has acted as an emetic, and has carried the black bile off. (Roars of laughter.) ... With you, my lovely one, my honeysuckle, my incomparable 'Maid Marion', as my wife and partner in all my joys and sorrows, I will be an English Ajax, defying the thunders and lightnings of mundane tribulation in our wedded life, darling – and oh! Do I not wish the happy, auspicious day of our nuptials was now at hand? (Continued laughter.)'

Montague Druitt was certainly having fun but it has to be noted it is also chilling for us to read this sentimental blather causing such courtroom merriment knowing that within two years, the same handsome charmer would be strangling and massacring women and provoking a very different kind of public uproar.

My Sweet and darling Marion, – when I take my solitary walks abroad I am ever fondly thinking of you. (Continued merriment.) At church yesterday, when the parson preached from the old familiar text, 'Love one another', my thoughts were wandering from the subject of his discourse, and where were they? Aye, where? They were nestling in your fond bosom. (Roars of laughter.) ...

The letters concluded, said the learned counsel, with 60,000 kisses, and with a number of geometrical figures that he understood were, in the language of love, emblematic of undying attachment and perennial love. (Laughter.) Druitt closed his case by sternly denouncing the 'amorous swain' for not giving any excuse for the 'despicable treatment of this poor young woman and for such disgraceful trifling with the affections of a chaste and virtuous woman'. He asked the jury to find in her favour and award her compensation proportionate to her 'wounded feelings and the wrong done to her womanly pride'. They heartily concurred, and she was awarded the considerable sum of £50 in damages. Yet there is a sting in the tail; Druitt could not resist being patronising about his client: '[Miss Mildon] was the honoured guest of [Mr Binstead's] numerous friends and relatives in Hampshire and Sussex, who invited her to balls, dancing parties, penny readings, and *other forms of mild dissipation in which unsophisticated country folks like to indulge'.*[18] (Our italics)

Was Druitt simply playing to the prejudices of the middle-class all-male jury? Or did he reveal a glimpse of a sincere, pitiless contempt for 'lesser' people. As he could so ably defend a 'chaste and virtuous' woman, despite her supposedly unsophisticated dissipation, so could

Druitt just as effectively wield a rapier against the female gender – at this point only rhetorically. In his opening address to the Poole jury there would be no occasion for light-hearted mirth, not in a murder trial. Instead Montague Druitt may have opened by flattering the jurors and the whole Poole community. With concentrated fury he could have pointed to the Sunday-school-teaching, one-legged shoemaker standing quietly in the dock and proclaimed that the neighbour they all thought they knew as incapable of such evil was, indeed, incapable of being a child murderer. The locals had been completely correct in their common sense judgment of Henry, whose very life hung in the balance. Whereas Elizabeth Young, he might have alleged, was an unfaithful spouse who was carrying another man's child – for a second time. It was a ruthless deflection; Montague Druitt accused Elizabeth of having callously murdered one of her own. Being an adulterer and a prostitute she was already depraved and damned and therefore, Druitt might have counter-accused, capable of ... anything. Druitt's courtroom demolition of this poor woman, who had just lost two children in succession, seems to have contributed to the wrath of many of the Poole townspeople. In a report of the trial by the *Western Gazette* of 20 May 1887: 'the then seemingly heartless manner in which she regarded the proceedings gave rise to a great deal of [adverse] popular feeling'. It is outrageous that a woman who was seeking justice after her spouse had bludgeoned and strangled her child to death was turned into the story's villain. Even after Henry was convicted, the backlash unleashed against her was so ferocious that Elizabeth reportedly had to hastily leave town for her own safety.[19]

By contrast, favourable newspaper accounts show that Druitt's advocacy skills had impressed the judge. For example, in the *Bridport News* of 29 April 1887: 'Mr Druitt's defence that the woman had more motive for committing the murder ... the judge complimented the learned gentleman [on] his ability as the prisoner's advocate.' And in greater detail in the *Hampshire Advertiser* of 30 April 1887:

> Mr Druitt's defence was that admitting the child's death was caused by violence by either the man or the woman, *the latter was the guilty party*. The prisoner invariably treated the child with tenderness and affection. *The woman had a motive* to remove the child of shame, as she was about to be confined with another which was legitimate [sic]. The *judge complimented Mr Druitt on the excellent way* in which he had watched the prisoner's interest for which the court and the prisoner were obliged to him. (Our italics)

There are indications that Mr Druitt's venomous eloquence may have been a little too ripe even for the learned judge who had appointed and later praised him. Perhaps fearful of the jurors being unable to see the wood for the trees, Judge Denham took no chances. He strongly advised them to find Henry William Young guilty of murder and saw no need for the jury to even leave their box to confer. The Poole men swallowed any doubts they may have had and dutifully returned the verdict the judge had all but demanded.[20] Our research at The National Archives in Kew, London, revealed the file on Regina v Young for the murder of Percival John Ings still survives [HO 144/196/A46955]. Judge Denman has written:

> Mr Druitt (at my request) for prisoner... Mr Druitt – to the jury for the prisoner, after conference with the prisoner, suggested that there was a doubt as to whether the prisoner or his wife did it. I summed up. The jury find the prisoner guilty – sentence death to be executed in Dorset.

In the margin Judge George Denman, perhaps a little defensively, has written: 'I think the verdict was quite right – G.D.' In the same file, the notes from a police interview with Henry Young reveals information that apparently was not raised in court as a reason for the murder, as Montague Druitt has strategically presented Young as totally innocent and his wife, a part-time prostitute, as completely guilty of Percival's murder. The record of the interview explains that Young was upset that his wife was pregnant with what he believed to be another child fathered by one of her clients. Young, it was explained, had felt neglected by his wife and believed her child Percival already received more attention from her than he did.

As Judge Denman passed a sentence of death Henry meekly protested his innocence while the judge, somewhat perplexed, chastised him: 'Some sense of selfish desire of some sort or another came into your head to destroy the life of that child, which you did in a terribly brutal and savage manner.'[21] Having done all he could for his client Montague Druitt may have quickly decamped to his next case – at least, there is no further mention of him again in extant records about this case. The sympathy aroused by the barrister for the murderer enjoyed a longer shelf life. On behalf of the condemned man, the somewhat hysterical townspeople organised a petition to try to gain a reprieve from the State. It was sent to Henry Matthews, the Home Secretary. This Tory minister will appear later in the narrative being traduced by Liberal-supporting tabloids for neglecting to personally catch 'The Ripper'. Predictably and, in this case, justly, the British Secretary of State for Domestic Affairs turned down flat the petition for clemency.[22]

Once the end was nigh, Henry Young seems to have oscillated between a pious and candid repentance for his crime and, at other moments, the same rage at his wife's infidelity that had caused his act of infanticide in the first place. As the *Hampshire Chronicle* reported on 14 May 1887 Henry made a full confession of his guilt to his parents and the prison chaplain, 'and also gives the reasons which induced him to commit the crime'. Henry apparently felt he had no choice but to squeeze the life out of a baby. The condemned man left behind a letter warning other young men not to follow his example to a premature grave – but it remains unclear if he meant by succumbing to sinful, violent impulses or by associating with a woman of the night.

Either way, what a bunch of prize chumps barrister M. J. Druitt had made of the outraged people of Poole. They had worked themselves into quite a collective lather over a shocking murder by shamefully siding with the murderer. All press sources nonetheless agree that Henry went to his execution with some stoicism and not a single stumble.

The previous Saturday the condemned man's barrister had also suffered a setback: Druitt's Blackheath cricket team had been defeated by a team at Bickley Park – though the blow was somewhat softened by Montague taking an impressive three wickets as a bowler.[23] On reflection perhaps Montague John Druitt, who in just over a year would join his deceased client by winding up as a month-old, well-dressed, rotting piece of human jetsam in the Thames River, might have done well to have taken counsel from Henry Young's warning.

II

Perfect Family...

Originally hailing from Wimborne, Dorset, Dr Robert Druitt (1814–1883) was the first born of Dr Robert Druitt Snr and Jane Mayo. Coming from the distinguished Druitt-Mayo clan of physicians, Dr Druitt was lauded in one of his many obituaries as 'a man of large culture and marked distinction'. He had written what was widely regarded as the physician's bible, *The Surgeon's Vade Mecum*, and for eight years he had been president of the prestigious and influential Metropolitan Association of Medical Officers of Health. Among his other notable achievements, he became a Fellow of the Royal College of Surgeons of England and a member of the Royal College of Physicians, London. He was vice-president of the Obstetrical Society and, for a few years, edited the *Medical Times and Gazette*.[1]

On the subject of alcohol Dr Robert Druitt's name was practically a cliché of Victorian popular culture. His official report on the cheap wines flooding England from France, Italy and Hungary (1873) almost single-handedly convinced many of the populace to switch from 'strong and fortified' wines to lighter beverages. He commented on all aspects of alcohol consumption. As his biography written in 1883 by Dr Cholmeley explained, 'He held and taught that "total abstinence" might be and doubtless often was, a useful and necessary discipline for desperate and confirmed drunkards, for dipsomaniacs.' During the mid- to late-Victorian era the social and health effects of public drunkenness in impoverished areas, such as Whitechapel, and within the home was being discussed as a public health issue. The Temperance Movement rejected the opinions of Dr Druitt and advocated total abstinence not just for alcoholics but for all citizens. Conversely, Dr Druitt's advice – that lighter, more pure wines rather than fortified wines could be beneficial to the health of men and women – was seized upon by brewers and drinkers of all classes, as proof that drinking light wine was a health elixir. Dr Druitt's poetic words must have comforted every over-indulger who read his popular work:[2]

A man must feel that he has taken something which consoles and sustains. Some liquids, as cider and some thin wines, leave rather a craving, empty, hungry feeling after them. To wine, above all other kinds of food, we may apply the phrase of the Hebrew poet, 'It satisfies the hungry soul, and fills the empty soul with goodness'.[3]

The wine industry continued to exploit Dr Druitt's good reputation long after his death and advertisements continued to appear quoting his endorsements well into the Edwardian era. Shamelessly the wine industry presented the good doctor as still alive and happily recommending their particular brand. For example, during the winter of 1888, an advertisement appeared in the conservative London newspaper *The Morning Post*:

MAX GREGER'S CARLOWITZ, THE CELEBRATED
HUNGARIAN CLARET, IS THE PUREST.

Dr Druitt writes:– 'A patient of mine who is a good judge of wine, writes to me that the wine which suits him best is Max Greger's Carlowitz. It gives renewed strength and improved digestion.'– Max Greger (Limited), Wine Merchants to the Queen, 66, Sumner St, Southwark, London. S.E. – (ADVT.)

A fascinating aspect of this advertisement is that by Wednesday, 5 December 1888, the day of its publication, not only was the good doctor by then deceased for five years, but so too was one of his nephews, Montague John Druitt, who had waded into the Thames at Chiswick the previous day.

Dr Druitt was much quoted in the press for his views on other social issues too, such as on how to improve the sanitary conditions of the poor and strategies to protect the community from communicable diseases. Pamphlets such as *Houses in Relation to Health; The Prevention of Cholera; Opium vs Grog; On Dancing Girls, Prostitution and the Contagious Diseases Act* and *Fresh air and better health for Children* (a scheme sanctioned by Dr Druitt to send sick London children to the local parks) were widely quoted and referenced in the media of the day. A panacea against the scourge of drunkenness, *Intemperance and Prevention*, had extensive circulation among all classes – upstairs and downstairs.

When analysing the Whitechapel atrocities it is perhaps not a coincidence that Dr Robert Druitt, backed by the full weight of the law, persistently advocated on the grounds of public health for the discouraging of all forms of prostitution: 'Now, I should prefer the repression of public prostitution, the incarceration of open and notorious women ...'[4]

Robert married Isabella Hopkinson (1823–1899) in 1845 and had found in her for himself not only a loving and devoted wife and mother (the couple had four sons and four daughters) but also a woman of great intelligence and strength of character, which would prove fortuitous for the extended family. The Druitt family took up residence at 8 Strathmore Gardens, Kensington, and the large, impressive home was, according to surviving sources, a happy and welcoming one.[5] The extended Druitt clan of Kensington, Christchurch and Wimborne were very close and Montague Druitt seemed particularly fond of his Uncle Robert and was a regular caller at the Kensington address.

When persistent illness saw Dr Robert Druitt sent abroad for recuperation (on and off for years) Isabella was left to raise their children and see them into adulthood as educated men and or women of good character. After her husband's death in 1883 she was unofficially elevated to the role of matriarch of the Druitt clan. Letters contained in the West Sussex Record Office reveal a beloved and respected woman who was a confidante to her siblings, in-laws, as well as nieces and nephews, and who enjoyed a close and easy relationship with her children.[6] She was the type of mother for whom kindness and common sense went hand in hand. It is clear her children and extended family sought her advice and approval. Necessity had fashioned her into a woman who would go out of her way to make things right for those she loved when they found themselves in distress. Even her outspoken brother-in-law James Druitt kowtowed to her. She was, like her husband, single minded and independent. This she would later demonstrate by the lengths she would go to in order to protect her much-loved son, the Reverend Charles Druitt, and the reputation of the Druitt clan.

For Charles Druitt (1848–1900), known as 'Pope' to his family, the year 1888 had started well. Although he was close to 40 and, like the other Druitt men of his generation, an Oxonian, he had found it difficult to secure a substantial living. Ordained into the Church of

England, he had already acted as a curate at Penistone in Yorkshire and at Weymouth and Parkstone in Dorset. His quest to secure his own parish and a home to accommodate a wife had thus far been unsuccessful. However, this year was to prove pivotal in his life, bringing him both happiness and later, excruciating anguish. He had finally secured a position as the vicar of East and West Harnham and with it a cosy parsonage suitable for married life.

Charles had formed an attachment to the sister of his best friend the Reverend Arthur du Boulay Hill. Isabel Majendie Hill (1856–1925) was also a friend of Charles' younger sister Emily who adopted the role of go-between for the smitten but very shy couple.[7] Charles was prone to illness and self-doubt throughout his life but was known to take his vows seriously. The nickname of 'Pope' – while humorous for an Anglican Vicar – had not been flippantly given. Even when he finally secured the position of vicar of his own parish, he was unsure of what Isabel's response would be. His sister Emily must have privately conferred with Isabel to ascertain the nature of her feelings and upon receiving a positive response, she gave her brother a big-sisterly push to hurry up and ask the poor girl for her hand in marriage. Charles summoned the courage on 7 June 1888 and Isabel happily accepted. The following Monday, Isabel's mother Mrs Maria Hill wrote a letter to Charles' mother Isabella Druitt about her joy and concerns over the betrothal of their two children.

> Downton Salisbury
> June 11 1888
>
> My dear Mrs Druitt,
>
> We have both so deep an interest in all this, that I feel we ought to exchange some words of affectionate greeting.
>
> I give my dear child to your son with entire confidence. I believe he will be a true loving husband to her and what greater blessing can a woman have?
>
> I know what it is and am so thankful that my darling Isabel should know it too –
>
> I think I may add without too much motherly pride – that your son has won for himself a jewel – Pure minded and holy from her childhood and superior to many women in mental gifts.
>
> I am very glad that her future husband is so good and able a man that she may be content to sit at his feet – as a woman should.
>
> I feel there are some causes for anxiety in this engagement on account of health and worldly prospects – I wish both stronger.

I can only trust they will become so. There seems to be just enough for their present needs – I wish there had been a rather wider margin – we can only look on with trust and hope, to the future –

Ever dear Mrs Druitt

> Yours most sincerely and affectionately,
> Maria E. Hill[8]

Mrs Hill needn't have worried about the pair as, even though they were to face tremendous challenges in their sadly short married life, Charles and Isabel would remain devoted to one another and, financially, they would manage well. Isabel was immediately anointed by her husband with the nickname 'schonstis', a playful variation of the German word for beautiful. As the daughter of a vicar, Isabel well understood the important role a clergyman's wife played in parish life.[9] She also shared Charles' love of music and was herself a talented musician and singer. She was pivotal in supporting her husband and ensuring his clerical career was a success.

On 15 September that year the happy couple married in the Parish Church, Downton, Wiltshire. Downton was the church where Isabel's brother the Reverend Arthur du Boulay Hill (1850–1938) was vicar. The Druitts were in good company that day and although they had tried to keep the event modest (the Hill family had only recently completed the mourning period for their beloved father the Reverend George Hill) the couple would have been very flattered by the presence of the Bishop of Salisbury, who officiated at the ceremony. He was assisted by Isabel's uncle (and the Deputy Head of Winchester College who was well known to Charles' cousin Montague Druitt) the Reverend J. T. H. du Boulay. Isabel was given away by her brother Reverend Arthur du Boulay Hill (a former Winchester master well known to Montague). It was by all accounts a happy day for the popular couple and Charles was pleased to now call his best friend Arthur his 'brother' and Isabel had gained three more 'sisters' in Ella, Emily and Gertrude Druitt.[10]

Reports of their wedding day would have been read by many people who may not have known the couple personally but would have been interested to read of the union of a son of the famous Dr Druitt into the equally famous Majendie family. Isabel Majendie Hill had, like her new husband, a well-known family name. Her mother Maria was the product of the Du Boulay-Majendie clan, which had many noteworthy members. Colonel Vivian Majendie (1836–1898, knighted 1895) was the bomb disposal hero who was Chief Inspector of Explosives for the

Home Office. Like Dr Druitt, his name was recognisable to members of all classes of society. He counted among his closest friends the famous writer and amateur criminologist George R. Sims, as well as Sir Melville Macnaghten, later head of CID during the sunset of the Edwardian era.[11] Vivian Majendie was a widower and regularly risked his life by examining and disarming the bombs, known then as 'infernal machines'. Colonel Majendie would certainly have considered the possibility of his only child Henry Grylls Majendie being left an orphan due to his dangerous vocation. The Majendie/Du Boulay family was a close and supportive clan. Isabel Majendie's mother Maria had entrusted the education of her sons to her brother the Reverend J. T. H. du Boulay and Winchester College, while their cousin Colonel Majendie was convinced that this could also provide the security he sought for his own son. Henry Grylls Majendie was thus given the comfort of family life by living with Reverend J. T. H. du Boulay and his family at Winchester College, providing a safe home and good education for Henry and peace of mind for his father.[12]

Colonel Majendie's skill as a bomb disposal expert and his knowledge of explosives helped to keep Londoners safe during a time of terrorism from militant Irish nationalists (called Fenians). On 24 January 1885 his expertise was called upon to examine no fewer than three explosions in one day. In an event that would come to be known as 'Dynamite Saturday', Fenians – in their determination to force Britain to relinquish control of their homeland – bombed the House of Commons chamber, Westminster Hall and the Banqueting Room of the Tower of London. In a later interview published in *The Sketch* of 25 April 1894, Majendie stated that the perpetrators of the outrageous acts had by that time changed from the 'Fenians or Clan-na-Gael; now they are due to the Anarchists.' He also discussed hoaxers, and showed he did not suffer fools gladly. In fact, he seems more incensed by those who perpetrated a hoax than by the actions of authentic criminals: 'In any case they are very negligent, and they help to cause us a great deal of trouble ... I know, if I caught one of them, I should try to make him feel sorry about it. The very least such people deserve is to be flogged or lynched.' The journalist shifts the grim focus of the interview by signing off with a flattering assessment,

> I could not help being impressed by the modest, unostentatious bravery with which he does his arduous duty. He served with distinction in the Crimea and the [Indian] Mutiny; but, like another famous officer he 'doesn't advertise', and it is very difficult to induce

him to talk about himself. On all other subjects he converses with grace and wit, and for my part I must say that I have rarely spent two hours so pleasantly or so profitably as those I passed in his company.

Later in 1898, Henry Grylls Majendie did suffer the loss of his famous father. Against expectations, it was not an explosion from an 'infernal machine' he was trying to disarm that claimed the colonel. Instead it was a heart attack after a church service in Oxford while visiting his sister. He was 61. Tragically it was his son who would die prematurely in the service of his country. In 1900, at the age of 35, Captain Majendie died from gunshot wounds in South Africa during the Boer War.[13]

Also acquainted with Colonel Majendie was another of Montague's uncles, James Druitt (1816–1904) who resided in Christchurch, where he operated a legal practice with the brother of Reverend Charles Druitt, Robert Druitt. Like his brothers, Uncle James was a significant contributor to his community. He served five terms as mayor and he was regularly called upon to act in the role of coroner. It is in this capacity that Uncle James came to know Colonel Majendie. In 1884 he called the Colonel to Bijou Hall, in Bournemouth, to provide expert evidence in an inquest into the death of Harry Gray in what was described as a 'Fatal Firework Explosion' on a steamer operated by the Bournemouth Steam Packet Company.[14]

James Druitt married twice and had fifteen children. He was a Conservative and a Freemason and one of his sons, James Druitt Jnr, went into legal practice in Bournemouth with his cousin William Harvey Druitt, the older brother of Montague. These Druitt cousins had a successful practice and at times passed legal work Montague's way. From his large family, it would only be Uncle James and James Jnr who were at Montague's sparsely attended funeral in January 1889 in Wimborne, Dorset.[15] On Friday 9 November 1888 at noon, only hours after Mary Jane Kelly was mercilessly slain in Miller's Court, Whitechapel, by the murderer known as 'Jack the Ripper', Montague's Uncle James was elected mayor of Christchurch and duly described as a man of 'high respectability' (*Christchurch Times* 10 November 1888). Like his brothers, he also possessed a determined and somewhat self-righteous character, which is revealed in his obituary from the same newspaper in 1904:

In the many local controversies of the last half-century, Mr Druitt has taken a prominent part and was a leader of a considerable following. He possessed a pungent and sarcastic power of speech and he often caused laughter among those who disagreed with him, as well as those who agreed with him, by his turning a point with a shaft of ridicule.

Of note, one controversy on which James Druitt preferred to close the chapter for the sake of his reputation and political career was the death by suicide of his nephew Montague. It is probable that his son, James Jnr, via Montague's brother William Harvey Druitt, told James Snr the truth behind Montague's death. James Jnr and William had both been working with Montague on a very significant court case, Druitt vs Gosling, just days before his suicide on 4 December 1888.[16] It is recorded that in early November 1888 James Snr, perhaps anticipating another term as mayor, had decided to record a memoir of his life and arranged for one of his daughters to act as secretary. What started with a flourish was abruptly abandoned and it was not until six years later that he resumed his life story. The man who was so proud of his history airbrushed Montague and his branch of the family out of it by simply lamenting, 'Now alas, no representative of the family is to be found' at Wimborne.[17]

It was James who wrote to his brother Thomas Druitt (1817–1891) about Montague's death. When Montague was a child, Uncle Thomas and his wife had emigrated to Australia. He became a schoolmaster in Sydney, and later the Archdeacon of Monaro in New South Wales. Thomas advised his sister-in-law, Isabella Druitt, of his awareness of the death and asked for Montague's sister's address in a letter from Cooma, in New South Wales, dated 27 February 1889: 'We have the sad news about poor Montague. It came fresh from Christchurch and I saw the particulars in the *Dorset County Chronicle* afterwards. Can you give me Georgie Hough's address?'[18]

The only sister of these prominent men who died unmarried at her brother's residence in Christchurch in 1880, was Jane Druitt (1822–1880).

This brings us to the youngest brother of the family, Dr William Druitt (1820–1885) who was the father of Montague. This Dr Druitt was perfectly content to remain a country physician in Wimborne, Dorset, as some of his forebears had been from as early as 1689. Dr William Druitt was the leading surgeon of Wimborne and its surrounds. Upon his death in 1885, he was described in *The Salisbury and Winchester Journal* of 3 October 1885 as a 'staunch Conservative'. He had been a stalwart of the local Anglican Church (Wimborne Minster), a justice of the peace and had sat on the Wimborne bench of magistrates. In addition he was a member of the Church of England governing body and a governor of the Queen Elizabeth's Grammar School in Wimborne, a fellow of the Royal College of Surgeons and of the London Society of Apothecaries.[19] *The Southern Times and Dorset County Herald* of Friday 2 October 1885 illustrates the depth of grief felt by townspeople at William's death:

> At midday on Sunday 27 and between the morning and evening services, which were conducted in thanksgiving for the late harvest, the town was startled by the death knell from the Minster tower, ill according to the joyous character of the day's celebration. Consternation was visible on every countenance when it became generally known that Mr William Druitt had died almost suddenly in the course of the morning. ... His integrity and high principles commanded the respect of all. He has ended a valuable and honourable life with the affection, respect, and regret of all his fellow townsmen who deeply deplore his loss and most sincerely sympathise with his widow and children in the unexpected bereavement which has overtaken them. They, with all who loved him, have at least the sweet consolation of the memory of the just.

The Salisbury and Winchester Journal further described the good deeds of the man, 'he will be much missed, especially by the poor.'[20] It is certain that the destitute of Wimborne and surrounding environs would miss the charitable doctor as those without sufficient funds were treated free of charge by this generous local surgeon. What this report fails to record is the devastating impact that Dr William's death had on his wife. He had medically attended to her for many years, as a caring and capable doctor who was also a loving husband he had brought through her ever-more-frequent bouts of depression.

Dr William Druitt's widow, Ann Druitt (1830–1890) was a woman with a delicate nature who was prone to melancholy. Montague was born in 1857 – he was her third child in three years. William and Ann Druitt were to have four sons and three daughters during their thirty-nine year marriage. They lived a very comfortable upper-middle-class life at Westfield House, by far the largest and arguably the most impressive house in Wimborne. There were extensive grounds and gardens, stables, and individual cottages were provided for the servants' accommodation.[21]

Ann Druitt (née Harvey) was a Dorset girl who had chosen well when she married into the accomplished Druitt clan of Wimborne. Her family had already known the tragedy of mental illness; her mother had committed suicide and her sister had spent time in an asylum after having attempted the same. Sadly, one of her daughters, Georgiana ('Georgie') also took her own life. As an elderly woman, she threw herself from an attic window. Since she had married a clergyman who had risen to become, from 1918 to 1932, the second Bishop of Woolwich, the suicide was treated as an unfortunate accident by the respectful press.[22]

As shown by letters written by Ann Druitt to her sister-in-law Isabella Druitt, the former experienced some lucidity before, eventually, succumbing to ever more frequent bouts of deep depression and paranoid delusions. Ann Druitt's four sons – William, Montague, Edward and Arthur – had by then left the family home to either study or pursue careers. Her firstborn daughter Georgiana (1855–1933) was living in London with her husband Reverend William Hough – then merely a humble vicar – and their children. She assisted William to run the busy Corpus Christi College Mission at Old Kent Road. The two youngest girls Edith and Ethel were too inexperienced to take on the burden of caring for their mother. Consequently when Ann took an overdose of laudanum, a difficult decision had to be made. Her eldest son William, with medical advice, agreed to place her in a discreet private asylum for the close monitoring of her condition. In July 1888 she was admitted to The Brooke House Asylum, which was located in Upper Clapton Road, Clapton, and was certified insane by Dr William Pavey.[23]

William Harvey Druitt Jnr (1856–1909) enjoyed a thriving legal practice in Bournemouth and quickly became financially secure, even affluent. In addition to the income from his legal practice William, with his mother and sisters, was a major beneficiary of his father's will. As the new head of the family, he took on the role of arranging and paying for the care of his mother (and we argue, later in 1888, covertly of his younger brother Montague too – *see* Chapter XII). During the 1880s, it had become the custom for gentlemen like the young Druitt brothers and their male cousins to delay marriage for financial reasons. The Archbishop of Canterbury commented on this trend in the *Huddersfield Chronicle* February 20 1888: 'Early marriages did not appear to take place among the upper classes, for he had heard it said that the young men seemed inclined to give up the idea of marriage. They put it off until they possessed enough to keep a wife and children.'

By 1888, William Harvey Druitt had not married, nor had any of his three brothers. On the other hand, Edward Druitt (1859–1922) and Christina Weld had certainly planned their upcoming wedding during 1888 for early 1889 – when news arrived of his brother Montague's ghastly suicide in the Thames. Perhaps a curious element here is that the couple chose not to observe a period of mourning for their tragic sibling and almost in-law. They decided to go ahead with no change to the timing of the nuptials. Edward's conversion to Catholicism had certainly created much angst within the Druitt clan and this might be the reason for not observing this particular social convention; it could also be that his conversion and the effect it had on their mother had long ago caused the estrangement of Montague and Edward. Edward's bride Christina came from an aristocratic Catholic family; her father was Sir Frederick Weld (1823–1891). English born, he enjoyed a distinguished career in the Antipodes. He held the positions of sixth Prime Minister of New Zealand, eighth Governor of Western Australia and fourth Governor of Tasmania. The union of Edward and Christina received congratulations from no less than His Holiness Pope Leo XIII (who would never know, and presumably never want to know, that he was blessing the nuptials of the brother of the late 'Jack the Ripper'). In attendance were Edward's surviving brothers, William Harvey Druitt and Arthur Druitt. They were the only family members to do so.[24] The newly married couple soon left for Australia where Edward had arranged a position with the State of Queensland's defence force. As with his Uncle James, Edward seemed to erase both his deceased brother Montague and his mentally ill mother Ann from his family biography. On returning to Britain, he would have a successful military career rising to the position of Lieutenant Colonel, followed by a role as an Inspecting Officer of Railways. Edward was never again to live in the West Country, instead choosing to distance himself from the past by living mainly in Edinburgh for the rest of his life.

The youngest Druitt brother, Arthur (1863–1943) became a schoolmaster at Jeffrey House, Edinburgh Academy, at 13 Kinnear Road. In 1894, he married Isabella Chiene the daughter of the Professor of Surgery at the University of Edinburgh. Arthur, like his brother Edward, made a life for himself and his new family in Edinburgh, although he remained close to his Aunt Isabella and his cousins who lived in Kensington.[25]

The two youngest Druitt daughters, Edith (1867–1943) and Ethel (1871–1950) arguably bore the brunt of the family disintegration caused by the death of their father. It was the two youngest girls who remained living at home with their mentally ill mother, until older brother William relieved their burden by placing her in an asylum. Edith married Reverend Frederick Vaughan in 1892 and went on to have a family of her own. The youngest sibling, Ethel, married when she was 44 to a widower and doctor Mr James Bond.[26]

For William Harvey Druitt the responsibilities and repercussions of caring for his unbalanced mother and, we believe, the almost unendurable strain of the last months of his brother Montague's double life and suicide, seem to have emotionally frozen him in place. A man with what must have felt like the weight of the world on his shoulders, he never married or left Bournemouth to live and work anywhere else. William died in 1909 at the relatively young age of 52 from a devastating heart attack as he was rushing for his afternoon train.[27]

III

...Perfect Gentleman

Montague John Druitt, referred to affectionately as 'Montie' by his large extended family, was indeed as he was later to be described by a 'West of England' Member of Parliament in 1891 who had posthumously learned the truth of his bestial crimes, 'the son of a surgeon'.[1] Such horror lay very much in the future when the infant was baptised by his Great Uncle William Mayo at the historic and picturesque Wimborne Minster on 30 September of 1856. As a boy, Montie commenced his education at Queen Elizabeth's Grammar School in Wimborne, an old prestigious school founded in 1497 by Lady Margaret Beaufort, the mother of Henry VII. Montague's father Dr William Druitt was a governor of the school and Montie proved to be a competent student, ranking fourth in history and third in geography. For his senior education, Montie sat a very competitive examination for a scholarship place at Winchester College. As his schoolmasters at Queen Elizabeth's Grammar must have anticipated, Montie breezed through his exam and was rewarded with a scholarship to Winchester, one of the oldest and most prestigious public schools in England.[2]

As with the other boys and young men at the college, Montie was known as a Wykehamist. He embraced the many extra-curricular offerings at Winchester, both sporting and academic. He excelled at all types of sports, including Fives (which required hand strength), football and athletics. During his school years he was several times the Winchester College Fives champion. His arm strength was legendary, although he appeared to push rules to the limit in competition. *The Wykehamist* reports on the Under-15 Cricket Ball Throwing Championship of that year with the winner throwing 72 yards, 8 feet,

8 inches, however, 'Druitt who was second, threw a foot or two further than the winner but was disqualified from having stepped on the tape in throwing.'[3] The gentleman's game, cricket, was Montie's favourite and during his time at Winchester he earned a position in the First XI. By the age of 18 he was acclaimed in the school journal for his frighteningly venomous fast bowling: 'The bowling of Druitt on the second day was extremely deadly, for he got a "White Hat" bowling three wickets with three successive balls.'[4]

As a member of the Shakespeare Society, Montague was cast in *Twelfth Night* but it seems as a thespian he was not up to the standard expected. Consequently the review of his performance published in *The Wykehamist* magazine was severe: 'But of the inadequacy of Druitt as Sir Toby what are we to say? It can be better imagined than described.'[5] By 18 years of age, Montague, under the tutelage of Reverend J. T. H. du Boulay and Reverend Arthur du Boulay Hill – the cousins of Colonel Vivian Majendie – seemed to have improved:

> The opening meeting of this Society was held on Saturday October 2, before a numerous audience. The play read was *Othello*... Mr Du Boulay, as Brabantio, and Mr Morshead as Cassio, were both admirable. A word of commendation must be given to Druitt for his careful reading of different minor parts; we should like to hear him in a more important character... A feature of the evening was the singing of some four-part songs, which had been worked up by Mr [Arthur du Boulay] Hill (to whom the best thanks of the Society were due) and which were introduced as interludes between the Acts.[6]

During the next meeting, *The Tempest* was read and the pertinent issue of *The Wykehamist* observes,

> This play is perhaps not very well adapted for reading aloud; it should be either seen on the stage or studied in private... Mr Du Boulay struck us as being very good in the part of Ferdinand. Druitt to whom it appears to be always necessary to give more than one part, read his different characters well enough; under the circumstances it is but natural that he should be unable to mark any difference between a king and a boatswain.

Clearly Montague was not first choice for leading Shakespearean roles but it appears he was a dedicated society member. In his final year at

Winchester he donated several texts to the school library including *Ulrich's Shakespeare's Dramatic Art* (two volumes) Coleridge's *Shakespeare Notes and Lectures*, Skeat's *Shakespeare's Plutarch* and finally, Bucknill's *The Mad Folk of Shakespeare*.

Montague's talents were more suited to the Winchester College Debating Society, for which he was elected secretary.[7] He competed in debates throughout his schooling and although at times lauded for his ability to mount a convincing argument, it was in this society that a few cracks appear, perhaps anticipating some unsavoury aspects of his character. Montague Druitt was admonished by the writer for *The Wykehamist*. Covering the latest debate, this reporter seems affronted by Montague who is listed as a 'visitor', and his approach to the occasion which could be interpreted as either aloof or ill-prepared, or perhaps both:

> The topic of debate was 'That in the opinion of this House the abdication of the late King of Spain was a cowardly and unjustifiable desertion of the post he had accepted'. The speeches of the opposers of this motion require but little comment, all of them being more or less true and sensible, and the arguments adduced in each being as good and conclusive as the subject, not we think a very extensive or well-chosen one admitted of.
>
> The last speaker on their side was a visitor, who though we are very glad to see members of the School, if not of the Society, willing and ready to come forward and speak, should scarcely have begun by announcing that he 'had nothing particular to say'.[8]

Noteworthy is that the following year another report appears in this publication which again suggests moments of aggression and the pushing of boundaries in the young man's developing character. Now 16 years of age, Montague chose to ignore the protocol of debate and presented his argument in an offensive manner. He was called to task by an opposing speaker. The topic of debate was: 'That the execution of King Charles I was in every respect unjustifiable'. Montie Druitt opened the proceedings as the first speaker and immediately riled his opposition with his ungentlemanly conduct:

> Druitt in proposing the motion, relied on strong and intolerant language, (for which a subsequent speaker on the other side called him severely to account...)[9]

Montague was an all-rounder and in what could often be the brutal, hyper-masculine world of boarding school, it is possible that his peers at the college admired his edge on the cricket field and in the debating room. Certainly he was popular enough to be elected in his final year to Prefect of Chapel, one of the most prestigious honours to be bestowed on a Winchester student. In this role, the son of a Church of England stalwart would wield considerable authority over other students. He would confer with Mr Du Boulay and his nephew Arthur du Boulay Hill, both ordained ministers and, coincidentally, the uncle and brother of Isabel Majendie Hill, who would later marry Montague's cousin, Reverend Charles Druitt. To top off his final year, Montague was awarded a scholarship to New College, Oxford. Before leaving for university, in acknowledgement of the sport that had brought him such accolades, Montague donated a cup to be awarded to the winner of the under-16 Fives competition. It would be known as the Druitt Cup.[10]

As previously mentioned, Montague came from a family with strong male role models. There was a family expectation that the Druitt men would be hard working, well educated and God fearing; they would choose a profession, train for it and make a success of it; they would make a good income from their vocation and be self-sufficient. Upon his graduation from Winchester, the senior Druitt men must have felt confident that Montague was well on his way to fulfilling their expectations.

Montague was fond of his uncle Dr Robert Druitt and his Kensington-based family. A surviving letter postmarked 16 September 1876, reveals Montague as a 19 year old, ready to commence studies at Oxford. He corresponded with his famous uncle, who had asked him to tutor his daughter Katherine in Latin while they were on holiday with Montie's family in Wimborne. He also revealed some discomfort about what he believes was a less than exciting country holiday for his Kensington cousins, for which he unashamedly blames his mother. A custom of this era was to formally refer to an aunt by their husband's name, in this case 'Aunt Robert' referring to his Aunt Isabella Druitt:

Dear Uncle Robert,

In the two short bits of Vergil Kitty translated for me vii (105–118) and xii (342–356)) there was no grammatical mistake of any sort except perhaps a very doubtful use of the dative – 'place near the food' – subjicient spulis. A dictionary was used, which I did not intend, so that the pieces which would otherwise have fairly tested a knowledge of words did not do so.

The construing in the second piece was plain sailing, but the really hard passages vii: 109–11 and 117–8, which would have been a great thing to have done rightly, Kitty quite misunderstood...

It is evident that Kitty has a sound knowledge of grammar rules, but does not know that the idioms of the two languages are so different that change of form in translating Latin to English as well as English to Latin is indispensable.

I was sorry to hear that you were not so well again and hope you will soon be better. I am afraid Emily and Kitty had a very dull time of it at Wimborne; an attempt of ours to make it less so was met by the assurances of their hostess that she should take care of her own guests herself!

I hope you will be able at some time to see me for a day or two in Oxford; I hope very soon to earn something independently. With love to Aunt Robert and Ella,

V. affect. nephew
M. J. Druitt[11]

At Oxford, Montague immersed himself in sports and clubs. Judging by his final results, he had become distracted from his academic pursuits. He again excelled at Fives and played rugby and cricket but with more competition at the elite college level, Montie was elevated to the Oxford Second XI cricket team. He was popular enough to be elected Steward of the Junior Common Room. He was also a participant in many social activities and events, and was recorded in the 'Oxford Journal' at the wedding of a close friend, Thomas Stubbs, to a Miss Evelyn Risley at a local Oxford church.[12] The 'elegant' wedding breakfast was served in a tent on the rectory lawn. Into the evening a garden party turned into a dance. A large number of visitors from the neighbourhood happily joined the occasion. It seems that the exit of the newlyweds to their honeymoon did not deter the Oxford chums from continuing their carousing:

Dancing commenced after supper at 9pm, and was kept up with spirit until midnight, when the wedding festivities were brought to a conclusion by the departure for Oxford of the bridegroom's College friends on their drag, amid loud and vociferous cheering for Mr and Mrs Risley, the happy pair, and the bridesmaids.[13]

Mr Montague Druitt was recorded as having gifted a velvet album with silver mountings to the newlyweds.[14] He was a regular attendee at many of the glittering events of the regular Dorset social season. In 1881, for example, Montague was at an important event, a ball took place at Crichel House to celebrate the royal visit of the Duke of Connaught. The Druitts celebrated alongside Henry Richard Farquharson, a future Tory Member of Parliament and, ten years later, the person behind the initially unnamed 'West of England' MP who breathlessly proclaimed that he knew the identity of the Whitechapel murderer.

During his time at Oxford, Montie became well versed in art of social climbing. He understood that without the advantage of a title and old money, like some of his privileged Oxford colleagues, he would have to be both a wily strategist and a flexible tactician to make a success of his life in a very competitive world. He would need to make appropriate social contacts who could aid his progress when a position was sought or a reference was required. On this front, Montie launched himself into a promising social life spearheaded by his cricket prowess; a fast bowler of his ability was always in demand for the many gentlemen's teams that toured around the country. Teams such as the 'Gentlemen of Dorset' often included middle-aged and older men who were happier being entrenched at the wicket with a bat in hand (rather than running in to bowl, for hours on end, on a warm, summer afternoon).[15] Montie played with many notables of the era including Lord Harris and later the greatest cricketer of the Victorian era: W. G. Grace.

To advance his social ascent Montague followed the example of his father and uncle's 'staunch' Conservative leanings and in 1879 became a member of The Oxford Canning Club. The club's secretary was George Curzon – Lord Curzon who would later serve as Viceroy of India and Secretary of State. The members of this club were the type of young men who would expect due to their background and exalted family reputation to become in due course members of the ruling elite of England.

The History of Oxford Canning Club 1861–1911, was written and privately published by Horace Hart in 1911 and is held by the British Library. It describes the rules and purpose of the club and gives an insight into the club meetings. To be accepted into the exclusive club Montague would have been required to be a paid-up member of the British Conservative Party. He also needed to be nominated by a proposer and a seconder and then voted in by ballot. The elected member would be admitted upon signing the following testament: 'The duty of the Conservative Party is to watch over and preserve in its integrity the British Constitution as at present established in Church and State. I the undersigned as a member of the Conservative Party, feel myself bound to this duty.'[16]

Meetings had to be held every week at 9 p.m. in the rooms of one of the members and during each weekly meeting a paper on politics had to be read and discussed. The book also reports that the club meetings could often rapidly degenerate into an all-night card game or 'whist party'.[17] A photograph of the group, taken at Oxford in 'Midsummer 1879' and held by the British Library, is we believe the oldest surviving depiction of Montague so far discovered and has never been published before, in a book on this subject (*see* plate section). In the crisp and atmospheric photograph, Montie in his 22nd year, is shown looking pensive and pious, his head bowed in repose. Dressed in a salt and pepper jacket, Montague and his fellow club members are standing or sitting in front of the ornate door of an ivy-covered Oxford building. Faint graffiti, the number 79, either scratched or chalked for the occasion, can be seen on the solid stone wall behind the men. Little could any of them have known that among them was a future, socialistic incubus who would commit himself to breaking the apathy of these same gentlemen towards the poor of the East End through murder and terror (and a chalked message on a wall will also play its part in the story of the fruitless police hunt for the murderer).

Graduating without a first class degree from Oxford did not trouble Lord Curzon's career trajectory – but this was not so for Montie, the once outstanding student and all-round success story of Winchester College. He graduated with a third class Bachelor of Arts in Classics in 1880 and his once-bright future looked to be all at sea. Perhaps facing limited options, he took a position as an assistant schoolmaster at Indian missionary George Valentine's small boarding school located at 9 Eliot Place, Blackheath. It had two modern features: separate sleeping accommodation for the students and a swimming pool.[18] Almost nothing but scraps have survived about Montague Druitt as a school teacher, except that he paid the school to lodge there and, presumably, taught the Classics and coached some sport. In the time between Montague completing his first degree in 1880 and commencing his legal studies in May 1882, there is an approximate eighteen-month gap.

We suggest that Montague may have started, but never completed, some studies in medicine. Those contemporaneous to him who believed in his guilt as 'The Ripper' would persistently claim he did have some surgical knowledge. This included a police-chief, a field detective, a clergyman, a famous writer (and the politician who would allude to the significance of 'Jack' being a surgeon's son). Too many writers, researchers and commentators on this much-misunderstood subject, however, have peddled a crudely reductionist interpretation of these Victorian and Edwardian sources. They treat as a fact that since Druitt was neither a doctor nor a medical graduate, any primary source that mistakenly asserts he was one *ipso facto* obviates their parallel claim he was a serial murderer. What has been missed is that a number of the same sources also qualified what they meant; they qualified 'doctor' to mean a medical *student* – and not necessarily a graduate. We found many examples in which medical students, despite not having graduated, were still being described as a 'doctor' or 'surgeon' – or still as a 'medical student' years after they had dropped out. Compared to how these words would be used in the twentieth century, in the nineteenth they were used more broadly – even, to our eyes, quite imprecisely.

For example, the famous writer who would fictionalise [the unnamed] Druitt as a middle-aged, fully qualified surgeon had also years earlier revealed the murderer to be really only a 'dabbler' in science. The aforementioned clergyman told a journalist that [the unnamed] Druitt was 'at one time a surgeon', arguably a cryptic way of saying that any career in medicine was cut short. The field detective mentioned above oscillates between saying [the unnamed] Druitt was a 'young doctor' or a 'medical student' (he is the only one of these sources who did not think Druitt was the culprit, an understandably erroneous opinion due to being kept under-informed – *see* Chapter XIX). Even the police chief who went to his premature grave believing in Druitt's guilt – the cornerstone of too many modern works is the persistent caricaturing of this well-informed, hands-on sleuth as an incompetent, homophobic ignoramus – also hedged his bets in an official file on the Whitechapel case. He names the long deceased suspect, M. J. Druitt, as having been 'said to be a doctor' implying this was a factor one had to learn verbally as there was no official documentation to verify it (in the same document 'Mr', not 'Dr', Druitt is characterised as unquestionably gaining erotic fulfilment from acts of ultra-violence; therefore, his being a medical man was provisional whereas, by contrast, his status as a sexually motivated psychopath was not.)

As previously mentioned, between graduating from Oxford with a mediocre degree, and taking up a poorly paid teaching position, there is a gap of about eighteen months before he resumed his post-graduate studies to train as a lawyer. It is entirely possible that during this interval Montague considered a medical degree, and took practical steps to emulate both his distinguished father and illustrious uncle. He could have easily attended some anatomy classes for a few weeks or months before abandoning this vocation to become a barrister. Lists of such academic transients have not always survived in the extant record. For example, some of the medical teaching colleges relied on 'occasional students' to bolster their numbers as reported in the *Leeds Mercury* of 25 June 1880:

The Victoria University

From the report of Principal Rucker for the session 1879–80 we make the following extracts: A very gratifying increase in the number of students has taken place during the past year 1879–80. Registered students, 142, Medical students 52, *occasional students 148*. (Our italics)

Upon his graduation from Oxford, a somewhat deflated Montague would have had a difficult conversation with his father and perhaps his Uncle Robert. What was Montie to do? Any doctor would expect to have at least one son follow him into the same profession and Dr William Druitt, so far, had none. One was a solicitor, one a soldier and another who would become a teacher but Montie was at a bit of a loss. Being 'extremely deadly' at cricket was all very well but it did not pay the bills or attract a suitable wife.

While it may initially have seemed an obvious choice for Montie to become a medical student, in practice the idea must have soon fallen flat. In an 1880's version of the generation gap the reality of medical training for Montague and his cohort was entirely different to that taken by his father and uncle. Dr Robert Druitt was apprenticed to his uncle Mr Charles Mayo at Winchester Hospital and then continued to study while working within a hospital setting. An expectation that Montie could achieve the same outcome as his father or uncle must have quickly been shown to be implausible, especially for a young man who seemed happier socialising than studying. *The London Evening Standard* of 1 October 1881 published an extensive article about the difficult life of the then modern medical student in comparison with previous graduates:

Thirty or even fewer years ago, the student came to town 'bound apprentice' to some country practitioner, who had not improbably passed into the profession at a day when examinations were not required... He had learned to bleed and to bandage, gather herbs... compound drugs more with an eye to the commercial aspect... than to their therapeutic action. In London he 'walked' a hospital, and in due time, armed with what tough practical knowledge he could pick up, was dispatched to kill or happily to cure.

The burdensome load placed on the modern student is then detailed:

The student must pass a preliminary examination in Arts, considerably more difficult than that to which University Graduates were subjected some years ago... Chemistry, Physiology, Anatomy, Chemical Analysis, Botany, Materia Medica, Zoology, Surgery, Pathology, Medicine (Systematic and Clinical), Gynaecology, and Forensic Medicine must all be mastered ... Finally should he aim at practicing as a consulting physician, he must learn German and French... It may be doubted whether the practitioner's remuneration is always equal to his merits. ... *his earnings are not greater than those of a well-briefed barrister* ... Nevertheless, *at no period were medical students more plentiful than now ... piled tier above tier in the Hospital theatre.* (Our italics)

If during the eighteen months after Montague completed his first degree he dabbled in medicine as a post-graduate 'occasional' student who already had a job, it would be likely that the sheer weight of study could have sunk the young man's ambitions, especially with his track record of a third class degree yet a first class social and sporting life. Ultimately, if the police chief, the famous writer, the field detective and the clergyman can be shown to be reliable sources about Montie Druitt, then they are the proof that he had acquired enough surgical knowledge to have promoted himself to be, macabrely considering his background, 'Chief of Surgery' in Whitechapel during 1888.

In 1882, Montague would have again found himself in the unenviable position of facing his father Dr William Druitt and discussing once more what on earth he was to do. The Druitt elders would not have been impressed with Montie's flailing career prospects. Perhaps his early success at Winchester had unrealistically raised their expectations. At Oxford and beyond he would not enjoy the close academic nurturing and oversight provided by Reverend J. T. H. du Boulay, Reverend Arthur du Boulay Hill and Dr George Ridding he had at Winchester. Perhaps Montie was the type of young man who had peaked in his senior years of school and was now firmly on the downward slide.

Even if this was so, it was not in the nature of the Druitt men to allow one of their own to surrender to mediocrity. When Montague discussed his future with his father, in all likelihood he mounted a convincing case that his true and natural vocation was the study of the Law. His past success as a debater and his proven interest in politics may have given Dr William Druitt some hope that Montie might indeed have finally found a viable vocation. The life for a student at the Inner Temple was an expensive one as there were compulsory dinners to attend, wine accounts to be paid – and that was apart from tuition fees and, upon graduation, the establishment of chambers from which to work. Dr William Druitt, despite perhaps having been previously burned by Montie's less than convincing attempts at a lucrative career, did agree to his son's request for the financial assistance he would need to study Law at the Inner Temple. However, rather than handing over the money and hoping for the best, Dr Druitt shrewdly gave his son an incentive to work hard and complete his studies, sacrifice some of his social and sporting life and, if all went to plan, emerge with a profession. Dr Druitt would furnish the £500 required on condition that Montague understood it was in fact his own inheritance from his father's estate, provided in advance. Montie, with no avenues for complaint, agreed to his father's proposal and was admitted to the Inner Temple in 1882.[19]

A glimpse of this period is given in a letter written by Montague's father Dr William Druitt, to his brother Dr Robert Druitt at his residence, 8 Strathmore Gardens, Kensington.

> Westfield Wimborne Minster
> 13 Dec. 1882
>
> My dear brother,
>
> We hear from Monty (sic) that the fog prevented his calling on you on Sunday which he hoped to have done.
>
> I hope his profession may be a success but it involves some sacrifices at present.[20]

The London fog was ferocious that December 1882. Montie's decision not to visit Dr Robert Druitt and his family of Kensington was a smart one. The fog in many areas of London was a noxious mixture of water vapour and pollution, causing many residents to have respiratory problems and, with their vision obscured, there were often dangerous mishaps. *Punch* published a ditty about the London fog soon after Montie's decision to delay his trip because of it.

> Mad as a March hare or hydrophobic dog,
> You feel in fact intensely suicidal:
> Such things befall us in a London fog![21]

Montague presumably made some sacrifices in 1882 and his father's strategy seemed to pay dividends because Montie applied himself to his studies and lived on his income from part-time teaching at Valentine's School at Blackheath, where he continued to lodge. On 29 April 1885 he was called to the Bar, as a full-fledged special pleader (a clerical legal assistant) and as a barrister arguing in court. At some expense, he rented chambers at 9 King's Bench Walk, Inner Temple. Within a few months this professional achievement was overshadowed by private bereavement – the death from heart failure of his father who left a considerable estate. Montague, as previously agreed with his father, received nothing.[22]

* * *

William Gilbert Grace (1848–1915) was the quintessential Victorian success story. Like Montague Druitt, he was the scion of a modest country doctor. One of nine children, he grew up to be a colossus with a fearsome beard to match. Through diligence and discipline, W. G. Grace transformed a latent athletic prowess to become the perhaps the greatest player in the history of the game of cricket (rivalled only by Australia's Donald 'The Don' Bradman in the twentieth century). Grace was one of the most famous men in Victorian England. Playing in a record forty-four seasons, W. G. Grace set precedents and created conventions that reinvented and refined the sport, ones that have lasted into the twenty-first century. The year before the Poole murder, Grace, though an all-rounder, had bowled out an astonishing 100 players of opposition teams. He was frequently captain of the first class English team and, among other clubs, he was the most illustrious member of the Marylebone Cricket Club (MCC). Grace was only nominally a doctor like his father (another example of how elastic that designation was in the Victorian era). Controversially – for the era – he earned a fortune from his fame despite retaining, at least officially, his amateur status.[23]

Mr M. J. Druitt was a notable county cricketer for Dorset County Cricket Club and a variety of sporting clubs including Kingston Park and the Blackheath Cricket, Football and Lawn Tennis Club (where Druitt was elected club treasurer and made a company director). Montague was a fast bowler with stamina and sought after by members of several gentlemen's touring teams including Incogniti and Butterflies. Many of these 'wandering' teams included gentlemen with time on their hands and the matches were often social affairs, with the local moneyed gentry hosting an afternoon tea, or dinner and a ball, for the players. Montie had been a member of the Incogniti wandering team during their West Country tour. Playing four matches in a week, the team moved about the county enjoying cricket and social life. These tours were described as 'Bread and cheese for lunch, dinner at six and then a great dance with the ladies'.[24]

In 1885, before the death of his father, Montague was finding success in both his professional and sporting life. His years of dedication to cricket were finally paying off. Any ambitious cricketer of the era like Montague understood that to play for the MCC could be the stepping stone to playing, like W. G. Grace, for England. The first challenge was to impress two influential members of the club who would take the next step and nominate you. In the Butterflies team Montague found two such supporters, Charles Seymour and Vernon Royle. Both were first-class cricketers and Royle had played one test match for England. In 1884, Seymour recommended and Royle seconded Montague's nomination.

It must have been a proud day for Montague and his family when he was selected to play alongside W. G. Grace against Wiltshire at Trowbridge cricket ground on Tuesday 11 August 1885. At the same time it was probably an exciting but nerve-wracking debut for Montague as whenever Grace appeared on a cricket pitch, a large crowd followed.[25] *The Bath Chronicle and Weekly Gazette* reported that 'the weather being again fine there was a large attendance of spectators.'[26] Perhaps overwhelmed by the occasion, Druitt who was never a reliable batsman was bowled out without scoring (in cricket parlance he 'made a duck'). It appears that he was not even given the chance to display his talent for bowling, as W. G. Grace commandeered the ball and took a total of 12 wickets for the match.

Montie Druitt was truly out of his league at this level of cricket. Still, the would-be barrister could boast to his future clients and friends that at least he had *once* played with the most acclaimed gentleman sportsman of the century. However, he probably would have been disappointed with his time playing for MCC. His years of dedication to the game, making contacts of influential people and his consistent success in his various teams, in the end stood for nothing. He played a handful of matches for the club but by 1887, it was appearing less likely that he would be selected regularly to play for the MCC and, by 1888, his chance at a first class cricket career was over. He continued to play for his other clubs but would never play at the top level again.

***

The period during 1887/88 saw Montague's family involved in a schism. A letter written by Montague's cousin, Reverend Charles Druitt in May 1887 from the 'Palace' at Salisbury Cathedral, and recently uncovered by the authors in the West Sussex Records Office, shows this. With their influential father Dr William Druitt, the devoted Anglican, by then deceased for two years, Montague's younger brother Edward did the unthinkable and converted to Catholicism. Reverend Charles Druitt was staying with Montague's family when the truth was revealed to him in confidence. Once he realised the news was common knowledge, he decided to share it. He acted in 1887 as he would in 1888 by confiding distressing news to his mother Isabella Druitt of Strathmore Gardens Kensington. In this letter of May 15 1887, he writes:

> ... Have you heard of Edward's foolish and treacherous conduct? It was a great blow to his mother, (who heard it direct from him last Mon or Tues) that he had been 'received' into the Church of Rome. I was told to keep it a secret; but before I left Wimborne I found that the fact had been common property so that it was a secret no longer! So far as I know the only reason that he alleges to justify his act is that in Singapore the Anglican Mission is less active than the Roman one ... It is a painful subject. I was not surprised when I heard it for Edith had told me the sort of rubbish that Edward had been talking since his return home from the East.[27]

The level of grief, anger and distress this action of Edward's caused his mother cannot be overestimated. It is a fair assumption that it would also have caused Montague disappointment or even anger as he had, at least outwardly, demonstrated his devotion to Conservative principles and the Anglican faith. For Ann Druitt the news was devastating. She would later be described by Dr Gasquet as suffering from 'melancholia with stupor', as being 'obstinate' and 'with an unreasonable refusal to spend money'.[28] As her second son would be described many years later without being named, Ann was constantly on 'the borderline of insanity'. Without her husband, and the medical support he could discreetly provide, upon hearing from her son Edward of his 'treacherous conduct', Ann was pushed too far. A letter dated June 13 1887, written by another of Montie's cousins Gertrude Druitt to her mother Mrs Isabella Druitt, suggests that less than a month after Edward's announcement Ann Druitt was placed in psychiatric care.[29] Ann would be in and out of private asylums for the rest of her life. In the summer of 1888 she attempted suicide and in July was placed in Brook House Asylum at Clapham. Ann Druitt, showing no sign of improvement was released from Brook House, and on the cusp of the autumn of 1888 and the beginning of the Whitechapel murders said to be by an elusive assassin soon to be known as 'Jack the Ripper', Ann was sent, for the benefit of sea air, to Dr Gasquet's asylum at Brighton.

IV

A Call to Rescue the Degraded

London of the early 1880s had become a hotbed of social upheaval. Many people with good intentions had been alerted to the conditions in the East End through newspaper reports, literature or from the pulpit of their local church. A patchwork quilt of social reform movements grew up in the metropolis, often promoting simplistic solutions to very complex problems. While the militant socialists championed worker's rights in rallies of tens of thousands in Trafalgar Square, there were numerous smaller gatherings promoting social purity and moral reform. These groups included The Ladies Association for the Care of Friendless Girls and the Temperance Movement. The former group tasked themselves with the rescue of young women who had turned to prostitution and the latter promoted a total abstinence from alcohol, becoming in time a large and financially powerful movement.[1] The university settlements of Toynbee Hall and Oxford House had also established their presence in the East End, in Whitechapel and Bethnal Green. There they offered lectures, recreation and hot meals to the impoverished residents with the aim of improving them physically, intellectually, and in the case of Oxford House, morally, through Biblical instruction.

The 'long depression' commencing in 1873, had been sharply felt throughout the United Kingdom and caused a slow burn of economic downturn with its consequence of irregular casual work and unemployment. Many artisans in London, who had previously managed to support their families with a regular income from their skilled labour, had been doubly undercut by this circumstance. Numerous dwellings previously inhabited by these workers had been demolished to make way for railways and large warehouses, pushing them further into the impoverished regions of London such as Whitechapel, where they found themselves living side by side with the lowest of the lower orders; the starving and the destitute. In 1887, a Congregational minister for Trinity Church Poplar offered a telling eyewitness account of the effect the downturn had on the workers of his parish:

> I hope you will allow one who has been a minister in the East-end of London for the last seventeen years to bear testimony from personal knowledge to the existence of deep and exceptional distress in our midst. These Trafalgar-square meetings indicate correctly the present condition of things in Poplar at least.
>
> Yesterday I walked through the East India Docks, and the place, instead of being a hive of busy workers, looked like a wilderness. There were acres of water empty of ships. The Isle of Dogs and Blackwall, usually ringing with sounds of work, are silent as cemeteries.
>
> It is distressing to walk through the yards. Samuda's where I am informed, between 2,000 and 3,000 artisans have been employed, does not give work today to 20 men. The Blackwall yard whose prosperity has been the prosperity of Poplar is empty. Yarrow's yard I am informed is about to be closed. During the last seventeen years I have known Poplar intimately, but no winter of these years has approached in distress the pressure of today. If frost comes, our sufferings will be terrible.[2]

George Robert Sims was one of several prominent writers who with their trenchant exposés alerted the citizens of London to the plight of the poor. Sims wrote daily newspaper columns as well as a series of articles published for *The Pictorial World* in 1881. Two years later a compilation of these pieces would become a widely circulated book titled, *How the Poor Live and Horrible London*. Sims was a man who was a full participant in life and he believed his experience had taught him that peoples' circumstances were determined mostly by luck, or the lack of it. Born into an upper-middle-class family, Sims enjoyed a good education firstly in Eastbourne and then at Hanwell Military College and the University of Bonn. His political beliefs, championing the rights of the worker, were strongly influenced by his Chartist grandfather John Dinmore Stevenson and by his mother Louisa, who was President of the Women's Protective and Provident League (one of the first trade unions for women). His father, also named George Sims, was a policeman and later a successful businessman. The father's former profession inspired in the son a life-long fascination with crime and mysteries.[3]

George R. Sims spent his early working years in his father's business and, bored with the monotony, he began to write insightful, witty theatre reviews on the side. This led to his employment as a journalist for the comic paper *Fun*. His employer Harry Sampson soon founded *The Referee* for which Sims, from 1874 and right up until his last breath in 1922, wrote a regular social commentary column called 'Mustard and Cress'. He wrote under the Shakespearean-inspired pseudonym Dagonet, even long after it was an open secret he was the author. Dagonet/Sims pushed and prodded his fellow Englishmen with bombastic observations that often amused – and just as often were not hostage, as its author conceded, to exacting factual accuracy.[4] Intellectuals were never won over by Sims and they derided his column as 'Custard and Mess'. It is in these *Referee* pieces, nonetheless, that Sims would both reveal and conceal the truth about the Thames suicide Montague J. Druitt, albeit never named, as being 'Jack the Ripper'. He also exploited the details of the murderer's saga as the genesis of several short stories – *see* chapters XII and XVII.

George Sims led a remarkable life. He married three times and was widowed twice. None of the unions produced any children though he was reportedly a doting uncle. A prolific novelist, poet and playwright, his hit play *The Lights of London* – a thriller about an innocent man falsely accused of murder – was a sensation and made his name in London's West End. (The play was twice adapted for silent film, once in 1914 and then again in 1923). He was a seasoned traveller and travel writer, and an early crusader for the rights of animals. Though an inveterate gambler, he became an extremely wealthy man and was noted for his generosity and practical philanthropy.[5]

Sims was also one of the leaders of the National Sunday League and its campaign for the opening of art galleries and museums on Sundays, which finally saw success in 1896. A lover of boxing, cricket and horse racing, he was a regular at the National Sporting Club – often accompanied by two of his closest friends: Sir Melville Leslie Macnaghten, later Head of CID at Scotland Yard, and Colonel Sir Vivian Dering Majendie. With much affection, Macnaghten called Sims 'Tatcho' because the celebrity writer endorsed various commercial products for a fee. The most famous product tie-in was a bottled lotion, the aforementioned 'Tatcho', that supposedly made a lady's hair more luxuriant but whose real selling point was that it claimed to cure, or at least significantly arrest, the ravages of baldness in men. With his squat rotund frame, naval beard, and hooded eyelids, Sims bore a striking resemblance to Albert Edward (Bertie) the Prince of Wales. He was regularly mistaken for Victoria's affable, if controversial heir (later to become Edward VII) as described in *The Era* of July 9 1888:

> Sometimes Mr Sims is taken for the Prince of Wales. That is not another of Mr Sims' jokes but an actual fact. The facial resemblance between the Heir Apparent and Dagonet is something remarkable, and it is possible that in some of the photographers' shops in London, when the portraits of the Prince of Wales run out, they sell Dagonet's counterfeit presentment, and the customers never know the difference. Mr Sims had not been in Birmingham half an hour before the rumour got abroad that his Royal highness had run down to the Hardware Village to get a relief from the Jubilee.

Characteristically Sims became the Vice President of the Eccentric Club. The generous and good humoured members of this association were also regular contributors to one of Sims' other great causes, *The Referee*'s Children's Free Breakfast and Dinner Fund, a charity he had founded in 1880 to provide nourishment for the poor children of London. It is testament to Sims' drive and genius for publicity that this became the largest charity of its type.[6]

George R. Sims was also a member of the Garrick Club (a gentleman's club in London with a membership of writers and actors, and aficionados of the theatre world). So was his close friend Macnaghten whom he affectionately called 'Mac', as did most of the police chief's friends and colleagues.[7]

As an amateur criminologist who had his own crime museum, Sims was highly respected enough to also be invited, again with his friend Macnaghten, to join Arthur Conan Doyle's Crime Club. Upon his death, George R. Sims, among many testimonials and reverential obituaries about the passing of a giant of British culture, was described by one newspaper as 'a man of notable character and wide human sympathies, who attained to a position in the popular esteem which no other writer since Dickens has ever quite filled.'[8]

The most famous and lasting of Sims' poems is *In the Workhouse – Christmas Day*, which was first published in *The Referee* in 1877. Its unqualified condemnation of the conditions endured by poor children set the tone for his willingness to confront the 'better classes' with the brutal truth about the poverty on their doorsteps. What would become a standard for school children to recite was initially greeted with disdain by the 'better classes' when it was first published. Sims noted in his autobiography that it was 'for a time vigorously denounced as a mischievous attempt to set the paupers against their betters.'[9] The workhouse was a regimented and cruel means of State-funded relief for the poor. With no other means of survival, families would enter the workhouse and as the name suggests, work long hours for their meagre rations and State-issued clothing. The government and the majority of the population baulked at giving handouts to the poor, many believing that these people had brought their unfavourable circumstances upon themselves. The concept of this institution was that better habits and a work ethic would be instilled in the residents enabling them to leave the establishment and fend for themselves.

In 1881, George R. Sims joined Arthur Moss, a local School Board officer, and the artist Frederick Barnard to walk the streets of Whitechapel and the impoverished East End to enlighten his readers as to what 'lies at our own doorstep ... a dark continent that is within easy walking distance of the General Post Office'. A place where '...it is dangerous to breathe for some hours at a stretch, an atmosphere charged with infection and poisoned with indescribable effluvia.'[10] Sims is scathing about the inaction of politicians in addressing the issue of home-grown poverty and their willingness to take on causes abroad at the expense of their own citizens:

It is to increased wealth and to increased civilization that we owe the wide gulf which today separates well-to-do citizens from the masses. It is the increased wealth of this mighty city which has driven the poor back inch by inch, until we find them today herding together, packed like herrings in a barrel, neglected and despised and left to endure wrongs and hardships which if they were related of a far off savage tribe would cause Exeter Hall to shudder till its bricks fell down. It is the increased civilization of this marvellous age which has made life a victory only for the strong, the gifted, and the specially blest, and left the weak, the poor, and the ignorant to work out in their proper persons the theory of the survival of the fittest to its bitter end.

Sims and his party entered a lodging house and described the scene before them:

Men, women and children are lolling about, though it is mid-day, apparently with nothing to do but make themselves comfortable. The company is not a pleasant one. Many of the men and women and boys are thieves. Almost every form of disease, almost every kind of deformity, seems crowded into this Chamber of Horrors... Among all the cruelties practised on the poor in the name of Metropolitan improvements this one deserves mentioning—that the labourer earning a precarious livelihood with his wife and his children have been driven at last to accept the shelter of a thieves' kitchen and to be thankful for it... Drink is the curse of these communities; but how is it to be wondered at?

The gin-palaces flourish in the slums, and fortunes are made out of men and women who seldom know where tomorrow's meal is coming from... Drink is the sustenance to these people; drink gives them the Dutch courage necessary to go on living; drink dulls their senses and reduces them to the level of the brutes they must be to live in such sties... A copper or two ... will buy enough vitriol-madness to send a woman home so besotted that the wretchedness, the anguish, the degradation that await her there have lost their grip...

I have often wondered that the advocates of temperance, with the immense resources of wealth and organisation they command, have not given more attention to the overcrowding and the unsanitary condition of the dwellings of the poor, as one of the great causes of the abuse of stimulants... It is not only that crime and vice and disorder flourish luxuriantly in these colonies, through the dirt and discomfort bred of intemperance of the inhabitants, but the effect upon the children is terrible. The offspring of drunken fathers and mothers inherit not only a tendency to vice, but they come into the world physically and mentally unfit to conquer in life's battle. The wretched, stunted, misshapen child-object one comes upon in these localities is the most painful part of our explorers experience... The drink dulls every sense of shame, takes the sharp edge from sorrow, and leaves the drinker for a while in a fools' paradise.[11]

A report from a local health officer is quoted to illustrate the full horror of the situation.

PROLONGED RETENTION OF A DEAD BODY IN A ROOM OCCUPIED BY A FAMILY

Mr Wrack reports that, upon visiting No.28 Church Street, Spitalfields, on the 5th December last, he found in the second floor front room the dead body of a child which had died of scarlet fever on 1st of the month. The body was not coffined, and it lay exposed on a table in one corner of the room.

The room was occupied as a living and sleeping room for five persons, viz, the grandfather and grandmother of the child, who were engaged at tailors' work. The child was playing on the floor. The room was about fourteen feet square and eight feet high, thus affording only 260 cubic feet of space to each person. The smell on entering the room was most sickening. Upon remonstrating with the people for keeping the body so long unburied, and especially for not having it coffined, they replied that they were waiting to raise the means for burying it; and, being Irish, said that it was not their custom to coffin their dead until the day of the funeral. The body was not buried until the 9th of December, and then it had to be buried by the parish authorities.

Sims was beside himself with anger at the inaction of those in power:

... It is necessary a great many things were done. It is necessary, above all, that the direct attention of the State should be given to the whole question, but the Home Secretary says there is 'no time 'to attend to such matters.

Sims issued a warning to the better classes by bringing the issue closer to home. Pointing out that the tailoring being performed in the room with the deceased body of a young scarlet fever victim in it may well be on a garment that would be carried 'with the germs of disease in it to the homes of well to do and prosperous people – a class which too frequently objects to be worried with revelations of the miseries of the masses.'

An excerpt from *Horrible London* sets the scene for us of what a walk through the streets of Whitechapel on a Saturday night in 1888 may have been like:

Between twelve and one it is a long procession of drunken men and women, and the most drunken seem to be those whose outward appearance betokens the most abject poverty. Turn out of the main thoroughfare and into the dimly lighted back streets, and you come upon scene after scene to the grim, grotesque horror of which only the pencil of a Doré could do justice. Women, with hideous, distorted faces are rolling from side to side, shrieking aloud snatches of popular songs, plentifully interlarded with the vilest expressions. Men as drunk as themselves meet them; there is a short interchange of ribald jests and foul oaths, then a quarrel and a shower of blows. Down from one dark court rings a cry of murder, and a woman, her face hideously gashed, makes across the narrow road, pursued by a howling madman. It is only a drunken husband having a row with his wife.

As Sims anticipated in a city beset with poverty, unemployment and neglect, its victims would soon 'start a crusade of their own to demonstrate in Trafalgar Square, and to hold meetings in Hyde Park'. From 1886, protests by the unemployed and destitute had become a regular occurrence; however, by 1887 the situation reached a peak. The poor and homeless had joined the unemployed in Trafalgar Square. Traditionally a gathering place for Londoners for all sorts of recreation or rally, the public square sat centrally between the better classes of the West and the poverty of the East. This time, however, the better off of the city had been dismayed to see their beautiful fountain and monuments festooned with washing, the paving littered by all sorts of unmentionable debris, human and otherwise. The lower classes sat slumped between the feet of the mighty lions, iconic representations of England's pride at the defeat of Napoleon at the Battle of Trafalgar in 1805 (Lord Horatio Nelson luckily sat high upon his column and was untouched by the great unwashed). Speeches were made by prominent writers such as George Bernard Shaw, and progressive churchmen, while socialists and reformers mingled among the masses.

The Lord Mayor's Day of November 1887 was gearing up for an uprising. The poor although grateful for one day's free lunch, were cynical at the token effort and at the pomp and ceremony that the day entailed. General Charles Warren banned public gatherings in Trafalgar Square before Sunday 13 November. This decision resulted in an uprising of a 70,000 to 100,000 strong crowd defiantly marching from all directions towards the square. The 4,000 police were outnumbered and hit back brutally at the crowds. Many protestors were injured with more than 150 taken to hospital. 'Bloody Sunday' would not be forgotten in London as it served as a warning that there was a social time bomb ticking in the very heart of their town.[12]

* * *

In April 1886 a meeting was held in King's Bench Walk in London where, among other lawyers, Montague Druitt had his chambers. Convened by Conservative politician Mr J. G. Talbot, he called together barristers from the Inner Temple – particularly the Oxonians among the group such as Montie – and urged them to join the mission at Oxford House, Bethnal Green. In effect it was a recruitment drive. Oxford House had opened in 1884 and the number of participants in the various clubs and sports that the establishment offered had grown so rapidly that more help was needed.[13] It was opened by a group from

Keble College, Oxford, who had felt that Toynbee Hall (which had also opened in 1884) in Whitechapel, founded by Reverend Samuel Barnett and his wife Henrietta as a non-sectarian institution, was not religious enough. As reported in *The Pall Mall Gazette* of 17 April 1886, the Hon. J. G. Adderley from Oxford House spoke of the need for these men to help in 'men's and boy's clubs, Sunday schools and district visiting, entertainments, lectures and classes, cricket and football clubs, serving on committees, charity organisation, housing of the poor, society for relief of distress'.

Adderley had previously stated that in regards to Oxford House, the 'primary object was to provide a place where Oxford men could go down and live among the poor and help them'.[14] It may be safe to say that the advocates for Oxford House were far more zealous than those of Toynbee Hall. While offering similar programmes to help the poor, including offering shelter within their premises, Oxford House also doled out their charity with a dollop of doctrinal 'political correctness'. The Bishop of London in 1888 explained to Oxonians, whom he was urging to join the cause, that the low-living people of the East End would recognise the sacrifice the Oxford men were making by mingling with them in their attempt at rescuing their bodies and souls, as reported in the *Oxford Journal* of May 19 1888:

> Self-sacrifice, the very foundation of all true honour, that one thing which all men alike even the wickedest and the basest, could not help respecting; the one thing before which human nature was sure to bow. It was for such sacrifice that they now called, begging those who had the strength who had the power who had the means, to do a work which could by only done by such men.
>
> If they indeed would undertake it there was before them a noble thing to do the noblest of all possible purposes to give themselves to: There was before them the *rescuing of thousands from moral degradation* by simply the contact of their own lives with theirs, to live amongst them because they cared for them; not to pander to any of their low tastes, not to lower themselves in any degree to their level. (Our italics)

By the time the Oxford House meeting at King's Bench Walk was held to recruit the learned Old Boys of Oxford to practice some self-sacrifice and help the poor and the fallen of the East End, Montague John Druitt was entrenched as a practicing barrister in his chambers at 9 King's Bench Walk. It has always been a curious factor in the description of 'Jack the Ripper' by a 'north country vicar' in 1899 (*see* Chapter XVIII) the maniac in his lucid state was part of some organised, reform movement committed to 'rescuing' the poor women of the East End – who later became his victims. But for which charity did Montague work?

We believe Montague had an involvement with Oxford House, whose advocates had ended up proselytising to help the poor of the East End. It is significant that the young barrister had a friend who had travelled a parallel path. Herbert Ross Webbe had attended Winchester College with Montie; and also had been an accomplished college cricketer, later playing for Oxford and the MCC. They both attended New College, Oxford, and Webbe also became a barrister at Lincoln's Inn. Montie and H. R., as he was known, worked cheek by jowl for several years when they established the Old Wykehamists Cricket team at their old school.

Montie also played cricket with H. R.'s brother, Alexander J. Webbe, who was a committee member and captain of the MCC. Herbert Webbe was already active in the Oxford House settlement and teaching in one of the St John's church schools on Sundays. Sadly and surprisingly, Herbert dropped dead from heart failure while conducting such a Sunday school class just one month after the aforementioned meeting at King's Bench Walk in 1886. It must have been a shock for Montie and his cohort of Wykehamist friends to lose one of their own so unexpectedly. By October of 1886, a fund had been set up to raise money for a memorial to the late H. R.'s memory. The honorary secretary of the fund was yet another of Montie and H. R.'s mutual friends on the Old Wykehamist committee, Mr T. R. Toynbee. The idea of the fund was to raise enough money to erect a tablet dedicated to him at both Winchester and Oxford, with the remaining funds directed to Oxford House at Bethnal Green. All of these tributes were achieved by 1888, with the Webbe Institute opening in Oxford House later that year.

Montie Druitt contributed to the fundraising of this memorial by organising a charity cricket match in Blackheath, one which was firmly linked with Oxford House. H. R. Webbe having died teaching at a St John's 'National School' (National Schools were part of the Anglican National Society for Promoting the Education of the Poor), Montie held a fundraiser for the St John's National Schools so this outreach could continue. He was able to gather an impressive list of players; one team was made up of Anglican clergy and the other was eleven MCC members, including Lord Throwley. Montie, with his own first class cricket career with the MCC by this time on the wane, was nonetheless able to gather a group of listed players, who were like him – not the first choice for selection for the MCC teams that weekend – and pit them against the Anglican clerics.[15]

As Montague was close to and naturally influenced by his uncle Dr Robert Druitt – an outspoken commentator on all things morally, socially and scientifically wrong with life in the East End – he would have formed strong opinions about the problems within the district. Likewise, he would have been familiar with the frustrations of those, the hardliners like his uncle and the more charitable such as Oxford House, Toynbee Hall and his own brother-in-law the Reverend William Hough who ran the Corpus Christi Cambridge Mission on the other side of the river on Old Kent Road, who had all tried with good intentions to remedy these wrongs. A walk around the streets of the East End was practically a rite of passage for Oxonians and similarly the Cantabs, who were graduates of Cambridge. Their college elders showed great insight by urging these privileged young men to witness first hand 'how the other half live'. What they saw was shocking as well as dangerous. The only friendly face was that of the desperate prostitute offering cheap, unwashed sex to the well-bred young men. Walking the streets of the East End, Montie must have been dismayed and disgusted that for all of his uncle's dedication and well-informed advice over so many years, he could not find evidence that even one of his recommendations had sincerely been acted upon. The area had neglected or non-existent sewers, the stench of polluted air mixed with that of unwashed humans, there was public drunkenness at all hours, street brawls and flagrant public displays of prostitution, dirty crowded dwellings and sickly neglected children.

As an Oxonian and 'doing his bit' for Oxford House, a series of current and cross-currents must have buffeted Montague's sick yet high-functioning mind. On the one hand he harboured homicidal urges towards so-called 'fallen women'. On the other hand, he could also see that establishment polices, whether Tory or Liberal, were barely making a dent in the degraded lives of the men, women and children of Whitechapel. We think Montague Druitt, who lived in an era of bomb-throwing militants – unless disarmed in time by Colonel Majendie and his team – absorbed the effect of nameless violence and the socialistic calls for radical action to alleviate mass suffering. It would just take an example, an inspiration or a trigger that would cause his depraved yet egocentric mind to justify the slaughter of alcoholic, homeless women who had never done him the slightest harm. Montie needed a mission.

V

'Rip' Murders not by
'The Ripper'

It is curious that before the murder of the first recognised victim of the madman who would come to be known as 'Jack the Ripper' there were not one but two previous such crimes in the Whitechapel/Spitalfields slum. These were not just ordinary homicides, as they involved poor women driven into prostitution who were violently attacked very much as were the subsequent tragic figures. The focus of many writers on this topic is the five victims ascribed to a single killer, whereas the murders before and after are given relatively short shrift. The two or three murders after the final one of the five are often seen as having been committed by imitators or copycats – an opinion with which we concur.

But what about the pair of atrocities committed *before* the infamous five? By the same logic does that not make 'Jack the Ripper' a copycat too? Did Druitt need somebody else to show the way towards his own atrocities? Despite his busy life of work and play, it is hard to believe that Druitt did not read newspapers. For example, the *East London Advertiser* of 14 April 1888 contained a report with a headline that could have been enticing for Montague's 'secret self':

BARBAROUSLY MURDERED

On Saturday the East Middlesex coroner held an inquiry at the London Hospital, Whitechapel, on the body of Emma Elizabeth Smith, aged 45, a widow, who was brutally assaulted when returning home along the Whitechapel-road on Bank Holiday night. Mary Russell, the deputy of a common lodging-house at which the deceased had been a lodger for some months, said that on Bank Holiday, the deceased left the house in the evening, apparently in good health. She returned between 4 and 5 o'clock the next morning, and she had been shockingly treated by some men. Her face was bleeding, and she said that she was also injured about the lower part of the body.

The deceased had often come home with black eyes that men had given her. – Mr George Haslip, house surgeon, deposed that the deceased was admitted suffering from severe injuries, which he thought had been caused by some blunt instrument. She had been drinking, but was not intoxicated. She had a ruptured perineum of very recent date, and also some bruises on her head. Her right ear was torn and bleeding. She told a witness that at 1:30 that morning she was going by Whitechapel Church when she saw some men coming, and she crossed the road to get out of their way, but they followed her. They assaulted her and robbed her of all the money she had.

She could not describe the men, except that one looked a youth of 19. After her admission she gradually sank, and died two days later. The deceased stated that she had not seen any of her friends for 10 years. – The Coroner said from the medical evidence it was clear that the woman had been barbarously murdered. Such a dastardly assault he had never heard of, and it was impossible to imagine a more brutal case. The jury returned a verdict of wilful murder against some person unknown.

By her own dying testimony in the hospital, Emma Smith had almost certainly been the victim of a 'High Rip' gang or some such organised band of marauders who were targeting prostitutes for rape, robbery and assault. In Emma's case these sadistic men brutalised her so mercilessly that she could not be saved. This might have been seen as an anomaly, this sudden positive press coverage of a 'fallen woman' had it not been consolidated, even escalated, by another, unconnected homicide. In the early morning hours of 7 August 1888, coincidentally another Bank Holiday, Martha Tabram (a.k.a. Turner) was last seen carousing with a couple of soldiers. Her horrifically mutilated corpse was next stumbled upon on the first floor of George Yard Buildings.

Druitt could have read all about the crime and subsequent investigations, for example, in *The Pall Mall Gazette* of 24 August 1888:

THE SHOCKING MURDER IN THE EAST END

Mr George Collier, coroner, resumed his inquiry yesterday, at the Working Lads' Institute, into the circumstances attending the death of a woman, supposed to be Martha Turner, aged thirty five, a hawker, lately living off Commercial road, E., who was discovered early on the morning of Tuesday, the 7th inst., lying dead on the first floor landing of some model dwellings known as George yard buildings, Commercial street, Spitalfields. The woman when found presented a shocking appearance, her body being covered with stab wounds to the number of thirty nine, some of which had been done with a bayonet.

How the body came to be there is a mystery which the police as yet have not solved. It is a singular coincidence that the murder was committed during Bank Holiday night, and is almost identical with another murder which was perpetrated near the same spot on the night of the previous Bank Holiday. The victims were both what are called 'unfortunates', and their murderers have up till now evaded capture. One witness examined yesterday was another woman of the same class, who seems to have been the last to see the deceased alive, and then she was with a soldier.

The coroner, in summing up, said that the crime was one of the most brutal that had occurred for some years. *For a poor defenceless woman to be outraged and stabbed in such a manner was almost beyond belief. They could only come to one conclusion, and that was that the deceased was brutally and cruelly murdered.* The police would endeavour to bring home the crime to the guilty party. The jury returned a verdict of wilful murder *against some person or persons unknown.* (Our Italics)

The Times of 10 August 1888 published shocking medical testimony that could have aroused those dark urges in the young barrister as he read the account on a train, or at his desk in his chambers, or before changing into his white uniform for a cricket match:

[Martha Tabram] had 39 stabs on the body. She had been dead some three hours. Her age was about 36, and the body was very well nourished. Witness had since made a post-mortem examination of the body. The left lung was penetrated in five places, and the right lung was penetrated in two places. The heart, which was rather fatty, was penetrated in one place, and that would be sufficient to cause death. The liver was healthy, but was penetrated in five places, the spleen was penetrated in two places, and the stomach, which was perfectly healthy, was penetrated in six places. The witness did not think all the wounds were inflicted with the same instrument. The wounds generally might have been inflicted by a knife, but such an instrument could not have inflicted one of the wounds, which went through the chest-bone. His opinion was that one of the wounds was inflicted by some kind of dagger, and that all of them were caused during life.

Again the treatment of the victim by the press had been sympathetic and the depiction of her blighted life before her murder perhaps by drunken soldiers as a social disgrace. These accounts inspired condemnations of the poverty that had led Martha to her eventual death.

In his memoirs, the police chief Sir Melville Macnaghten, who will loom large in this narrative as the sleuth who solved five of the dozen Whitechapel Murders, mentions these two earlier murders. Yet for all his bracing modernity, when it came to the anonymity and sexual drives of serial killers he did not consider their implications. We argue that Montague Druitt must have been influenced by these well-publicised murders:

> The attention of Londoners was first called to the horrors of life (and death) in the East End by the murder of one Emma Smith, who was found horribly outraged in Osborne Street in the early morning of 3rd April 1888. She died in the London Hospital, and there is no doubt that her death was caused by some young hooligans who escaped arrest. On 7th August the body of Martha Tabram was discovered lying on the stairs of a house in George Yard. Her death was due to a number of wounds in the chest and abdomen, and it was alleged that a bayonet had been the weapon used upon her. The evening before she had been seen in the company of two soldiers and a female friend. Her throat as not cut, and nothing in the shape of the mutilation was attempted. I think I am right in saying that the soldiers were detained, but that available witnesses failed to identify them.[1]

Despite Sir Melville's intimate knowledge of the true solution to five of the dozen or so Whitechapel Murders here he shows a total lack of nous regarding these earlier, unconnected slayings. If the same maniac did not commit one or both of these crimes therefore he must be imitating or have been inspired by them. And since he did not live in the vicinity, the *next* murderer must have had another agenda in operation that was narrowly focused on the East End – a motive apart from a twisted erotic need to kill and defile 'fallen women'.

Unless Druitt had tried to kill before these two murders and found the experience unsuccessful, ironically because he was scared, then the Smith and Tabram murders might have been a blueprint for him on how to do it and not get caught. Interestingly, there is recorded an assault on a woman in early 1888 who was almost certainly a prostitute that, at least circumstantially, points to Druitt's first, fumbling effort to kill. On 28 March 1888, just past midnight, a man later described to the police as 'aged *about 30*, height five foot six inches; *face sunburnt*, with *fair moustache*; dressed in dark coat, light trousers, and wideawake hat' (our italics) knocked on the door of 19 Maidment Street, just south of the Bow Road, Mile End. The locale was cohabited by a woman who would later, for propriety's sake, hide behind the fig leaf that she was a 'seamstress'; the ever-ready cliché cover for a Victorian 'unfortunate'.[2]

The victim's name was Ada Wilson. Her version of events was that she went into her parlour after hearing somebody at her front door and finding, to her shock, a complete stranger standing there. This unknown man immediately produced a clasp knife and demanded money – or she would forfeit her life. Bravely she refused, and the cad stabbed her twice and deeply in the area of her throat. Ada, nonetheless, could still scream and did so, panicking her assailant who fled empty-handed.

Gushing blood but still conscious, Ada was found by two women who ran and fetched a pair of constables. They took down what they must have assumed was the wounded woman's dying declaration, before she was rushed off to hospital. Miraculously Ada Wilson survived. As Ada recovered, however, she would find her underground life exposed by her nosy, judgmental neighbour, a Miss Rose Bierman, who lived upstairs with her mother. As reported in *The Eastern Post and City Chronicle* of 31 March 1888, Rose said that Ada was on notice to quit the lodgings and although she liked to describe herself as married, the neighbour had never, she said, seen any husband. With passive-aggressive malice Miss Bierman revealed that Ada had many male visitors, and, 'Last evening [Mrs Wilson] came into the house accompanied by a male companion, but whether he was her husband or not, I could not say.' That same night Miss Bierman heard 'the most terrible screams' and said she saw a 'partially dressed' Ada collapsing in the parlour. She was screaming for somebody to stop her gentleman caller from fleeing as he had just cut her throat. As the victim fainted and the assailant bolted out the door Rose Bierman described him as 'a young, fair man' who exited as if he was 'accustomed' to opening and closing this particular latch.

If Montague Druitt was the man who tried to kill Ada Wilson, did he want to again feel power over a so-called harlot but this time to make her physically suffer? Was he, as suggested by the snitch of a neighbour, a regular gentleman caller of Ada's; a toff client who liked his coitus rough and, perhaps, lost control of his dark urges during a violent tryst? Did witnessing the distress he had caused Elizabeth Young, a part-time prostitute in Poole whose activities he had used to cast doubt on whether her respectable husband could be the one guilty of murdering a baby, awaken some kind of dormant and deviant sexual desire in the young barrister; a desire to fatally harm 'fallen woman' which had its first fumbling expression in this assault on Ada Wilson?

In his 1914 memoirs this is how Sir Melville Macnaghten expounds on 'sexual mania', a redundant Victorianism for a disturbed person who is erotically fulfilled by acts of ultra-violence, or by watching such acts:

> Students of history, however, are aware that an excessive indulgence in vice leads, in certain cases, to a craving for blood. Nero was probably a sexual maniac. Many Eastern potentates in all ages, who loved to see slaves slaughtered or wild beats tearing each other to pieces, have been similarly affected.

The police chief also displays a notably modern and prescient grasp regarding a psychological paradox – homicidal psychopaths who walk among us can assume, all too easily, a persuasive mask of mundane normality:

> The disease is not as rare as many people imagine. As you walk in the London streets you may, and do, not infrequently jostle against a potential murderer of the so-called Jack the Ripper type. The subject is not a pleasant one, but to those who study the depths of human nature it is intensely interesting.[3]

What the upper-class Macnaghten missed, however, was that Druitt did not have to return to the vile slum of Whitechapel-Spitalfields ever again to satisfy his 'sexual mania'. He could savage poor women in Hyde Park, or Blackheath where he lodged, or just about anywhere in London. Instead Montie had discovered his self-justifying mission. This was to force the 'better classes' that had produced him and which he secretly despised, to be confronted by the poverty of the slums. Everybody knew they were responsible and they had to do something about it. He wanted the cosy elite to feel not only the dripping viscera, but that his victims' lives had already been robbed from them by the callous and criminal neglect of those with plenty.

Something else needs to be mentioned at this point. Culturally speaking, the groundwork had been laid for the possibility of a gentleman maniac by a best-selling novella of two years before: *The Strange Case of Dr Jekyll and Mr Hyde* by the Scottish author of adventures and thrillers, Robert Louis Stevenson. It has a diabolical twist to its ending that could work only once. Close friends of the scientist, Henry Jekyll, spend most of the plot anxious about their middle-aged, morally upright pal associating with a low-life named Mr Edward Hyde (who is younger, smaller and, somehow hard to define, innately repulsive). Is he being blackmailed by Hyde, they fear? The inappropriate crony becomes a murderer and, appallingly, is found a cowardly suicide in the missing doctor's lab. Has Jekyll been done away with too by this monster? It can only be imagined the collective dropping of jaws around the entire country when the truth was finally revealed: Jekyll and Hyde are the same person; they have been split by the scientist inventing a potion to carve off his evil side as a completely independent alter ego. After a time, Jekyll tries to go 'cold turkey' but it is too late: he begins transforming into Hyde without administering the drug.

Victorians did not realise what genre they were reading – what seemed to be some sort of thriller involving the collision of high society with the criminal underclass turned out to be a science fiction story, or romance as it was called then. *The Times* hailed Stevenson as a genius. The book was an enormous success everywhere it was published. Overnight the titular characters' names became clichés for a person with a dual personality. Yet from the start stage versions of the novel dispensed with much of the plot, particularly the mystery of how Jekyll and Hyde are intertwined, because it was assumed that it was hopelessly redundant: the audience already knew. Dr Jekyll was thus moved to be the protagonist *and* antagonist of the tale and provided with a fiancée-in-peril – an awkward structure that has bedevilled plays, movies and television adaptations ever since (as has been the crudity of depicting Hyde as like something that has escaped from a zoo).

During the 'Ripper' murders of late 1888, a version of *Jekyll and Hyde* was doing 'boffo box office' at the Lyceum Theatre. It starred the actor-manager Henry Mansfield, a popular ham, and his transformation scene, accomplished with lighting effects, garish make-up and much writing was, by universal consensus, the show's high point. As the real murders began, letter writers to newspapers were convinced that the East End assassin was some kind of Jekyll-and-Hyde – a few even accused the production of inspiring such brutal crimes.

The analogy with Druitt only goes so far, however, as the latter's handsome face never changed. His family seemed to have believed he suffered from an epileptic illness that meant he could barely recall his crimes. Perhaps the more accurate literary allusion is *The Portrait of Dorian Gray* by Oscar Wilde; the titular character remains angelic of face and bearing while his picture congeals and decays in the upstairs attic. We argue that another novel about a gentleman with a dual identity was created in order to grant Montie Druitt a measure of literary immortality in the form of Marie Belloc Lowndes' 1913 *The Lodger* (*see* Appendix 1).

VI

From Tory to Terrorist

Montie Druitt was one of hundreds of other donors who had contributed to the establishment of the People's Palace on Mile End Road. A large recreational area, offering both culture and amusement to the folk of the East End, had been sadly lacking. Oxford House needed more space and opening this new facility meant that in 1888 it could stage, among other cultural events, an art show. The previous year had seen the opening of the Palace to much fanfare. Queen Victoria had agreed to leave her 'tight-drawn bonds of seclusion' and join her East End subjects in celebration of their newfound refuge, offering them a more wholesome brand of entertainment than could normally to be found on the streets or in public drinking houses of Whitechapel.[1]

The men of Oxford House welcomed an easy evening of fellowship now and then, and a walk around an art exhibition was more attuned to their tastes than some of the other less savoury rescue work they were expected to do. It was an open secret that these men often drew the short straw compared to those volunteering for their 'friendly rival' Toynbee Hall; Barnet's volunteers had an easier charter to follow as the push to moral repair through religiosity was not their priority. If, as we believe, Montie Druitt was, with his old Oxonian friends, a contributor to the work of Oxford House he would have fully experienced the foul sights, sounds and smells of what was night time in the East End. As the *Northern Whig* newspaper put it on 6 December 1888: 'If you wish to see the most intelligent and cultured phase of East London life, you should ask to spend an evening at Toynbee Hall. If you would rather become acquainted with a rougher and less polished element, the Oxford House men will readily introduce you to it.'

It was the last Thursday evening of August and although cold, it was fine enough for the likes of Montague Druitt to venture out on foot to the People's Palace in the East End and spend some time viewing their latest Oxford House-sponsored 'picture exhibition'. From there, his walk into the heart of Whitechapel would have been easy but not leisurely. Upper-class gentlemen like Montie understood that the key to survival in this area was to dress like a proletarian, to be inconspicuous and, if the need arose, to run very fast.

Mary Ann Nichols, nicknamed 'Polly' by her family, was exactly the sort of person the good folk of Oxford House and the volunteers from any of the multitude of other moral reform leagues was trying to help. It was only days since her birthday and at 43, she found herself shabbily clothed, with three teeth missing, an alcoholic, and worn out and destitute. But like many of the women who of necessity walked the streets for day-to-day survival, she had once led a respectable life. At St Bride's Church in Fleet Street, she had, at the age of 18, married a machinist, William Nichols. They had remained married for twenty years. In the opinion of her father Edward Walker, her downfall began when she was pregnant with her fifth child. Her neighbour Rosetta Walls nursed Polly through her late pregnancy and the birth of a son and helped to look after the large brood of children. Polly's father believed that William, during this time, launched into an affair with Rosetta and this caused his daughter to leave the family home. However, William Nichols' version of events was different. He was adamant that his estranged wife had become, for no reason, a quarrelsome drunk. She had left him 'four or five times if not six' and abandoned her five children, the youngest only 16 months old. He had not taken up with Mrs Walls for at least two years after Polly had left him, he said. However, Mr Walker believed that while Rosetta was caring for the children, she had also offered respite to William while Polly was still living in the matrimonial home.[2] Which ever way it transpired, Polly found herself alternating between the workhouse and the street.

She had held a position as a domestic servant with Samuel and Sarah Cowdry in Rose Hill Road, Wandsworth, in May of 1888. Perhaps the confines of strict Methodist family life were too much for her, for after two months she absconded, taking with her clothing valued at

£3 10s, which she would no doubt have promptly pawned for cash. Polly's father conceded that his daughter had become a habitual drunk and that he had taken on the care of his oldest grandson in his own home. Rosetta became mother to the other children. For a woman of her time, Polly had not only evaded the regular sweeps of debilitating or deadly disease such as typhus, scarlet fever and cholera, a scourge which cut through the East End with relentless regularity, she had also survived five home births. Sadly, however, whatever the challenges of her former life, she would not survive the wrath of a fit and agile young barrister whose upper-class existence thus far had been as distantly removed as it possibly could from Polly Nichol's fall into a 'low life'.[3]

Montague Druitt, like Polly Nichols had observed his birthday in August. He was now 31 and if his father had lived to see his son launch into his 32nd year, his hope that 'his profession may be a success' would have been well realised. All outward appearances supported the view that now he was into his thirties, Montie was at last well on his way towards a bright future. This appearance, however, was false. Montague John Druitt was undergoing all kinds of inner turmoil. His mother was mad, his brother Edward had spurned the family religion, and his own first-class cricket career was defunct. His name would only appear in the best papers, on the MCC list, as one who had played less than three games in that year – hardly worth a mention. In the early hours of 31 August 1888, the dark side of his personality came to the fore.

The Buck's Row Slaughterhouse was the very type of establishment that Dr Robert Druitt had rallied against during his time as a President of the Medical Officers of Health. The late physician had been adamant that any application for slaughterhouse licences located either underground or within the vicinity of public dwellings should be flatly refused – on the grounds that the health of the public is put in peril when such establishments exist close to where people live. Dr Druitt had whooped and hollered about the likes of Barber's Horse Slaughterhouse in 1857, and here it was, over thirty years later and the 'cart loads of abominable filth, the refuse of slaughterhouses' still seeped into the streets of Whitechapel.[4]

Polly spent what would prove to be the final day of her life drinking. Any money she may have earned on the streets that afternoon she used to continue her daily binge. Her friend Ellen Holland, who had lodged with Polly at Thrawl Street, testified at the subsequent inquest that she had encountered Polly near the corner of Osborne Street and Whitechapel Road at 2.30 that final morning, very much the worse for wear. Ellen tried to persuade Polly to return with her to their lodgings but a determined and penniless Polly continued to make her own way, staggering on into the night and her impending doom.[5]

Montague Druitt like most surgeons' sons had a broad knowledge of the practice of surgery. For Montie and the other young men of the Druitt clan, the *Surgeon's Vade Mecum*, written by Dr Robert Druitt, was probably a wicked delight. Growing up within the confines of a stifling Victorian home in the country, the chance to partake in any literary 'forbidden fruit' was close by. After all, the book was a source of the family's pride that one of their own had written the 'Surgeon's Bible'. Montie would have had the opportunity to study its pages, resplendent with descriptions of the female reproductive system as well as of the results of venereal disease. Based on reliable and consistent Victorian and Edwardian primary sources, we also suggest that an unsettled Montie had attended some anatomy and surgical classes but only dabbled in medicine and did not graduate.

About 1:30 a.m. of 31 August 1888 Polly Nichols was told that unless she could find the necessary money, she would lose her bed in the flophouse she was frequenting. She was reportedly optimistic, saying in the very last hours of her life: 'Never mind,' pointing at a new, black hat she was wearing at a jaunty angle, 'I'll soon get the doss money. See what a jolly bonnet I've got now.'[6] Around 3.15 a.m., a staggering, intoxicated woman in the dim light of an early morning empty street in Whitechapel would stand no chance against the physically agile and sharp-minded Montague Druitt. The strength in the hands of Druitt, the champion of Fives, would have made the act of murder about which he must have long daydreamed, swift and easy. Barely upright, she would have offered no resistance to the 'gentleman' as he approached her. He would have been a class or two above the regulars and his cultured tone, even though he was dressed down for the occasion, would have imparted a completely false sense of safety. Did he bother to present himself as a rescue worker, as her deliverer from the streets? Or did she muse that a client of this class, if she could procure him in some way, could fund at least two nights in a flophouse?

Mercifully, Polly's end probably came quickly. Holding her tight against him, Druitt slashed her throat with two swift, forceful cuts. So determined was he that she should not cry out, his force drove the knife to such a depth it severed her windpipe and gullet right through to her spinal cord. In the murky darkness he lay the woman down and as he must have so often imagined, he lifted the dead woman's dress and set to work. He slashed her stomach with swift strokes of the knife and, mindful of being discovered, his performance lasted no longer than four or five minutes. Full of adrenalin but disciplined enough to call time on his murderous act, he dragged his victim to the entrance of a stable of the slaughterhouse not far from a row of terrace houses. Then, fleet of foot, he fled into the night. The horrendous scene was left and very soon two local workers would stumble upon it. It was Friday morning 31 August 1888.[7]

My devil had been long caged, he came out roaring.

Robert Louis Stevenson,
*The Strange Case of Dr Jekyll and
Mr Hyde*, 1886[8]

By Saturday 1 September, Montie Druitt would be back in Wimborne, playing cricket in the genteel surrounds of Canford, the cricket ground within Lord Wimborne's estate.[9] Tea with scones, jam and cream in the afternoon in a crisp white marquee – in those sunlit, civilised surroundings, the actions of the previous early morning, in fact Whitechapel itself, must have seemed like no more than a grotesque dream. Meanwhile, the press went into overdrive at this first murder by an unknown lunatic, which was immediately interpreted as the *third* atrocity after Emma Smith and Martha Tabram. It is possible of course that if it was Druitt who had attacked Ada Wilson in March, it may in fact have been the *second* homicidal assault by the same killer – this time successful.

Scotland Yard was under the bristling command of General Sir Charles Warren as Metropolitan Police Commissioner. He had ruthlessly put down the rioters and demonstrators in Trafalgar Square on what became known as 'Bloody Sunday', a thankless task – so nobody thanked him. (Warren had to settle for a knighthood.) He was a man of contradictions: charming and arrogant, reactionary and liberal, even progressive, a Napoleonic autocrat who could also be collaborative – a man who could absorb and act on expert advice.[10] Beneath Warren was the new Assistant Commissioner of the Criminal Investigation Department (CID) Dr Robert Anderson, a pious, Irish Protestant lawyer, incorruptible but conceited, whose one knack was managing to be away on holiday nearly every time the murderer struck (at one point enjoying the Swiss Alps). Below the hapless Dr Anderson were two dedicated public servants who worked tirelessly trying to catch a monster who would prove to be as cunning as he was elusive. The reliable and meticulous Donald Swanson, Chief Inspector of the CID, was in day-to-day operational control of the investigation into the Whitechapel Murders.[11] Below Swanson were several top detectives who did a lot of the fieldwork, the questioning of witnesses and the interrogation of suspects. The highest ranked – and regarded – was Inspector first class Frederick Abberline, who would work tirelessly to try to catch the killer.[12] Warren, Anderson, Swanson and Abberline, and the rest of the force, had to deal with intense media interest – and criticism. Perhaps as Druitt had hoped, *The Echo* of two days later emphasised the squalor in which the victim already existed:

AN OUTCAST IN TRAFALGAR-SQUARE

It has been ascertained that the unfortunate woman was one of those who, last year, *were in the habit of sleeping in Trafalgar-square; and when a clearance of the nightly visitors was made, it being found that she was destitute; and had no means of subsistence*, she was admitted as an inmate to the Lambeth Workhouse. After her discharge from the workhouse and subsequent disappearance from service at Wandsworth, little was known of her whereabouts by her relations. Lately, it seems that she had been lodging in a common lodging-house in Thrawle-street, Spitalfields, leading an immoral life, and known by her female acquaintances as 'Polly.' (Our italics)

On 11 September 1888, a letter writer to *The Star* conjectured a profile of the killer that was treated as hopelessly whimsical but which is eerily prescient – you only have to substitute cricket for golf:

'Meanwhile', writes an eccentric correspondent, 'you, and every one of the papers, have missed the obvious solution of the Whitechapel mystery. *The murderer is a Mr Hyde, who seeks in the repose and comparative respectability of Dr Jekyll security from the crimes he commits in his baser shape*. Of course, the lively imagination of your readers will at once supply certain means of identification for the Dr Jekyll whose Mr Hyde seems daily *growing in ferocious intensity*. If he should turn out to be a statesman engaged in *the harmless pursuit of golf* at North Berwick – well, you, sir, at least, will be able gratefully to remember that you have prepared your readers for the shock of the inevitable discovery.' (Our italics)

It would take ten years, but the unnamed letter writer must have felt vindicated when a couple of writers, both well-known to Chief Constable Melville Macnaghten of the CID, revealed that the murderer had indeed been a respectable, upper middle-class 'Jekyll-and-Hyde' figure – he was even, supposedly, a fully qualified surgeon, a recluse and so rich he did not have to work for a living. No golf, though, or apparently any sporting pursuits whatsoever. After being discharged from a private asylum this 'mad doctor' was idle; he spent his days at cafes or travelling aimlessly on buses, at least until the next homicidal eruption. Hardly anything like the by then late Montie Druitt?

VII

The Reign of Red Terror

Annie Smith would have been a perfect choice for a lady like Mrs Isabella Druitt to take on as a housemaid. In Victorian times, domestic service employed more women in England than any other vocation. With so many girls from poor or working class families to choose from, the problem was not a lack of applicants but rather finding a young woman suitable enough in habit and demeanour to live within the family home. In the case of the Druitts of Strathmore Gardens, Kensington, and families of a similar social standing, a polite, honest and intelligent girl was a highly prized employee.

Annie was unusually well-educated for a young woman from a working-class background. Her father being a soldier in the 2nd Queen's Life Guard had entitled her to a sound education at a regimental school. As a young woman, she found employment as a gentleman's maid in Westminster and later found love with John Chapman, a decent man with secure employment. Her domestic life included the birth of eight children and, courtesy of her husband's wealthy employer, comfortable living quarters in a cottage with him and her surviving children, on a grand estate, Leonard's Hill in Berkshire. Annie Chapman's early married life did not foreshadow her becoming one of many separated or widowed women of the Whitechapel district who had to rely on the proceeds of matchbox making or vice to find shelter for the night. The undoing of both Annie Chapman and her father was drink. George Smith's demise had come about in an insalubrious drinking establishment in Wrexham, his throat cut by his own hand.[1]

With an ability to read well it is probable that Annie, and probably her father, would have been familiar with the views on alcohol of

Dr Robert Druitt as it was a subject in which they both held an interest. Dr Druitt's widely publicised belief that the 'abuse of drink was one of the greatest scourges to mankind' somewhat contradicted his endorsement of drinking light wine for health. Nonetheless, Dr Druitt recommended sweet wines for consumption by women and children, 'for health' as the lesser of two evils – the other evil being total abstinence. For example, at a lecture given to an audience of mostly women, Dr Druitt explained: 'He had had an opportunity of becoming acquainted with teetotallers; he had seen their anatomical plates representing a drunkard's interior in different stages; they say alcohol is a poison; nothing shocked him more than the arguments brought forward against drink by the teetotallers; they had done good, no doubt; but he could not agree with their arguments on this question.'[2] From another arguably more clear-sighted angle, George R. Sims let it be known that it was surely poverty that drove poor men and women to drink, and not the reverse. He saw no other problem with alcohol that the eradication of a class system which neglected those at the bottom could not cure.[3]

Of the eight children born to Annie and John Chapman, six had died as infants, possibly the result from being born of an alcoholic mother and suffering what is known today as foetal alcohol syndrome. Annie had become well known to the constabulary of Clewer while she was living on the estate with John. She had a tendency to regularly take to the bottle and wander about the streets in an inebriated state: 'She had been in the custody of Superintendent Hayes for the offence, but had not been charged before the magistrates.'[4]

When considering the type of life Annie Chapman had enjoyed before her downfall, one might have imagined her walking along the High Street with her little girls, or taking them for a stroll through Kensington Gardens past the palace en route to visiting her mother. Unfortunately, for Annie, even a stint in a sanatorium for alcoholics did not prevent a relapse upon her discharge and soon she had left her husband and children and taken up with a man named 'Sievey' who worked as a sieve maker. Annie's social standing was by this time seriously on the downward slide, and soon to hit rock bottom when she became a resident of Dorset Street, Spitalfields. It 'had the reputation of being the most evil street in the whole of London.' It was said to be the 'first street to which the police directed their searches in the event of an untraced London crime. Although it was only a short thoroughfare, it was one vast brothel, with no fewer than 1,200 people crammed from cellar to roof in its common lodging houses and these included beggars, petty thieves, confidence tricksters and the dregs of whoredom.'[5]

The couple lived together and drank together. It was not by chance that when John Chapman died suddenly and his wife's ten shillings a week maintenance stopped, Sievey decided that Annie's charms had worn off. He high-tailed it back to his previous slum dwelling in Notting Hill and the increasingly forlorn and infirmed Annie remained in Dorset Street. For security, she began cohabiting with Edward Stanley, known as 'the pensioner'. He was a 45-year-old labourer and for part of every week he stayed with her, paying for their nightly bed at a doss house. This was a relationship seemingly based on a mutual love of drink and some weekend companionship. Annie took to wearing several brass circles on her finger as a copy of a wedding ring. She may have felt they gave her an air of respectability, albeit frayed. From the descriptions of Annie Chapman during the early autumn of 1888 it is almost certain that apart from suffering the physical decline and malnutrition brought about by alcoholism, she was also in the latter stages of tuberculosis.[6]

The kitchen of the common lodging house at 35 Dorset Street was at last quiet and mostly free of people by 1.45 a.m. on Saturday 8 September 1888. Annie Chapman was known to the deputy Timothy Donovan as a woman who 'gave no trouble'.[7] A fellow resident of the doss house would not have agreed as Eliza Cooper had quarrelled with Annie during that week. It was over a piece of soap she had loaned her to enable Annie's friend Edward Stanley to wash himself. The fight had taken place in a public bar and Annie had 'slapped her on the face' while Eliza replied with a strike 'on the left eye and on the chest.[8] Despite Annie's obvious bruising from this fight and her ill health, when the deputy Mr Donovan learnt that Annie had failed to secure the coins for a bed, he cast her out into the street in the early hours of that morning. Still hoping for a bed, she shuffled away, her weakened voice trailing off, 'I haven't enough now but I shan't be long.'[9]

Like all the residents of the area, Annie would have been all too aware of the grisly murder of Polly Nicholls a little more than a week before. The news boys screaming the headlines would have been unavoidable: 'Barbarous and Mysterious Murder. Horrible Mutilations'.[10] But for Annie, at this early hour of a very cold and dark morning, the scene of that crime, Buck's Row, was just another dingy, dimly illuminated street in the vicinity of where she now staggered.

Number 29 Hanbury Street was one of a row of three-storey tenements, originally built for Huguenot silk weavers a century or so before. By 1888, however, it had become just one among a long line of slum dwellings. By all accounts, the front door was always kept open and the short passage leading through to a relatively private, fenced backyard was often used by rough sleepers and rough types looking to use the secluded spot for an 'immoral purpose'. It is to this spot that Annie Chapman wandered on her last morning.

The sounds of a woman with a laboured gait shuffling along Hanbury Street, heavy of breath from consumption and weary of body from an over-indulgence in alcohol would not have failed to alert a predator that a sick and vulnerable human being was nearby. Whether it was from curiosity or intent, Montague John Druitt had returned that early morning to the scene of his first crime. Perhaps he had been aroused by the headlines he had caused and felt secure that the constabulary had not one clue to the identity of the perpetrator. Perhaps he had returned with a view to raise the level of hysteria another notch higher. In the dimly lit Hanbury Street on that Saturday morning he spied a sickly, desperate woman in dire need of a few coins to buy herself a bed for precious rest. The coroner speculated that Annie must have been seized 'perhaps with Judas-like approaches'.[11] Did Montie's cultured accent and courtly manner put Annie at ease? Did she lead him to the secluded yard where men and women were known to withdraw for short trysts? Did he speak to her reassuringly before wrenching up her chin and strangling her?

Neither sound nor scream was heard at the back of a house populated by dozens of people. Perhaps she suffered for but an instant before death overcame her. He lowered the now heavy, lifeless weight to the ground near the back steps and, checking for the sounds of any approach from the street, set about his business: 'Her throat was then cut in two places with savage determination and the injuries to the abdomen commenced.' With efficient speed the abdomen was slashed and small intestine extracted, still attached and placed above the victim's right shoulder. 'The left arm had been placed across the left breast, and the legs were drawn up with the feet resting on the ground and the knees turned outwards. The face, which was turned on its right side, was bruised, and the tongue was swollen and protruded between the front teeth but not beyond the lips.'[12]

This hellish scene was discovered by John Davis, a resident of number 29, just before 6 a.m. For reasons, perhaps symbolic, only known to Montague, Annie had been not only disembowelled, her uterus and ovaries had also been removed and taken away. After examining the body, the attending surgeon Dr George Bagster Phillips concluded that the murderer must have sound anatomical knowledge and that, at a minimum, it must have taken him 15 minutes alone with the body to carry out his cruel surgery. Dr Phillips said that if he had attempted what the perpetrator had done, as a surgeon it would have taken him 'the best part of an hour'.[13] *The Lancet* concluded that the work was obviously 'that of an expert – or of one, at least, who had such knowledge of anatomical or pathological examinations as to be enabled to secure the pelvic organs with one sweep of a knife.'[14] In a macabre postscript Annie's one physical sign of modest respectability, her fake brass wedding rings, were missing so her fall into the depths of degradation and indignity, even post mortem, was complete.

Montie had again brought horror and uproar to the district of shame and neglect that was Whitechapel. All eyes, even those of the better classes he associated with, were turned at last to that disgrace. The police were luckless but hardly idle. They arrested dozens upon dozens of men in Whitechapel and the immediate vicinity – of all classes – but none were charged, as the evidence was weak or non-existent. Without fingerprint identification, or the capacity to discern human from animal blood, the police needed to virtually catch the murderer in the act, otherwise, he was a total stranger to his victims and they to him. If Montie was following the police's lack of progress, he might have read *The Pall Mall Gazette* of 15 September 1888:

> They have not arrested any man against whom a reasonable prima facie case could be made out; but they have arrested more than one whom there never was the faintest warrant for suspecting ... We are entitled to express our surprise that the police have pounced on persons who were plainly innocent. That they have not succeeded in arresting the culprit is a pity; but that they have been energetic in the wrong direction is distinctly a reproach. There is a worse thing than doing nothing: that is, doing something that ought not to be done.

For Montie, that second Saturday in September 1888 had proved to be quite a victory. For the last match of the season his team had performed exceedingly well. On their home ground, Blackheath had defeated the brothers Christopherson for the first time in five years and Montie had used his 'extremely deadly' bowling skills to get out three of the opposing batsmen. It was a worthy celebration to be had for the wind up of the cricketing year. The Christopherson brothers, numbering enough to form their own cricket team, proved to be good sports by agreeing to join their vanquishers for their end-of-season celebrations.[15] That is what real gentlemen did. In the coming days, Montie could read of his personal performance in two very different theatres: cricket and murder.

A rumour spread like a brush fire through the East End that a notorious, violent character nicknamed 'Leather Apron' was the likely culprit. The man behind the nickname was a local man of the Hebrew faith named John Pizer. He strenuously denied the crime. He probably was a disreputable character[16] – and had been picked out of an identity parade, though by a witness judged to be unreliable – but he had an unbreakable alibi. The release of Pizer did nothing, however, to smother the incendiary sparks of sectarian hatred felt by too many Christian bigots against the East End's large Jewish minority, who had fled Czarist persecution.

In the mid-1960s, American journalist Tom Cullen discovered how other people at the time were making the connection between the crimes and revolutionary social democracy – but swiftly dismissed it as a coincidence:

> Still others had turned over in their minds the idea that the Ripper murders might have had a social or political content without realizing the full implications of this possibility. *The Lancet* even speaks of the murders as having 'served a good purpose', that purpose being to 'awaken the public conscience'. [Reverend] Samuel Barnett of Toynbee Hall held that 'the murders were, it may almost be said, bound to come'. 'The Whitechapel horrors', he added, 'will not be in vain if at last the public conscience awakens to consider the life which these horrors reveal.' His wife Henrietta Barnett... went further, commenting on how powerfully the murders had served as a stimulus for housing reform. Mrs Barnett wrote, 'Verily it was the crucifixion of these poor lost souls which saved the district.' Even *Commonweal*, the organ of William Morris' Socialists, was forced to concede that 'in our age of contradictions and absurdities, a fiend-murderer may become a more effective reformer than all the honest propagandists in the world.[17]

George R. Sims, as Dagonet, wrote copiously about the Whitechapel murders. He pilloried the police, the Police Commissioner and the Home Secretary for botching every aspect of the investigation – often in the form of rude poems. Within ten years, and as the chief scribe of the cover-up, Sims would heap praise on the constabulary for being diligent and efficient and for coming within inches of catching [the unnamed] Montague Druitt. (Sims never acknowledged this about-face). He was also a left-wing progressive, albeit not a Marxist or a radical. From 1888 right through to his last Whitechapel musings in his memoir of 1917, Sims was consistent in never suggesting that social reform was the motive of the fiend-murderer. The closest he came was to concede that the atrocious social conditions had 'foreshadowed' the crimes as mentioned in his column of 23 September 1888 in *The Referee*:

> A great many letter writers in the daily papers are pointing to the lesson of the Whitechapel horrors, and endeavouring to attract public attention to the conditions under which the East-end poor live. Under any civilised conditions it would have been impossible for these monstrous crimes to have been committed one after the other in the heart of a densely populated neighbourhood... in *How the Poor Live*, these murders which are now horrifying London were clearly foreshadowed.

There were a few voices raised in 1888 who did contemplate that the murderer was a 'scientific and philanthropic sociologist', as we see in *The Pall Mall Gazette* of 24 September:

THE POLITICAL MORAL OF THE MURDERS

> Meanwhile is there any reason to suppose that the lesson of the Whitechapel murders has been fully learned in London? Taking as the most faithful hypothesis that they were the work of a scientific and philanthropic sociologist, can we say that he has reason as yet to stay his hand? The police, we know from the proceedings at the inquest are at their wits end; do not expect fresh evidence and frankly waiting for a fifth murder to give them a clue to the preceding four.

A famous letter was written by the writer and critic George Bernard Shaw, then only 32. The Irish socialist wrote to *The Star* on 24 September 1888 what would become a seminal condemnation of the ruling elite's crimes against the poor. Satirically he congratulated 'some independent genius' for shaming the State into, at last, acting with some practical compassion towards the destitute. If only the maniac, Shaw jokily suggested, would switch targets to some tempting toff, poverty might be eradicated (*see* Appendix 3 for the full text):

> Whilst we conventional Social Democrats were wasting our time on education, agitation, and organisation, some independent genius has taken the matter in hand, and by simply murdering and disembowelling four women concerted the proprietary press to an inept sort of Communism...
> Indeed, if the habits of duchesses only admitted of their being decoyed into Whitechapel back-yards, a single experiment in

slaughterhouse anatomy on an aristocratic victim might fetch in around half a million and save the necessity of sacrificing four women of the people.

Montague Druitt must have been amused, perhaps thrilled, if he read those words. Shaw might not have been quite so jocular if he knew the 'genius' was not some slavering lumpen of the abyss, but rather a nominal Tory, a professional man and a noted sportsman who lived elsewhere in London. He was a sane and cunning murderer whose mission *was* to bring a kind of Red Terror in order to rattle and disrupt an establishment – of which he was a card-carrying member. He was not really a serious political actor; he joined no radical associations, attended no public rallies, wrote no manifestos and made no effort to contact the State with a list of demands. Like the legion of twenty-first century anomic terrorists who do not bother to adhere, even minimally, to the religious customs of the ideology they are prepared to kill for, Druitt was driven by a deranged appetite for horror, supplemented by a mere side dish of socialistic ideology – but it kept him in Whitechapel.

The police, public and press did not have to wait long for another atrocity, this time even more audacious as Montague Druitt would murder two poor, defenceless women on the same night – and once more vanish. Such apparent nerve would horrify and astonish the world. As Tom Cullen so acutely wrote utilising the same morally neutral word as Shaw:

> ... he had studied the terrain as a general might study a situation map. For his life depended upon his knowledge of the area. On the night of the double murder, for example, when the police were hot on his heels, one false turning, one sidestep would have landed him in the arms of the law... Jack the Ripper ... was omnipresent there. He hovered over the slum-ridden, crime-infested area like some evil genius.[18]

Demoniacal Work Disturbed

The summer of 1888 had tested the mettle of all of the children of the late Dr William and his wife Ann. They had each grappled in their own way with the sorrow, denial, hope and finally acceptance of their mother's mental collapse. For the elder siblings Georgiana and William, it was a case of thought and practical action being implemented. Georgiana had a husband and child to care for in London and could no longer be called on for lengthy periods to care for her mother in Wimborne. As the oldest son, and with a busy legal practice to attend to, William Druitt took the practical steps with the help of his medical contacts to find the best type of asylum into which to have their mother committed, one that would provide the appropriate level of care and respect for a woman of her standing. The two youngest girls, Edith and Ethel, had endured the attempted suicide of their mother and a feeling of hopelessness that she may never re-emerge as the woman they both loved. For Arthur there was a natural sorrow about the reality of his mother's situation but for Edward, who had previously upset his mother with his revelation about his conversion to Catholicism, a level of guilt must have been felt. It would have been about this time that Edward revealed to his mother and his siblings the real reason for his conversion the previous year – he would soon be taking a young Catholic woman for his bride.

For Montague, the upset and angst within his family must have also had a profound effect. Not only was his mother in a compromised state of physical and mental health, his younger brother Edward had flouted the expectations they had grown up with and even worse, he seemed to be thriving because of it. Edward too was an excellent cricketer, playing regularly for the Royal Engineers as well as a variety of gentleman's teams. Like Montie he was also accepted as a member of the MCC and was selected for a match. He had performed missionary work in Singapore and had a promising career in the military. The following year Edward would take up a position in Queensland, Australia, and not only that, he would take his new Catholic wife with him, as well as a hefty chunk of her wealthy father's money. Edward Druitt by all accounts was a likeable chap. He was described in *A History of Royal Engineers Cricket* as 'a dear good fellow and a very reliable bowler. He could bowl all day. He could generally be relied upon to make 20–30 runs in a dignified and sound manner.'[1]

Montie must have felt at least envious, if not completely affronted, that his younger brother was doing much better than he was, privately and professionally. At one time Montie was the golden boy of the family. Now the early high achiever in both sport and academia was looking decidedly second-rate compared to his younger brother. Although by thirty Montie's career as a barrister was certainly gathering a head of steam, perhaps for the impatient young man it was not quite fast enough. Of course, he was to become a skilful and undetected murderer, one whose blood-drenched exploits were to enthral the nation – but he could hardly brag about that 'hobby' to anyone.

In June and July of 1888 his performance as a cricketer, particularly for Blackheath, severely declined. His wicket taking dried up and his form slump may explain his exclusion from the team for an Old Wykehamist match, which for Montie, as a senior member of that club, was more than unusual. What may also be inferred from this, however, is that his state of mind rendered him not up to the task. Perhaps he was just not in the right frame of mind to run around a cricket field with his old schoolmates while his mother was settling, badly, into asylum life.[2]

The London newspapers continued to cash in on the latest, often rehashed, stories of the dreadful state of things in Whitechapel – murders, mutilations, prostitutes, debauchery – all fare providing a jolly good read. Montie's family who had always enjoyed following his progress as a sportsman or a barrister via the various news publications would have been pleased to learn that by autumn, for Montie, things were looking up. He had been given a brief to defend a clerk, Christopher Power, 32, of 12 Halliday Street, Hackney, who was charged in the Central Criminal Court with 'feloniously wounding' Peter Black, a draughtsman, living at 1 Canterbury Terrace, Canterbury Road, Kilburn, by stabbing him with a table knife. Possibly due to Montie's negotiation, the charge had been downgraded from one of attempted murder. Druitt had experienced the attention and responsibility of such cases, having previously defended the child murderer Henry Young. In what seemed like an open-and-shut case, Power would need Montague's proficiency as a barrister to save him from years of imprisonment. The prosecutor explained that Power and the victim, Mr Peter Black, had been in the same employ and were well known to one another. Mr Power had come to believe, however, that Mr Black was harassing him and as a consequence had written two threatening and incriminating letters. The court heard that:

> On Friday, evening, the prisoner came into his room, and accused him of following him about, and circulating reports about him. He used bad language, and witness noticed that he had his right hand behind his back. The prisoner then said 'I will cut your throat,' and struck at him with a knife, Witness seized his wrist, and a desperate struggle ensued. Witness called for help, and several people came, followed by the police, and the prisoner was given into custody.[3]

The Times reported on 20 September 1888: 'Assistance was obtained and the prisoner was arrested, and he denied that he had used the knife.' The prosecution called Mr Black's landlady as a witness: She testified,

> She heard a violent knock at the door, and on opening it she saw the prisoner, who asked if Black was home, and rushed past her into his room. She afterwards heard a great noise there, and the [victim] called out Murder. She ran up and saw the two men struggling, and tried to separate them. She heard the prisoner threaten to kill the [victim].

Montague Druitt, for Mr Power, called several witnesses. This time it was Mr Power's landlady to offer mitigating evidence that her lodger was acting strangely suggesting some kind of mental impairment was at play. The other witness was Dr Gilbert, the surgeon from Holloway gaol. He explained that the prisoner sincerely believed he was 'being followed about by people who heard and repeated everything he said'. Dr Gilbert, upon examination by Mr Druitt, concluded that he believed Christopher Power to be suffering from delusions and was unaware of 'the nature and quality of the act'. Without hesitation, Dr Gilbert declared the defendant to be clinically insane. Mr Justice Charles summed up for the jury, who followed his lead and found Power to be guilty of the act but while suffering from madness at the time: 'Mr Justice Charles directed the prisoner to be detained as a lunatic during Her Majesty's pleasure.'

Montague had achieved for Power the best outcome he could from a very 'sticky wicket'. He must also have entertained some deep and uncomfortable thoughts about the consequences Power faced. He would be indefinitely locked up in a State institution for trying to cut a man's throat. A diagnosis of lunacy would get any man off the hook – but at what price? Life in a dingy, overcrowded, stinking asylum was not an attractive prospect. An infamous criminal was unlikely to be afforded a term in a comfy private asylum, even if he was a gentleman whose family had deep pockets. Montie probably spent at least some time contemplating that there would be nothing other than Broadmoor or the hangman's noose for the Whitechapel murderer, if he was ever caught.

Montague's Aunt Isabella from Kensington would have been most interested in reading the report of the Power case in *The Times* of Thursday 20 September 1888. She was a woman diligent at clipping out anything from newspapers to do with her clan. She may have, like the majority of her fellow readers, also read the next story which appeared in the same edition, just near the report of Montie's qualified success. This story was beneath the heading 'Inquests'. It detailed the resumption of the inquest into the shocking murder and mutilation of Annie Chapman earlier that same month. The report revealed two things, one being the manner of the murder and the other obvious conclusion that thus far, they were no closer to identifying the murderer. The shocking aspect of this report for the reader was that *The Times* deemed the details of the murder to be 'totally unfit for publication, of the deliberate, successful, and apparently scientific manner in which the poor woman had been mutilated.' The editor of the story further added, 'No further arrest in connection with the Whitechapel murders had been made up to last night, and the police are still at fault.'

Whereas the summer of 1888 had been less than satisfactory for Montie Druitt, autumn was certainly looking up on a number of fronts both overt and covert. This was, however, untrue for Mrs Elizabeth Stride who lived in the lodging house at 32 Flower and Dean Street,

Spitalfields, within the 'evil quarter mile'. The story of how Elizabeth Gustafsdotter, a good Lutheran girl from a hard-working farming family in Torslanda, Sweden, ended up in this godforsaken place is a tale of tragedy, heartache, fantasy and re-invention and then, as its finale, pure horror.

Born in 1843, Elizabeth had a conventional rural upbringing consisting of robust religious instruction and church attendance with very little formal education. As a teenager, she moved to Gothenburg to commence work as a domestic servant and became burdened with an unwanted out-of-wedlock pregnancy – in a country where adultery had until the mid-nineteenth century remained illegal. To top off Elizabeth's troubles she had contracted syphilis. The standard treatment of the day included the ingestion of mercury with a solid dose of humiliation. She was forced to comply with public health legislation, similar to the Contagious Diseases Act in England, which forced women of low moral standing, as Elizabeth was now considered to be, to endure regular pelvic inspections performed by a police-appointed doctor, to check on the progress of their venereal disease. The treatment for her affliction was probably the cause of Elizabeth's miscarriage. With nowhere to go and having lied to authorities that both of her parents had died, she eked out a living as one of the many prostitutes who serviced the men of the Gothenburg seaport and town.[4]

By 1866 Elizabeth, a pretty and petite woman, applied to emigrate to England. Her application was successful and once she arrived in her new homeland, she attempted to start a new life. She gained employment as a servant in a Hyde Park home and later married John Stride, a man in his late 40s and a carpenter by trade. John and 'Liz' Stride moved to lodgings at Poplar in the East End and opened a coffee shop but, unable to compete with all the public drinking houses in the area, the business soon lost money. John's father was a wealthy man and the Strides would have anticipated receiving a substantial inheritance from him. When he died leaving them nothing, they could no longer prop up the business and so it became as untenable as their partnership; both business and marriage were abandoned. Liz left John and headed for accommodation in a part of London she could afford to live, Whitechapel. Thus began a merry-go-round of arrests for vagrancy, admission to a workhouse, and returning to her husband. Once on the streets or in the lodging houses of Whitechapel, Elizabeth would be known as 'Long Liz'.[5]

On 3 September 1878, a paddle steamer used as a pleasure cruiser named the *Princess Alice* had been transporting 800 men, women and children along the Thames near North Woolwich Pier. She was returning from a day cruise from near London Bridge, down to Kent and back again. The already polluted Thames was particularly toxic that day, having had 75 million imperial gallons of raw sewage just released into it. With light fading, and the steamer slightly off course, the *Princess Alice* collided with a destructive force in the shape of a coal freighter, *Bywell Castle*. The cruiser broke into three parts, sinking quickly into the syrupy, suffocating waters. As no passenger list was kept for the day trip, the number of dead was never accurately known but an estimate of 600–700 nevertheless was compiled. Liz Stride told everybody who would listen how she was both a survivor and a victim of the *Princess Alice* disaster. Among those drowned, according to the Swede, was her first husband and her two children, one of whom died in its father's arms.[6]

Liz escaped only by climbing up a rope as the vessel was sinking. A man who had climbed onto the rope ahead of her slipped and kicked her accidentally in the mouth, knocking out her front teeth – so she said. Only after she became the next victim of Montague Druitt did the truth emerge: the alleged names of her late husband and children were not to be found on the list of the dead as compiled by a meticulous West Kent enquiry.[5] Liz Stride was not known to have given birth to any children other than stillborn, and she had almost certainly lost her teeth due to the effects of syphilis.

With her on-and-off relationship with John Stride being, by 1881, permanently off, Liz moved into lodgings at 32 Flower and Dean Street. It is likely that Liz received some small maintenance payments from John and supplemented this with work as a charwoman, the lowest level of honest employment. John Stride died in 1884 and with him the modest pension. Elizabeth had taken up residence with Michael Kidney in lodgings in Fashion Street. He shared two of the same drawbacks as his new partner: syphilis and a love of drinking.

By the end of the summer of 1888 Michael Kidney and Liz Stride made for a desultory couple, living from hand-to-mouth like hunter-gatherers of the Neolithic Age rather than citizens of a wealthy industrial metropolis. Mr Kidney and Mrs Stride were by this time more often apart than together. He would later present his view of their unstable relationship to the coroner. 'During the three years I have known her she has been away from me about five months all together ... it was drink that made her go ... she always came back again. I think she liked me more than any other man.'[8]

Liz was frequently arrested for drunk and disorderly behaviour and was a familiar figure at the Thames Magistrate Court. On her final night she was in the vicinity of the International Working Men's Educational Club, at 42 Berner Street. This was a socialist club for debate, friendship and entertainment, mostly frequented by Russian and Polish Jews. Late on the night of Saturday 29 September a debate on 'Why Jews should be socialists' had wound up and by midnight a majority of the ninety or so attendees had departed into the wet and gloomy night. One member, Morris Eagle, entered the yard at 12.40 on Sunday morning 30 September. From the time Mr Eagle walked through the gates of Dutfield's Yard and back into the club he noticed nothing amiss.

Liz Stride was seen by a passing witness being pushed to the ground by a drunken, broad-shouldered man. She screamed, but not very loudly. The witness, a Hungarian Jewish man named Israel Schwartz, saw another, thinner man seemingly emerge from a nearby pub and yell at the drunk to stop hurting the woman. He ran over brandishing a knife. Suitably terrified, the witness and the drunk ran off in the same direction.[9] Presumably the young man asked if the woman was alright. She would have been pleasantly surprised to discover that her saviour had a posh accent; he was a gentleman, but dressed down rather like a sailor with a peak cap and a salt and pepper jacket. After a few words and the proffer of money, the couple slipped further into the darkness where Druitt immediately slit her throat before Stride could have sensed she was in mortal danger (so swift was his knife that she was discovered still grasping cachous breath mints). Without a sound he lowered her body to the ground. Before he could even tear open her clothes, however, he heard the sound of the clopping hoofs of a horse.

At 1 a.m. Louis Diemschutz, a Russian immigrant of the Jewish faith, drove his horse and cart into the yard. As he entered, his horse hesitated and moved to the left. Leaning to the right, Diemschutz looked down and through the darkness and light rain saw an object on the ground. He poked it with his riding crop. Finding no reaction, he stepped down and took a closer look, as Druitt stood perfectly still watching him from the gloom. There was no reason to panic or flee, not yet. Shocked to discover it was a figure of a woman either unconscious or deceased, Diemschutz immediately feared it was his wife. Abandoning his horse and trap, he ran into the lodging house and was relieved to discover her quite safe, sitting with other people in the ground-floor dining room. The panicked Russian told them what he had found and the lodging house dwellers, having procured a candle began following him back into the yard.[10]

By then Montague Druitt had bolted, loping through the streets and back alleys with which he had become so familiar. He was angry, frustrated and determined to satisfy his thwarted urges – and his gruesome signature was missing. He needed everyone to know that the non-mutilated body in Berner Street was *his* work and not just some random attack by a drunken client. He knew that the window of opportunity between the discovery of the body of his latest victim and the police mobilising to sweep the area would be tight. Could he dispatch another 'fallen woman' and feel her warm entrails in his hands before the entire East End lit up like a Catherine wheel? Within less than half-an-hour he would be near Mitre Square, propositioning another poor woman with his silver tongue and loose change.

Panic Sweeps 'Slumopolis'

By 1888, John Kelly had cohabited with Kate (Catherine) Eddowes for seven years, yet he knew little about her. In the vicinity of 55 Flower and Dean Street where they had first met, this was not unusual. Their shared love was drinking and once that daily ritual took hold, there was little need for talk about what had been or what might have been. On the streets of Whitechapel women like Kate Eddowes with their stories of woe were a dime a dozen. Like Kate, most of them were also mothers, sisters, wives and daughters and similarly had fallen out with most of those who could have helped them before they hit the bottle, then hit the skids as they morphed into the stereotype of the drunken, screeching, slovenly woman synonymous with the inhabitants of the East End. Kate and John had been on their annual hop-picking sojourn in Kent. The journey on foot was long and arduous but staying on a farm provided food and a place to sleep for a few weeks and, in a good season with plenty of hops to pick, some money to bring back home. But 1888 had not been a good year. Returning from Kent, penniless, John Kelly pawned his boots for a pittance and he and Kate promptly drank away most of the proceeds.[1]

On Saturday 29 September Kate, delusional and destitute, wandered off with a vague notion that she could seek out her married daughter and ask her for money. An unidentified maniac offing women in the street had created a heightened level of concern for John. He was worried about Kate's safety, so with some small concern, but not enough to accompany her for protection albeit barefoot, he admonished Kate to be back before nightfall. To this she replied: 'Don't you fear for me. I'll take care of myself and I shan't fall into his hands.'[2]

Kate Eddowes somehow found money that afternoon but it was not from her daughter Annie. Tired of her drunken mother's scrounging, the previous year Annie had, with her husband's consent, packed up the family and moved, leaving no forwarding address. Wherever the money came from that day it was certainly sufficient to satisfy the needs of a seasoned alcoholic to the point of inebriation. By 8.30 p.m. Kate, with her singing and swaying, swearing and calling out, had attracted a crowd on the Aldgate High Street. Two police constables picked up the now collapsed woman from the pavement and escorted her, with difficulty, to the Bishopsgate Street Police Station. And this was not for the first time. The duty officer who was greeted with the sight of the slurring woman propped against the counter barely flinched as he was hit by the sharp smell of strong alcohol and stale perspiration. Nor was he surprised when, upon asking the prisoner's name she looked up to his expressionless face and replied indignantly, 'nothing'. Escorted into the cell to sober up, Kate fell into a deep slumber. When PC Hutt checked on her after midnight he found her awake, singing and demanding to be released. Eager to clear her cell for the next unfortunate who would surely soon take her place, she was released from custody and left the station at 1 a.m. calling back, 'Good night old cock'.[3]

Exiting the building Kate Eddowes walked towards Mitre Square, less than 10 minutes away. This large expanse of paved yard was bordered by buildings. It was close to St Botolph's Church where prostitutes paraded, and passers-by propositioned, or alternatively heckled, them. Mitre Square afforded privacy and darkness for women to take their clients for a hurried rendezvous. By now, Montague Druitt was high on adrenalin and compared to the carefully planned nature of his first two murders, tonight his need for a proper result, a proper display of his 'independent genius' was pushing out the boundaries of his calculated risk-taking. He may have been somewhat out of control after the previous interruption, though he could still deploy his easy-going manner to lure the unwary.

As a young man wearing a peaked cap emerged from the gloom, how noble and healthy must the face with the neat, fair moustache have looked to Kate. She must have thought her luck had changed – for here was a genuine toff slumming it in this stink – as some of them did – and hopefully with a toff's ready cash.

He asked her name – they never did, just how much. How typical of an educated gentleman to be so thoughtful. As they made small talk and she was sure the assignation would soon take place, she put her hand on his chest. Behind her, Kate could hear some men walking past, minding their own business, and so there was no need to turn around. Once they were out of sight, she informed the gentleman how long they had before the patrolling bobby would make his return: it might be less than 15 minutes. I know, Montie whispered.

Once in a dark corner of Mitre Square, Druitt strangled Catherine Eddowes with accomplished speed, dexterity and growing experience – he was getting better at murder. He carefully lowered her supine body to the ground. Not a sound had been emitted during the act, from her or from him. It was so quiet that Druitt could hear a slumbering person's heavy snore from an open window somewhere nearby (it would turn out to be an off-duty policeman – Scotland Yard really could not catch a break).[4] Removing his knife, Druitt ripped open his victim's filthy clothes and began tearing at her flesh. He may have noticed she was wearing a man's lace-up boots[5] or, in his moment of unleashed frenzy, maybe not. This woman, he was going to make sure, would be the most horrendously mutilated yet.

Police Constable Edward Watkins, on his beat, entered Mitre Square a mere 15 minutes since his last patrol. He was greeted in that dark space by a shocking and sickening sight. A woman lay on the ground in her own body organs and with her face slashed. Here is the report of Dr Frederick Gordon Brown, a police surgeon who examined Kate Eddowes' remains at the scene:

The body was on its back, the head turned to left shoulder. The arms by the side of the body as if they had fallen there. Both palms upwards, the fingers slightly bent. The left leg extended in a line with the body. The abdomen was exposed. Right leg bent at the thigh and knee. The throat cut across.

The intestines were drawn out to a large extent and placed over the right shoulder – they were smeared over with some feculent matter. A piece of about two feet was quite detached from the body and placed between the body and the left arm, apparently by design. The lobe and auricle of the right ear were cut obliquely through.

There was a quantity of clotted blood on the pavement on the left side of the neck round the shoulder and upperpart of arm, and fluid blood-coloured serum which had flowed under the neck to the right shoulder, the pavement sloping in that direction. Body was quite warm. No death stiffening had taken place. She must have been dead most likely within the half hour. We looked for superficial bruises and saw none. No blood on the skin of the abdomen or secretion of any kind on the thighs. No spurting of blood on the bricks or pavement around. No marks of blood below the middle of the body. Several buttons were found in the clotted blood after the body was removed. There was no blood on the front of the clothes. There were no traces of recent connexion.[6]

Though it is doubtful Druitt had planned for this, Catherine Eddowes had been nevertheless killed in the jurisdiction of the City of London. Now two separate police forces and investigations would be scrambling to solve two murders and, hopefully, catch the maniac. In Goulston Street, about three streets from Mitre Square and heading back into Whitechapel – and the jurisdiction of the Metropolitan Police – another bobby on his beat came across a torn and bloody piece of apron. It was near a doorway and he noticed on the wall of the building, written in chalk, a short message in double negative which apparently looked like this:[7]

> The Juwes are
> The men That
> Will Not
> be Blamed
> for Nothing

Police Constable Alfred Long swore black and blue that when he found the two artefacts at 2:55 a.m. neither had been there on his earlier round. Whether the graffiti was really scrawled by the killer – in a legible 'schoolboy's hand'[8] – or was just coincidentally above where the killer dropped his 'trophy', the apron fragment was certainly established to have once been part of Catherine Eddowes' pitiful attire.

This meant that Montie Druitt had not immediately headed back to Blackheath, or at least to the relative sanctuary of his chambers at King's Bench Walk a few miles away, or frankly *anywhere* that was not Whitechapel, but had remained in the centre of the growing and spinning Catherine wheel whose fuse he had lit by committing two atrocities on the same night. Why? The subsequent chapter postulates that there are hints in various sources by people who would know that Mr Druitt did not immediately leave the district despite it being like a city under siege. This was because he could not, because he was in custody. In a fatal blunder for the authorities, they may have arrested the murderer and let him go (probably with an apology).

The message itself was soon obliterated on the recommendation of Superintendent Thomas Arnold advising Commissioner General Sir Charles Warren, who made the final decision. Both high-ranking policemen showed admirable forbearance and compassion. With temperatures boiling, they were apprehensive that some fearful, sectarian and bigoted residents might focus on the East End's Jewish community and the message might trigger an explosion. Before a police photographer could reach the spot, a sponge was produced and the writing was wiped off in front of Warren and Arnold, and a pack of police – who had also read the words.[9]

Many at the time, and since, have second-guessed their admittedly difficult decision. For one thing, did they really think a Jewish murderer was outing his own ethnic and religious identity for... what purpose? Was it not far more likely that since the neat hand-writing was in English – not German, Hungarian, Russian or Yiddish, with just one word ostentatiously misspelt to *appear* to be composed by a foreigner – that the author was more likely to be a gentile and an Englishman? Apart from that conceptual conundrum there was no way the message would not leak to the press, virtually immediately – so they might as well have waited to have it photographed. As it was, Sir Charles Warren managed to put a foot in the worst of both worlds: the public learned of a message blaming Jewish migrants, and a potential clue was lost forever. The press reaction was predictably scathing – and now the killer had a name, one which thoroughly jettisoned the slimy prejudice inherent in 'Leather Apron'. Combining the name of a semi-legendary pest from the 1830s who had become known as 'Spring Heeled Jack'[10] with the savagery inflicted on this killer's victims, somebody created 'Jack the Ripper' and used it to sign a letter which they sent to the media. Here is the content:

Dear Boss,

I keep on hearing the police have caught me but they wont [sic] fix me just yet. I have laughed when they look so clever and talk about being on the <u>right</u> track. That joke about Leather Apron gave me real fits. I am down on whores and I shant [sic] quit ripping them till I do get buckled. Grand work the last job was. I gave the lady no time to squeal. How can they catch me now. I love my work and want to start again. You will soon hear of me with my funny little games. I saved some of the proper <u>red</u> stuff in a ginger beer bottle over the last job to write with but it went thick like glue and I cant use it. Red ink is fit enough I hope <u>ha. ha.</u> The next job I do I shall clip the ladys (sic) ears off and send to the police officers just for jolly wouldn't you. Keep this letter back till I do a bit more work, then give it out straight. My knife's so nice and sharp I want to get to work right away if I get a chance.

Good Luck.

Yours truly
Jack the Ripper

Dont [sic] mind me giving the trade name

PS Wasnt [sic] good enough to post this before I got all the red ink off my hands curse it

No luck yet. They say I'm a doctor now. <u>ha ha</u>

The Central News office, which sent copies of stories to a variety of newspapers, claimed to have received the above communication on 27 September 1888 – written in red ink. Two days later they forwarded it to the police dismissing it as probably nothing more than a 'joke'.[12] On 1 October 1888 nobody was laughing when the same office received a postcard this time smeared in real blood. It read:

I was not codding (sic) dear old Boss when I gave you the tip, you'll hear about Saucy Jacky's work tomorrow double event this time number one squealed a bit couldn't finish straight off. Ha not the time to get ears for police. Thanks for keeping last letter back till I got to work again.

Jack the Ripper

At least at first, Scotland Yard was convinced this was a genuine communication from the madman. There seems to have been some confusion as to *exactly* when the postcard was sent. If it was before the murders then the contents alone surely proved their authenticity – the killer was correctly predicting a 'double event' (and possibly the mutilation of Catherine Eddowes' ears, which were damaged by her assailant). On the other hand, there was no firm evidence it did exist before public knowledge of the crimes. The consensus was that it did not matter about the chalk message being wiped away as these letters were far superior; they had his handwriting on two separate documents. Reproductions were quickly made and sent to be displayed to police stations and to newspapers.[11] Yet sceptical voices were raised within days suggesting the two pieces of 'Jack the Ripper' correspondence were hoaxes. George R. Sims, in his Dagonet column of 7 October 1888, bluntly if jovially debunked them as obviously the creation of a fellow journalist:

> JACK THE RIPPER is the hero of the hour. A gruesome wag, a grim practical joke, has succeeded in getting an enormous amount of fun out of a postcard which he sent to the Central News... Of course the whole business is a farce. The postcard is an elaborately-prepared hoax... Murders and battles are... a boon and a blessing to men of the Press... How many among you, my dear readers would have hit upon the idea of 'the Central News' as a receptacle for your confidence? ...I will lay long odds that it would never have occurred to communicate with a Press agency... This proceeding on Jack's part betrays an inner knowledge of the newspaper world ... Everything therefore points to the fact that the jokist is professionally connected with the Press. And if he is telling the truth and not fooling us, then we are brought face to face with the fact that the Whitechapel murders have been committed by a practical journalist – perhaps by a real live editor! Which is absurd, and at that I think I will leave it.[13]

At some later point Scotland Yard must have soured on the whole 'Jack the Ripper' alleged breakthrough. In his memoirs, Sir Melville Macnaghten claimed, once he was Assistant Chief Constable of the CID from mid-1889, to have discovered the identity of the journalist who created the hoax after a year of investigating the matter (which meant that the chalk message *was* a potential clue thrown away for nothing):

> On 27th September a letter was received at a well-known News Agency, addressed to the 'Boss'. It was written in red ink, and purported to give the details of the murders which had been committed. It was signed, 'Jack the Ripper'. This document was sent to Scotland Yard, and (in my opinion most unwisely) was reproduced, and copies of same affixed to various police stations, thus giving it an official imprimatur. In this ghastly production I have always thought I could discern the stained forefinger of the journalist indeed, a year later, I had shrewd suspicions as to the actual author![14]

A private letter to George Sims in 1913 from the former head of the Special Branch, John George 'Jack' Littlechild, named the pair of unscrupulous hucksters who composed the letter and postcard whom Macnaghten modestly asserts to having identified: 'With regard to the term "Jack the Ripper" it was generally believed at the Yard that Tom Bullen [sic – Bulling] of the Central News was the originator, but it is probable Moore, who was his chief, was the inventor'.[15] (Obviously Littlechild did not realise that Sims had called it as a hoax in 1888, or that he probably already knew the name of the hoaxer from his close friend, Macnaghten).

A search of the local neighbourhood for any witnesses by police soon after the double homicides struck gold. They found three witnesses, Jewish immigrant men who were leaving a club that night and had seen Catherine Eddowes with her final client in the street. One of them, a respectable Polish-German cigarette salesman, Joseph Lawende (a.k.a. Lavender) had the closest view of the couple. Some writers put great store in Lawende claiming to some reporters and the police that he would not have been able to identify the man at some future line-up, not realising he was probably terrified of reprisals from the very same maniac.[16] Other sources show that Joseph Lawende was almost certainly the super-witness used to 'confront' major Whitechapel suspects; in 1891 and even as late as 1895 (and in the latter case, a man whom Lawende reportedly and remarkably affirmed – *see* Chapters XVI and XVIII). The other deafening silence over the past fifty years is that between Dan Farson's book of 1972 and our previous work in 2015 – with the exception of a few grudging concessions in Phillip Sugden's often brilliant book of 1994 – the striking, generic resemblance between Montague Druitt and Joseph Lawende's description of the man with Eddowes goes unmentioned and unacknowledged.

At the coronial hearing into Eddowes' murder, Mr Lawende, who was judged to be so valuable he was sequestered by the police, was allowed by an official present to testify only that the man he saw was wearing a peaked cap. The reticence of the authorities to broadcast their best eyewitness description – because Joseph Lawende's sighting was timed by a clock to be within mere minutes of Catherine Eddowes' mutilated remains being stumbled upon by a horrified PC Watkins – did not impress the newspapers. They collectively felt that adherence to stuffy protocol was hindering the killer being recognised and caught. *The Times* of 2 October 1888 was the first to reveal to the public the likeliest description of the prime suspect being 'of shabby appearance, about thirty years of age and 5ft. 9in. in height, of fair complexion, having a small fair moustache, and wearing a red neckerchief and a cap with a peak'. The full description was finally published by the *Police Gazette* on 19 October 1888:

> At 1:35 a.m., 30th of September, with Catherine Eddowes, in Church Passage, leading to Mitre Square, where she was found murdered at 1:45 a.m. same date – A MAN, *age 30, height 5 ft. 7 or 8 in., complexion fair, moustache fair, medium build*; dress, pepper-and-salt colour loose jacket, grey cloth cap with peak of same material, reddish neckerchief and in knot; appearance of a sailor. (Our italics)

This was still a description that might fit a dozen, a hundred or a thousand men, or more. A document survives which was written by Sir Charles Warren to the Home Office mentioning some suspects the police are endeavouring to locate and either clear or arrest. One he mentions is instructive about the way Druitt will later be designated as a medical man: '2. a man called Puckeridge was released from an asylum on 4 August. He was *educated as a surgeon* & has threatened to rip people up with a long knife. He is being looked for but cannot be found as yet.'[17] (Our italics) The author Phillip Sugden discovered that Warren was referring to Oswald Puckeridge, who was 50 at the time of the murders (and probably later exonerated in official documentation, now lost). On the suspect's marriage certificate he identified as a chemist. This does not mean that he had not studied anatomy and surgery, just that he had eventually switched courses and graduated as an apothecary.[18]

Other men the police were investigating were 'three insane medical students', only one of which the surviving sources allow us to identify. This was John Sanders and he was being investigated by Chief Inspector Abberline. Sanders has superficial parallels with Druitt, as the former was the son of a surgeon (in his case his father was an Army doctor) who had also died prematurely. John Sanders had five siblings, and was 26 at the time of the murders. He had become a medical student in 1879 at London Hospital but only studied for a few months before he was placed in a private asylum. He would spend the rest of his life in and out of institutionalised care. A detective called at his home and was told that the mother and her ailing son had gone abroad. Inspector Abberline's report about this suspect to Commissioner Warren on 1 November 1888 said: 'Searching enquiries were made by an officer at Aberdeen Place, St John's Wood, the last known address of the insane medical student named John Sanders. But the only information that could be obtained was that a lady named Sanders with her son at No. 20, but left there to go abroad 2 years ago.[19] In fact, Scotland Yard had blundered. The unnamed detective had the wrong address (the correct one was the similarly named 20 Abercorn Place, Maida Vale)[20] but Sanders periodic confinements made him an unlikely fiend anyway. The significance here is that again the term 'medical student' is bandied about in the present tense, yet Sanders had only been a student for a few months, had never come close to graduating and his studies had terminated more than six years before. It proves that even exposure to a few anatomy classes – plus a brush with madness – was enough for any man to be a possible 'Jack the Ripper'. Unlike John Sanders, Druitt probably never registered as a medical student – by then he was already working for a living and undecided about another career. By comparison, Montie was just passing through. It is a potentially incriminating factor, nevertheless, and Sir Melville Macnaghten writes that he was posthumously and *verbally* informed about it by members of the murderer's own family as there was no documentation to check (Macnaghten would write in 1894 that Mr M. J. Druitt was 'said to be a doctor' – *see* Chapter XVII).

Or was it Montie Druitt himself who had told the police he had once been a doctor?

X

Scotland Yard's Fatal Blunder?

'What is your name,' sir?

The young man of about thirty dressed rather like a working-class sailor in a salt and pepper coloured jacket removed his grey cloth cap with a peak. Beneath it he revealed that he wore his hair neatly parted down the dead centre of his head and slicked tight against the sides. Like many gentlemen of his class he had no whiskers, only a fair, smudge of a moustache cut off square at the ends (as facial hair goes, he need hardly have bothered). He had been arrested by an alert bobby chatting in the street with a young prostitute, and had been haughty and defensive at being questioned. Perhaps that was understandable. Respectable gents 'slumming' it in the East End and found to be in the company of a woman of ill-repute hardly danced a jig at the arrival of 'Constable Plod'. He also could not know there had already been two women dispatched that very night in horrific circumstances – assuming he was not their killer.

As he sat before two detectives in the police station, the aspect of his appearance that quietly excited them were the dark splotches of blood on his cuffs, incriminating stains which the gentleman made no effort to conceal – or acknowledge. Two women had been murdered, one horrifically mutilated and a veritable army of police were scrambling, in both the Met and City jurisdictions, to catch this infernal assassin who, by his latest audacious atrocities and miraculous escape, had once more made them all look like fools and knaves. That is unless this handsome, young man with the well-bred accent before them was the maniac; in that case the nightmare was over.

The suspect sat calmly in an office of the police station with his legs crossed and his carry bag nearby on a desk. He was certainly shrewd enough to dress down for his sojourn among the poor people of this neighbourhood. Far from concern or fear at being in custody, he exhibited all the insouciance of a member of the public school-educated elite – almost as if it was he who was interviewing them.

'Montague Druitt, Inspector,' the man replied. He reached into his jacket and produced legal documents with that name on them: Mr M. J. Druitt.

'What is your business in Whitechapel, Mr Druitt?'

'I'm a barrister with chambers at King's Bench Walk,' he replied, almost bored. 'But I regularly do charity work at Oxford House; to give what assistance I can to the degraded and the destitute. That woman the constable saw me with had been assisted by our group before. I was trying to convince her to line up at the night refuge on Crispin Street for her own safety, but we were interrupted by your man.'

Another Inspector spoke more harshly at this implied reprimand. 'There have been two unfortunates butchered tonight, sir, the young constable was only doing his duty.'

Then came the inevitable query which Montie was expecting – in fact, banking on.

'Are you related, sir, to the Dr Robert Druitt?'

'I'm his nephew.'

At that moment, we think it was all over as pulses in the room raced at the idea of detaining an upper-class professional giving up his free time to do God's work and one who had V.I.P. connections. If he could account for his bloodstains he would be go free – scot free.

'Those bloodstains on your shirt cuffs, sir – could you explain how you got them?'

Mr Druitt examined them with surprise but not alarm. His brow furrowed in that exaggerated, supercilious way of Oxbridge men, as if struggling to fathom how on earth he could be asked something so trivial. His eyes lit up and he grinned as he seemed to remember.

'I have dabbled in medicine and surgery,' Mr Druitt explained, 'like my late, illustrious uncle, and tonight I ended up treating a man with a wound in his leg and, rather than condemn him to a tedious wait at the public hospital, I did my best to stitch him up. But I'm no surgeon, officers, and may have done him more harm than good.'

The Inspectors looked at each other and communicated with their eyes: 'that will do.'

'Sorry to have troubled you, sir, would you like a constable to escort you back towards your chambers?'

'Thank you, no Inspector. I am sorry to have been the cause of all this fuss.'

Just as the barrister was exiting the station, a detective came bounding out towards him.

'Mr Druitt, stop!' Montague froze and turned slowly around, his face a blank.

'You forgot your bag, sir!'

'Thanks officer, I'm always doing that. I'd forget my own head if it was not so firmly attached.'

That bag may have contained organs, or at the very least clothing fragments Druitt had removed from Catherine Eddowes. If only the police had not been so intimidated by Montague's class and connections they might have opened it – and the nightmare really would have ended.

Is there evidence for the speculative, historical recreation above? Did Montague J. Druitt come to police attention when he was alive? Or, was he entirely a posthumous suspect and solution?

Though it has been missed by most people who have read Sir Melville Macnaghten's enjoyable autobiography, when it comes to incriminating evidence against [the unnamed] Montie Druitt, the retired police chief strongly implies that there had been two streams of information about him which had arrived separately at Scotland Yard. Also, by implication, this second stream flowed to Macnaghten personally bypassing normal channels. He wrote in 1914:

Although, as I shall endeavour to show in this chapter, the Whitechapel murderer, *in all probability*, put an end to himself *soon after* the Dorset Street affair [murder] in November 1888, *certain facts*, pointing to this conclusion, were not in possession of the police till *some years after* I became a detective officer.[1] (Our italics)

According to the first stream, in 1888, this suspect was almost nothing, whereas in the second stream, due to 'certain facts', he was everything. The original facts about this suspect must have been mundane, or unpersuasive. After all, if Druitt was an entirely posthumous solution, Macnaghten could have written that *all* the facts were only learned years later, which would be much less embarrassing for Scotland Yard. Instead, a suspect they had been aware of – to some undefined degree – was catapulted by incontrovertible evidence to the top of the list, though a solution that was beyond being tested with a jury (hence the appropriate caution of Macnaghten's 'in all probability').

There are other sources that point in this direction: Druitt being arrested or, at the very least, being questioned by police. Such an encounter would have to have been in the East End with his name being taken down. Otherwise, there would be no facts in the first stream of information to be measured against the second. In 1894 Macnaghten would write two versions of an internal memorandum about the Whitechapel Murders and name Montague Druitt as a prime suspect in both. He wrote there as if Mr Druitt had come to police attention while alive, though it has to be said that since he tells so many fibs in both documents this does not, evidentially speaking, amount to much (*see* Chapter XVII).

Sir Basil Home Thomson (1861–1939) was an Old Etonian who went to school with Sir Melville Macnaghten and succeeded him as Assistant Commissioner of the CID in 1913. He also attended New College Oxford with none other than Montague John Druitt. Sadly, in 1925 his rich and lengthy career of public service as a police chief, colonial and prison administrator, anti-Bolshevik activist and master of espionage, was extinguished by ignominious scandal. Sir Basil was arrested in Hyde Park soliciting a female prostitute. He tried bribing the arresting officer and, when that failed, later, claimed to widespread ridicule that he was merely researching a book. Sir Basil Thomson was convicted and disgraced.[2] In his writings on 'Jack the Ripper', Sir Basil may have slipped up again for he admitted, albeit in only the American edition of his 1936 history of Scotland Yard that [the unnamed] Druitt *had* been in police custody: 'His friends had grave doubts about him, *but the evidence was insufficient for detaining him with any hope of obtaining a conviction*'.[3] (Our italics) This strongly suggests Thomson knew, from Macnaghten, that Druitt – a man he had once known at New College, Oxford – had been arrested and, however briefly, investigated and freed. Or, since Thomson makes a number of 'errors' over the years about the Whitechapel case and the 'drowned doctor' suspect – deliberate or not – and seems to be reliant on second-hand sources, perhaps the arrest of the 'doctor' was just a guess on his part, and Sir Melville did not confide to his successor that he had attended university with the very fiend.

In 1903 the retired Chief Detective Inspector Frederick Abberline was happily telling a reporter that he was certain that a recently convicted wife poisoner, who had lived in Whitechapel during the murders, was almost certainly 'Jack the Ripper'. His disparaging comments, however, about the drowned man solution caused a spat with George R. Sims, which will be dealt with further on. What concerns us here is that Abberline did recall Montie Druitt and, while his memory is flawed and his knowledge is of only the *first* stream of facts on this suspect, his comments are instructive as we see in *The Pall Mall Gazette* of 31 March 1903 when he is asked about the doctor who killed himself. Abberline dismisses it out of hand:

> I know all about that story. But what does it amount to? Simply this. Soon after the last murder in Whitechapel the body of a *young doctor* was found in the Thames, but there is absolutely nothing beyond the fact that he was found at that time to incriminate him.... Then again, the fact that several months after December, 1888, when the *student's body* was found, the detectives were told still to hold themselves in readiness for further investigations seems to point to the conclusion that Scotland Yard did not in any way consider the evidence as final. (Our italics)

The most important aspect of Druitt that Abberline recalls clearly is that he was young and that he was a medical *student* (the word 'doctor' as argued earlier was used interchangeably with 'student'). We think the honest Abberline is almost remembering that the 'young doctor' had been on a suspect list as a completely minor figure because he had been arrested while alive and cleared. This is because the timing of Druitt's suicide was too early to have brought the drowned barrister into contention; as there were between two and four subsequent murders ascribed to 'Jack the Ripper' by police, press and public.

In the writings of Macnaghten's literary friends from 1898 there is mention of a bobby who allegedly encountered the murderer but missed his chance to make an arrest. We have to machete our way through a tough, fictional shield here, as the suspect involved is a Polish Jewish immigrant supposedly seen with Catherine Eddowes rather than the young, gentile-featured man dressed like a sailor – and witnessed by a Polish Jewish immigrant. We argue that two threads are being deliberately interwoven and obscured: Druitt was seen by a Polish man in Mitre Square and, a little later, he was confronted – and arrested? – by a police constable on the night of the double murder. Here is George Sims from a 1907 article on the true identity of 'Jack the Ripper':

> One man only, a policeman, saw [The Ripper] leaving the place in which he had just accomplished a fiendish deed, but *failed* owing to the darkness, to get a good view of him. A little later the policeman stumbled over the lifeless body of the victim... The policeman

who got a glimpse of Jack in Mitre Court said, when *some time afterwards he saw the Pole*, that he was the height and build he had seen on the night of the murder. (Our italics)

This policeman, claims Sims, saw the suspect later and was still unable to identify him, a disappointing outcome to say the least. In his 1914 memoirs Sir Melville Macnaghten more tightly fuses together the two threads: the Polish witness seeing Druitt and Eddowes before he killed and slashed her corpse, and some hapless, unnamed bobby who must have encountered the real killer – and who comes across, yet again, as ineffective. Macnaghten even has the real Jewish witnesses emerging from a club near Mitre Square transferred to the first murder that night. They are *all* improbably riding on the cart that interrupted Druitt from mutilating Liz Stride (was it a taxi service?). He even more starkly portrays the gentile policeman as comparatively useless:

When the public excitement then was at white heat, two murders unquestionably by the same hand took place on the night of 30th September [1888]. A woman, Elizabeth Stride, was found in Berners [sic] Street, with her throat cut, but no attempt at mutilation. In this case there can be little doubt but that the murderer was disturbed at his demonical work by *some Jews who at that hour drove up to an anarchist club in the street.* But the lust for blood was unsatisfied. The madman started off in the search of another victim, whom he found in Catherine Eddowes. This woman's body, very badly mutilated, was found in a dark corner of Mitre Square. *On this occasion it is probable that the police officer on duty in the vicinity saw the murderer with his victim a few minutes before, but no satisfactory description was forthcoming.* (Our italics)

It is an uncharacteristically officious, even jarring, putdown of a fellow Scotland Yard man by the usually sunny and affable 'Good Old Mac'. The Polish immigrant Joseph Lawende's description of a 30-year-old man of medium build and height, and with a fair moustache, chatting with Catherine Eddowes is completely buried and obscured by Macnaghten. It also means that the anti-Semitic graffiti can be explained as a *specific* message by the murderer, motivated by rage for having been interrupted by this handful of Jewish men travelling on a cart:

During this night an apron, on which bloody hands had been wiped, was found in Goulburn [sic] Street (situated if my memory is correct, about half-way between Berners Street and Mitre Square). Hard by was a writing in chalk on the wall, to the effect that 'the *Jews* are the men who will not be blamed for nothing'. The apron gave no clue and the chalk writing was obliterated by the order of a high police official, who was seemingly afraid that a riot against the Jews might be the outcome of the strange 'writing on the wall'. *This was the only message left behind by the murderer*.[4] (Our italics)

For the first time in his writings on this subject, Macnaghten confirms that the graffiti was written by [the unnamed] Druitt without explaining where the barrister was for nearly an hour between the murder of Eddowes and depositing her apron and writing the message. Since it was not a cartload of Hebrew men who interrupted him before he could mutilate Stride's corpse, why then did Druitt really pause to write this cryptic yet clearly anti-Semitic message?

Sims never once mentions the controversial 'writing on the wall', but he does repeatedly refer to another vital witness that night – a coffee stall owner. This never named Victorian barista claimed he had served a customer who had bloody cuffs and bragged of having knowledge of the two murders *before* it was publicly known. The witness also thought that the suspect bore an uncanny resemblance to none other than George Sims. Strangely, the police seemed to have been completely disinterested in this eyewitness – why?

We have only a single reference to this episode outside of Sims' multiple accounts. This is from *The North Eastern Gazette* of 21 September 1889:

'JACK THE RIPPER' SEEN BY EVERYONE BUT THE POLICE

The London edition of the *New York Herald* further says: – One of those innumerable *cranks* who have found 'Jack the Ripper' called at the *Herald* office yesterday. He has written a complete history of the case, and intends to offer himself as a witness at the inquest on Tuesday next. 'I am quite certain I know the man,' he said: '*I have talked with him many times*, and I can show you his photograph'; whereupon he produced one of Dagonet's poems, and pointing to the portrait of George R. Sims said, 'That's *like the man*, sir, as near as possible. There you get the contour, sir. My man's face was *bronzed*, and not quite so deathly pale, but travelling would produce that, sir. That's like the man, sir.' (Our italics)

According to this acerbic account, the witness (a 'crank') is not saying that the suspect looked exactly like Sims, or that he had a naval beard. Instead the 'contours' of his features are similar, and that he was tanned. He had also spoken to him several times; he is, or was a regular customer. After another Whitechapel murder of a poor woman in July 1889, perceived to be by the same maniac as the 1888 homicides, the coffee stall owner was trying again, apparently with no success, to interest people in his sighting. The only person who seems to have taken this man seriously, at least by 1891, was George R. Sims. In a 1904 interview (and the same 1907 article mentioned earlier) Sims explained exactly when and how he resembled 'Jack the Ripper' – because the famous writer was never in doubt it was an authentic sighting of Montague Druitt and not the ravings of a 'crank', lunatic or pest. He told this to a reporter from *The Daily Express* and his revealing comments were published on 1 August 1904:

DAGONET'S DOUBLE
STARTLING REMINISCENCES OF THE 'RIPPER' MURDERS

'A man who had seen Jack at a coffee stall in the small hours on the night that two women were killed, and had noticed his shirt cuff was bloodstained, took my portrait with him afterwards to Dr Forbes Winslow, and said, "That is the man; on the night of the murders, long before they were discovered, I spoke to him. In conversation I said, "I wonder if we shall hear of another Jack the Ripper murder?" "You'll very likely hear of two tomorrow," was the reply, and the man walked hurriedly away.'

WHO WAS THE MAN

Seen last night by an *Express* representative, Mr Sims said he believed that the coffee stall keeper came across his portrait on the cover of the first edition of *The Social Kaleidoscope*, in a shop in a side-street in Southwark. [*See* illustration in plate section.]

'It was a terrible portrait – *taken, when I was very ill*. My face was *drawn and haggard*, and surprisingly like the Ripper, whom only the coffee stall keeper *and a policeman ever set eyes upon* ... 'Mr Sims said that he had not the slightest doubt in his mind as to who the 'Ripper' was.

'Nor have the police', he continued.

'In the archives of the Home Office are the name and history of the wretched man. He was a *mad physician belonging to a highly respected family*. He committed the crimes after having been confined in a lunatic asylum as a homicidal maniac.' (Our italics)

In that picture on the cover of his first published writing from 1879, the usually rotund Sims does look quite different; he is atypically thin and his face is longer due, as he says in 1904, to being 'ill ... drawn and haggard'. He also has his hair parted in the centre (rather than his usual off-centre) and, with his high cheeks and his hooded eyelids he does resemble surviving pictures of Montague Druitt. He also mentions that a policeman also encountered this same man (by implication an English gentile). We think that all these various scraps – some further complicated by being deliberately semi-fictionalised – are trying to pre-emptively discredit a bobby who might come forward and say that he had arrested the suspect described as a 'mad physician'. A promising suspect – as he was bloodstained and had been seen consorting with a prostitute – was questioned in custody on the night of the double murder but quickly released.

There was no hard evidence against the medico toff, and yet according to all these sources in the late Victorian and Edwardian eras he must have been the 'The Ripper'. Perhaps this policeman might recall that the inquiry was a bit hasty, even perfunctory, due to the impeccable pedigree of the gentleman in question – and that over the years this putative bobby saw that a famous writer like George Sims had to all intents and purposes blamed an unnamed PC for letting them all down. He might at last have come forward and complained about this treatment. Such a source does, in fact, exist. This is again from *The Daily Express* of 16 March 1931:

'I CAUGHT JACK THE RIPPER'
EX-CONSTABLE AND A STRANGE NIGHT MEETING
MAN RELEASED

The cause of this intriguing headline during the Great Depression was an ex-police constable Robert Clifford Spicer, who had been fired from the force in 1889 for drunkenness on duty – an embarrassing fact he left out of his self-serving, bombastic letter to the newspaper.[5] Spicer had just retired from being the groundskeeper of a school sports field. In his letter he said he was inspired to write to the newspaper due to a recent article on the alleged psychic, Robert James Lees, and how he had once led the police to the very door of the mad doctor who was the killer and subsequently placed in an asylum for the rest of his days. But, he writes, the madman could have been taken off the streets much earlier as he, Spicer, had arrested him and bundled off him to be interrogated at Commercial Street police station.

Only 22 years old at the time, PC Spicer had, he wrote, stumbled upon the suspect in Henage Court, off Brick Lane, handing money over to a young prostitute (whom the copper knew by name):

> He turned out to be a highly respected doctor and gave a Brixton address. His shirt cuffs had blood on them. Jack had the proverbial bag with him (a brown one). This was not opened, and he was allowed to go.

Spicer says he saw the same man a few times afterwards – at a time when Montague Druitt would have been deceased – accosting women at Liverpool Street Station. The constable would cheekily tease him about searching for new victims. Recognising his intrepid pursuer – the one cop who could not be fooled – the doctor would turn and bolt. Or so the 64-year-old Spicer tells the yarn, complete with a 'Jack' wearing a high hat, black suit and a gold watch and chain. At first, it appears that Spicer's unverified tale could not to be a sighting of Druitt. At least not until you look a little closer at the former constable's account; it is expanded in the article by a reporter from the *Express* who went to interview the dyspeptic geriatric. Excitedly shaking a gnarled forefinger at the ghosts of the pompous detectives who thwarted him from enjoying that headline ('I Caught Jack the Ripper') over fifty years earlier, Spicer decries:

> 'I was so disappointed when the man was allowed to go that I no longer had my heart in police work', he said. 'The case was taken out of my hands by the detective branch but I am sure I would have been able to prove my suspicions if the matter had been left to me. As soon as I saw the man in that dark alley – way in the early hours of the morning I felt sure he was the Ripper. The woman to whom he was talking was a notorious character of the class to which all the Ripper's victims belonged. He evaded my questions when I challenged him. "That's no business of yours," he replied when I asked him what he was doing. "Oh isn't it?" I replied. "Then you come along with me", and I marched him off to the police station, with the woman following. The news that the Ripper was caught spread like lightning through the district. Women peered out of their bedroom windows and shouted and cheered. Some were so excited that they ran half-naked into the street. A crowd followed us to the station.'

Robert Spicer missed his calling: he should have been a Hollywood screenwriter. His epic march of the arrested villain through the now-safe Whitechapel streets by him, the triumphant young hero, complete with just enough – but not too much – exposed female flesh, would surely have impressed the likes of moguls such as Cecil B. DeMille and Irving Thalberg. At least until the disappointingly lame finale:

> 'I took the man before the inspector and said that I charged him on suspicion with being Jack the Ripper. There were about eight or nine inspectors in the station at the time – all taking part in the hunt for the criminal. Imagine how I felt when I got into trouble for making the arrest! The station inspector asked me what I meant arresting a man who proved to be a respectable doctor. "What is a respectable doctor doing with a notorious woman at a quarter to two in the morning?" I asked, but no one would listen to me. The man was released, and that, as far as I was concerned, was an end to the matter.'

We would happily leave this yarn as nothing more than that; a groundskeeper's unbelievable anecdote to prove that he was not just another forgettable labourer – except for two other intriguing details of his original letter. He writes as if he took note of the Edwardian revelations about the 'mad physician' solution, one of which reportedly involved a bobby meeting this suspect on the night of the double murder (although his memory has bent these sources into a pretzel). He also describes a man who resembles Druitt:

> There have been several articles and confessions from time to time in the newspapers. Jack the Ripper was supposed to have admitted he was *arrested by a young constable, but was released*. I claim to be that constable... [the suspect was] *about five feet 8 or 9 inches* and about 12 stone, *fair moustache, high forehead and rosy cheeks*... (Our italics)

Behind the Hollywood-style window dressing what actually happened is that Spicer arrested Druitt, who was the same man seen that night by the coffee stall witness. He turned out to be the *nephew* of a 'very respectable doctor' and could account for the bloodstains due to having studied a bit of medicine and doing charity work among the poor for Oxford House. Druitt's celebrity pedigree had indeed helped him out of a jam. And when the coffee stall keeper tried to get traction with the authorities for his legitimate sighting, the police shunned him because they knew of whom he was talking about: Dr Druitt's nephew, who had been 'cleared' and they did not want a 'highly respected family' embarrassed.

Initially Spicer thought no more of the incident, and was soon out of the force due to his own shortcomings. Nevertheless, he was bitter at his dismissal and these ill-feelings festered over the years. He also noticed in the writings of George Sims/Dagonet that the fiend had been allegedly identified as a doctor who committed suicide – and that a bobby had been less than effective on the night of the double murder. He assumed, correctly, that this referred to him – and he was incensed at this as it was his superiors who had released the suspect. Once he latched onto the story about the psychic in 1931, he *had* to say that his doctor was alive and kicking afterwards in order to align his account with the new story, and not the one Sims had repeatedly told.

Finally there is Sir Melville Macnaghten's strange comment at his 1913 press conference announcing his retirement. Though he would deny it in his memoirs, the police chief claimed that not being on the force in 1888 (to his acute embarrassment and frustration his appointment was delayed by a year – *see* Chapter XVI) was no less than the 'greatest regret of his entire life' because he had missed 'having a go' at 'Jack the Ripper'. But since nobody knew who the killer was then, what possible difference would it have made? Macnaghten seems to be sincerely saying that his presence as a police sleuth would have been decisive; the madman would have likely been caught. This is confirmed by his farewell police dinner where the *West Gippsland Gazette* of 2 September 1913 claims an emotional Macnaghten decried to the admiring throng: 'Had he joined the force earlier he might have *had a chance of catching Jack the Ripper*'. (Our italics) He sounds as much of an empty boaster as Robert Spicer. Unless what Macnaghten meant was that had he been on the force in 1888, he was *uniquely placed* to expose Montague Druitt. He thought, perhaps, that he would have spotted the name 'M. J. Druitt' on a list of arrests. Enjoying as he did a close friendship at the Home Office with Colonel Vivian Majendie – and knowing the latter had a relative who was marrying into the clan of the late Dr Robert Druitt – he would have, as a personal favour, discreetly checked out this Mr Druitt, and, he believed, tumbled to his game. For that to be true, at some point Druitt's name would have to have been officially registered as a suspect, one who was questioned or arrested in Whitechapel – and released.

In 1914, Macnaghten asserted without any qualifications that it was the unnamed Druitt who wrote the message in chalk; 'the only clue ever left behind by the murderer'. Clumsy as it was, a panicked Montie may have made this scrawl, leaving the apron fragment as the bait, after he had been questioned – and his name had been taken down. He needed to divert the investigation away from an upper middle-class gentile by throwing suspicion on a handy victim of sectarian and racial prejudice. By Arnold's and Warren's reported reactions, the wily barrister succeeded for a while. And as a part-time schoolmaster, he may well have carried pieces of chalk in his pockets (tantalisingly in the photograph we discovered of M. J. Druitt in the Canning Club there is a chalk scrawl on the wall behind the young gentlemen).

If Druitt was detained by the police and released, Scotland Yard had made a blunder which, sadly, would not be their last. In letting him slip through their fingers, they had doomed the mad barrister's next and final victim: Mary Jane Kelly.

Charnel House on Dorset Street

For Alderman Whitehead his elevation to Lord Mayor of The City of London had not turned out as he might have hoped. His predecessor Mr De Keyser, now safely back in his native Brussels, had weighed into the debate about Jack the Ripper and his comments, though unhelpful to Whitehead, were in hindsight chillingly insightful. The inauguration day, the Lord Mayor's Show, is held each November when the newly elected Lord Mayor is driven through the City to the Guildhall. Various city guilds and military regiments parade through the streets, which are closed to usual traffic. Even though Whitehead had announced that extra funds would provide more meals for the poor, hoots and abuse still greeted him from some of the crowd as his carriage progressed through the crowd-lined streets. The previous Lord Mayor, De Keyser, had happily bid farewell to London at the peak of the Ripper murders. Once safely abroad, De Keyser became a self-appointed expert on the Whitechapel crimes. His theories failed to entertain any acknowledgement that the murderer's deeds could become a catalyst for change in the East End; he rejected the social reformer angle that some sections of the press were adopting as the possible motive. Montague, scouring newspapers for reports on his crimes, would surely have become enraged at the insulting proclamations of the former mayor.

Seated with a journalist from *L'Indépendance Belge*, in his birthplace, Brussels, De Keyser casually shrugged off the prevailing theories as to the identity of the Whitechapel murderer. 'I do not believe him to be an enraged moralist or a man skilled in surgery and the scientific Socialist theory is just claptrap. This murderer is simply a maniac.' Then De Keyser grew animated, 'He is a kind of human mad dog, perhaps he could be of interest to Monsieur Pasteur, I do believe he can now cure rabies. I give him some credit he is intelligent but because his whole physical and intellectual being is so set on the single object of his monomania that he has been able to evade all the professional and amateur detectives.' The reporter braved one more question to the impatient and pompous official, 'Will he finally be caught?' 'Yes' replied the outgoing Lord Mayor, 'he will be caught when he commits his next crime. A whole army of bloodhounds [metaphorical and literal] will be on his track the moment he draws blood again. If he does not begin again, it is a corpse – the corpse of a suicide – that will ultimately be found. With a whole community against him, he cannot long escape.'[1]

Exactly a month after that article was published, the day dawned windy and cold. There had been heavy showers the night before and with the threat of further rain, the numbers lining the streets were deemed to be less than previous years. As the parade made its way along Fleet Street, the mayor was heckled and jeered 'by youths who held up the placards of the evening papers announcing the revolting murder in Whitechapel. These were flourished before them with yells of "Look at this!"'[2]

Montie Druitt was well aware of the derision the Lord Mayor's Show received from many quarters. Even among the upper classes it was seen as a bit of a joke. The new Lord Mayor, resplendent in all his regalia, was providing one free meal to the poor of Whitechapel for one day of the year, which was almost rubbing salt into the wound of what was politely called 'The Social Question'. What about the other 364 days? The parade swept around the streets of the legal district and the men of King's Bench Walk would endure the closing of streets and the infiltration of the common people onto their patch. Druitt, having had a busy month with his court case, could contemplate never murdering again. He may have calculated that as the police had no clue to the identity of Jack the Ripper, he might be able to recommit himself to a normal life, with his secret intact. He had made a difference, he had made them see! But he was panicked by some of the supposed eyewitness descriptions. This was understandable, even more so because of that bobby and the chief detectives. With his name on a file, another arrest for loitering in the vicinity of the crimes might prompt further investigation – and a case might be built against him. It would be a foolish gamble to ever enter that evil, quarter mile again. Self-interest should reign now. Yet Montie was unravelling.

He couldn't just revert to his old life now. With each murder he had become less of the old Montie and more of the madman with the nickname of 'Jack the Ripper'. His mania was becoming stronger and more frequent as was his obsession with reading news of the crimes – and the provocative comments of Mr De Keyser stoked his rage.

On the morning of Thursday 8 November, Mary Jane Kelly woke up in her one-room hovel at 13 Miller's Court, Dorset Street, with a thumping headache and a pressing problem. Her rent was now well over a month in arrears, to the tune of 29 shillings, and she could not avoid the landlord McCarthy for too much longer.[3] At the age of 25, Mary was used to working her way out of a sticky situation and just as promptly landing herself back into another. For eighteen months she had resided in various lodgings with Joseph Barnett. She had furnished him with a variety of stories about her former life, her real name was Marie Jeanette, she was born in Limerick, or perhaps she was Welsh. She had been or had worked for a West End madam and another time had lived like a lady with a gentleman in Paris.[4] Some of her story was undoubtedly plausible, for Mary Kelly stood out amongst the drabness and hopelessness of the East End due to her comely looks. Her beautiful face and shapely, rounded figure had not yet yielded to the rapid withering of youth which comes from a lack of food and washing facilities and too much alcohol. Regardless of her past, Barnett was happy to remain and with his regular wage from his work as a Billingsgate porter, she was happy to let him. It was in the summer of 1888 when he lost his job and the money dried up that the previously short hours they had spent together became all day and the couple, both heavy drinkers, began to quarrel.

Barnett later explained that Mary Jane 'was always very anxious to hear about the murders and used to make him read to her anything in the press about the horrors gripping the whole nation.'[5] Mary became so concerned that she took to allowing prostitutes who were her friends stay overnight for mutual protection. She seemed willing to let her relationship with Barnett slide once his wages dried up. In the heat of one of their all-too-frequent arguments, she threw an object at his head, missed, and instead broke a window.

Walter Dew would become famous in 1910 for intercepting and arresting the wife muderer 'Dr' Hawley Crippen, but back in 1888 he was a humble detective constable. He recalled Kelly as 'a good looking and buxom young woman'.[6] She knew she could employ her charms with a better standard of client, if one should come along. She believed she could still pass herself off as one who had lived as a Parisian courtesan and if she could find a better class of pleasure-seeking man, very soon, she could settle up with McCarthy and maybe even have money to spare. To Mrs Elizabeth Prater who lived in the room above Kelly, Mary Jane was 'a very pleasant girl who seemed to be on good terms with everybody'. Mary told Mrs Prater that she was looking forward to the annual parade the next day. 'I hope it will be a fine day tomorrow as I want to go to the Lord Mayor's Show.'[7]

As Thursday wore on, however, Mary became more morose. She spent the afternoon at the Ten Bells, one of her local drinking haunts, and on returning home, the worse for drink, she tearfully confided to another friend, Lizzie Albrook, 'This will be the last Lord Mayor's Show I shall see. I can't stand it any longer. This Jack the Ripper business is getting on my nerves. I have made up my mind to go home to my mother. It is safer there'.[8] Lizzie recalled the last words that Mary said to her, 'Whatever you do don't you do wrong and turn out as I have.'[9] That evening Barnett returned to Miller's Court wanting to speak with Mary so Lizzie discreetly left them alone. Barnett was sorry to have to admit to Mary that he had not found work and had 'nothing to give her'.[10]

Whatever further transpired in the early hours of Friday morning is speculative. Inspector Walter Dew, who had known Mary Kelly by sight, believed that whoever Jack the Ripper was, he must have had the 'power to quell the natural fear in the minds of women and especially to the type whom his coming meant an unspeakable death'.[11] The type of man who was well-spoken and not vulgar, dressed up or down but very clean regardless, controlled in manner and able to show a woman like Mary Kelly a substantial amount of cash when negotiating a 'trick'. He might as well be describing Montague Druitt.

Around 2 a.m. on what was to be Lord Mayor's Day, Mary Jane Kelly was trying to scrounge some money from an unemployed, young labourer named George Hutchinson, while he, homeless, hoped to share her bed for the night, with or without sex. Instead a very affluent-looking gentleman appeared and tapped Mary on the shoulder. He made her laugh and quickly negotiated a tryst. A very miffed Hutchinson took a good look at this client whom he deemed to be a little over 5 feet 6 inches, slim and with a waxed moustache. He looked like a prosperous man of the Hebrew faith – ostentatiously so. In his witness statement to Inspector Abberline, Hutchinson claimed the man was wore a long Astrakhan coat, a tie with a horseshoe pin, spats and a gold chain (with a red stone hanging from it).[12] If this was

Montie, he had pulled out all stops to disguise himself, an appearance far removed from a sailor but which also consolidated his sectarian chalk message – the Jews are to blame. The couple returned to her little room and shut the door. Hutchinson grew tired of waiting for the session to be over and sloped off to try and find another free bed. Did it amuse Montague that he was about to a massacre a beautiful young woman on a street that was the same name as his hometown district?

In the morning, as the crowds of London began to line the streets for the parade, the ill-tempered John McCarthy gruffly ordered his messenger, John Bower, to go to number thirteen and try to get some rent. It was now Friday 9 November 1888 and McCarthy, realising the rent arrears were heading towards two months' worth, had lost patience. Bower steeled himself and reluctantly set off to collect the debt, anticipating a reception of either abuse or tears. Arriving at the door he knocked, but got no response. He then banged with a closed fist. Again, there was no answer. Bowyer bent down to peer through the keyhole. The key on the inside was missing but even so, the room was so dark he couldn't see a thing. He walked around to the window and noticed it was covered on the inside by what remained of a cheap curtain. With the broken pane still unrepaired he put his hand in and pushed aside the curtain. 'He looked into the room and saw the woman lying on the bed, entirely naked, covered with blood and apparently dead.'[13] John Bower sprinted back to McCarthy, who returned as quickly as his stiff legs would take him. Bower urged him to look through the window while avoiding a second glance himself. After some confusion, as he tried to adjust his eyesight to what he was actually looking at in the gloom, the hardened landlord recoiled from the window in shock. He had just enough breath to coherently order Bower to fetch the police without delay. Walter Dew who was by then already hardened to viewing unpleasant crime scenes was one of the eye-witnesses called to the scene:

> When my eyes had become accustomed to the dim light I saw a sight which I shall never forget to my dying day. The whole horror of that room will only be known to those of us whose duty it was to enter it. The full details are unprintable. …There was little left of her, not much more than a skeleton. Her face was terribly scarred and mutilated. All this was horrifying enough, but the mental picture of that sight which remains most vividly with me is the poor woman's eyes. They were wide open, and seemed to be staring straight at me with a look of terror.[14]

What had been inflicted upon the body of Mary Kelly, after a quick and quiet strangulation, was almost beyond normal comprehension. The signature of 'Jack the Ripper', the throat cut from ear to ear and the mutilation and removal or displacement of organs was this time not enough. The grisly scene contained the mere remnants of a human carcass after it had been literally torn to pieces. Most of what made Mary Jane Kelly human, at least in appearance, was gone. Her ears and nose were removed, her breasts cut off and placed on a table by the side of the bed. Her stomach and abdomen were torn open with a sharp knife and the kidneys and heart placed on the side table of grisly specimens. The liver had been removed and placed on the right thigh and the once beautiful face was slashed, leaving only the eyes intact. As had occurred before in this series of murders, the uterus had been extracted and appeared to be missing. What lay before the sickened witnesses, the police and their photographer whose job it was to review the crime scene and to record an account of a murder, was the remains of a young woman, Mary Jane Kelly who had been described by her heartbroken friend Mrs Prater as 'tall and pretty, and as fair as a lily'.[15]

Without a record of why Druitt did this and how he felt about it, we have to turn to insightful fiction about the dark side overwhelming a civilized conscience. This is, once more, from Robert Louis Stevenson's *The Strange Case of Dr Jekyll and Mr Hyde*:

> Instantly the spirit of hell awoke in me and raged. With a transport of glee I mauled the unresisting body, tasting delight from every blow; and it was not till weariness had begun to succeed, that I was suddenly, in the top fit of my delirium, struck through the heart by a cold thrill of terror. A mist dispersed; I saw my life to be forfeit and fled from the scene of these excesses, at once glorying and trembling, my lust of evil gratified and stimulated, my love of life screwed to the topmost peg.[16]

The police chief Sir Melville Macnaghten, we argue further on, privately conferred with members of Montague's family. In early 1891 they told him what they knew about their maniacal member's reaction to what he had done to his final victim, and why. We think that their description of details of this crime scene convinced him that their Montie was the killer and they were not just delusional. They knew aspects of the crime scene known only to the police and the killer. They told him that they believed their deceased loved one suffered from an epileptic illness (*see* Chapter XVIII) and not just a psychological ailment. This is from the chief's memoirs of 1914:

On the morning of 9th November, Mary Jeanette Kelly, a comparatively young woman of some twenty-five years of age, and said to have been *possessed of considerable, personal attractions*, was found murdered in a room in Miller's Court, Dorset Street. This was the last of the series, and it was by far the most horrible. The mutilations were of a positively fiendish description, almost indescribable in their savagery, and the doctors who were called in to examine the remains, averred that the operator must have been at least two hours over his hellish job. A fire was burning low in the room, but neither candles nor gas were there.

The madman made a bonfire of some old newspapers, and of his victim's clothes, and, by this dim, irreligious light, a scene was enacted which nothing seen by Dante in his visit to the infernal regions could have surpassed. It will have been noticed that the fury of the murderer, as evinced in his methods of mutilation, increased on every occasion, and his appetite appears to have become sharpened by indulgence.

There can be no doubt that in the room at Miller's Court the madman found ample scope for the opportunities he had all along been seeking, and the probability is that, after his awful glut on this occasion, his brain gave way altogether and he committed suicide; otherwise the murders would not have ceased. *The man, of course, was a sexual maniac, but such madness takes Protean forms*, as will be shown later on in other cases.

Sexual murders are the most difficult of all for police to bring home to the perpetrators, for motives there are none; only a lust for blood and in many cases a hatred of woman as woman. *Not infrequently the maniac possesses a diseased body, and this was probably so in the case of the Whitechapel murderer.* Many residents in the East End (and some in the West) came under suspicion of police, but though several persons were detained, no one was ever charged with these offences. [Our Italics]

The newspapers across the country were saturated with this unprecedented escalation by the murderer. One example is the *Worcestershire Chronicle* of 17 November 1888,

LONDON'S LATEST HORROR.
Another of 'Jack the Ripper's' Victims.
Misery, Murder, and Mutilation

As was briefly announced in our city editions last Friday, a painful sensation has again been created in London—and indeed throughout the country—by the discovery that another woman of the unfortunate class has been murdered and shockingly mutilated in the East End.

All of the scrappy, semi-fictionalised sources agree that what Druitt did to Mary Jane Kelly's remains broke his mind – at least for a while. Wherever he went, we think that he ended up in the presence of his cousin, Reverend Charles Druitt, who must have been visiting his mother in Strathmore Gardens, Kensington. Under the comparatively limited protection of the Church of England's version of this sacrament – both in terms of law and custom – Montague confessed all his crimes to Charles. The latter wasted no time in contacting his other cousin, William, Montie's older brother. The cool and calculating Bournemouth solicitor, the Dorset clergyman found, had already taken covert, even criminal, steps *before* the Miller's Court explosion to get his insane sibling out of the country.

Right: Dr Robert Druitt (1814–1883), Montague Druitt's famous uncle. (Photograph by Moira & Haigh Courtesy of Wellcome Collection CC)

Far right: Montague's aunt Isabella Druitt, née Hopkinson (1823–1899) tried to tell the authorities 'The Ripper' had died. (AM 865-1-4 By courtesy of the County Archivist, West Sussex Record Office, and with acknowledgements to Causeway Resources)

Right: Dr Robert Druitt and family. Back row, third from right, is Charles Druitt, the future clergyman whom we believe took Montague's confession of guilt. (AM 865-1-27 By courtesy of the County Archivist, West Sussex Record Office, and with acknowledgements to Causeway Resources)

Above left: Reverend Charles Druitt (1848–1900). (AM 865-1-7 By courtesy of the County Archivist, West Sussex Record Office, and with acknowledgements to Causeway Resources)

Above middle: Isabel Majendie Druitt, née Majendie Hill (1856–1925). Her marriage to Charles united the Druitt, Du Boulay and Majendie clans. (AM 865-1-12 By courtesy of the County Archivist, West Sussex Record Office, and with acknowledgements to Causeway Resources)

Above right: Gertrude Druitt (1862–1901) (AM 865-1-5 By courtesy of the County Archivist, West Sussex Record Office, and with acknowledgements to Causeway Resources)

Above left: Dr William Druitt (1820–1885), father of Montague John Druitt. (AM 865-1-54 By courtesy of the County Archivist, West Sussex Record Office, and with acknowledgements to Causeway Resources)

Above middle: Ethel Mary Druitt (1871–1950), Montague's youngest sister. (AM 865-1-9 By courtesy of the County Archivist, West Sussex Record Office, and with acknowledgements to Causeway Resources)

Above right: William Harvey Druitt (1856–1909), older brother of Montague and the leader of the first phase of the cover-up. (Stewart P. Evans)

Far left: James Druitt senior (1816–1904), Montague's uncle.

Above left: Lt Col Edward Druitt (1859–1922), a younger brother to Montague.

Left: Queen Elizabeth's Grammar School in Wimborne, Dorset. Montague Druitt attended this school in his early years. (Courtesy of Wellcome Collection)

Above left: Montague John Druitt (1857–1888) as a young schoolboy. He can be seen in the centre of the group staring directly into the camera. (Courtesy of the Warden and Scholars of Winchester College)

Above middle: Montague at Winchester College in 1869, aged 12 or 13. (Courtesy of the Warden and Scholars of Winchester College)

Above right: Winchester College outer gate from College Street. Founded in 1382, Montague won a scholarship to this prestigious college. (Courtesy of the Warden and Scholars of Winchester College)

Below left: Montague (middle) at 16 years of age. (Courtesy of the Warden and Scholars of Winchester College)

Below middle: Montague at 18, sporting a fair moustache. (Courtesy of the Warden and Scholars of Winchester College)

Below right: Montague at 19, as a cricketer in Winchester's first XI team, 1876. (Courtesy of the Warden and Scholars of Winchester College)

Left: Montague as Prefect of Chapel in 1876; he was 19 and in his final year at Winchester. He was a high achiever and won a scholarship to New College Oxford. (Courtesy of the Warden and Scholars of Winchester College)

Above: Clowning for the camera, Montague poses for his final year school house photograph in 1876. (Courtesy of the Warden and Scholars of Winchester College)

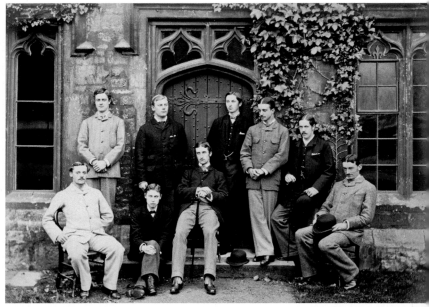

Oxford University Canning Club, Midsummer 1879. Montague is standing, third from right, wearing a salt-and-pepper jacket; he is 22 in this previously unpublished picture, making this the most recent photograph of him. (The Canning Club, [Oxford], Midsummer, 1879/British Library, London, UK/© British Library Board. All Rights Reserved/ Bridgeman Images)

Right: Dr William Gilbert 'W. G.' Grace (1848–1915) was one of the most famous men in England and the most famous cricketer of the nineteenth century. Montague Druitt played alongside him for the MCC. (Courtesy of Wellcome Collection)

Below right: Colonel Sir Vivian Majendie (1836–1898). Engineer, bomb disposal expert and Chief Inspector of Explosives seconded to the Home Office. A close friend of the police chief Sir Melville Macnaghten and the author George R. Sims.

Bottom right: Melville Leslie Macnaghten (1853–1921) as a young man. (Christopher McLaren)

Below: Macnaghten served as a senior police administrator from 1889, and as Assistant Commissioner of the CID from 1903 to 1913. He was knighted 1907. From 1891 until his premature death in 1921, the Old Etonian charmer orchestrated the cover-up of the Druitt family secret while simultaneously giving the public enough snippets of information to indicate that the person behind the Whitechapel murders was now dead. (Christopher McLaren)

George Robert Sims (1847–1922) pictured in 1884. As the popular columnist 'Dagonet', he had a column every Sunday in *The Referee*. He was a liberal advocate for the poor. A famous playwright, a poet, novelist and a true crime aficionado, he propagated the 'Druitt solution' to the Edwardian public – albeit disguised.

PRICE ONE SHILLING

HOW THE POOR LIVE

By GEORGE R. SIMS

With Sixty Illustrations by FREDERICK BARNARD

London
CHATTO & WINDUS, PICCADILLY

THE
SOCIAL KALEIDOSCOPE.

SERIES OF
TWENTY-FIVE FIGURES.

Price SIXPENCE.

London:
R. J. FRANCIS & CO., WINE OFFICE COURT, E.C.

Above left: The son of a successful businessman, Sims never lost his progressive identification with the working class and the poor. He was one of the prominent writers who documented London's systemic poverty and this piece of hands-on journalism from 1883 proved to be very influential.

Above right: Sims as he appeared in his first publication of 1879. Due to being ill, the author is much thinner than usual and his hair is parted in the centre. In 1888 a Whitechapel witness asserted that this picture of Sims strongly resembled the murderer, minus the beard. With hooded eyes and this hairstyle, it does resemble surviving photos of Montague Druitt.

THE NEMESIS OF NEGLECT.

Above left: The Riot in Trafalgar Square, 19 November 1887. The mob were put down by the police led by Commissioner Sir Charles Warren. (Stewart P. Evans)

Above right: *Punch*, 29 September 1888. 'The Nemesis of Neglect', a famous cartoon linking the 'Ripper' murders with the district's systemic poverty. (Stewart P. Evans)

Below left: St Bride's Church, Fleet Street. In 1864 Mary Ann 'Polly' Nichols married William Nichols in this church. Polly was believed to be the first murder victim of Montague Druitt in August 1888. (© Sarah Agius)

Below right: St Botolph's, Whitechapel, was in 1888 known as the prostitute's church as women would walk around its boundary hoping to attract clients. From there, it is a short walk to Mitre Square where Catherine Eddowes was murdered. (Authors' collection)

Providence Row Night Refuge, Crispin Street, a Catholic institution that provided shelter for homeless men and women in Whitechapel.

PROVIDENCE ROW NIGHT REFUGE
MALE AND FEMALE APPLICANTS.

Into the abyss; a grim photograph of poor citizens on a Whitechapel street *circa* 1888, (Stewart P. Evans)

The original Oxford House in Mape Street, Bethnal Green. Various connections point towards Montague Druitt having an association with this charity, which was part of the University Settlement Movement in the East End. It was more conservative and had more religious vigour than its sister settlement Toynbee Hall. (Oxford House)

H. R. Webbe (1856–1886). Herbert Webbe was a friend of Montague's and a fellow Wykehamist, Oxonian, barrister and first class cricketer. His involvement with Oxford House, we believe, was also shared by Montague Druitt.

Above left: King's Bench Walk, in the heart of the legal district of London and weighted heavily with Oxford graduates such as Montague. In 1886 a meeting was convened here by Oxford House to recruit Oxonians to go into the East End and rescue 'thousands from moral degradation'. (© Sarah Agius)

Above right: Montague Druitt's legal chambers at 9 King's Bench Walk stand today as they did in 1888. Situated in the Inner Temple legal district, they were within walking distance of the poverty and dysfunction of the East End. (© Sarah Agius)

Above: The discovery of the murder of Mary Ann 'Polly' Nichols on 30 August 1888. (Stewart Evans)

Below left: Henry Mathews, Tory Home Secretary from 1886 to 1892, later Viscount Llandaff of Hereford. He denied the petition by the residents of Poole to reprieve child murderer Henry Young from the gallows. A year later, Matthews, unknowingly, set up a reward for the capture of Young's lawyer, a multiple murderer.

Below right: The backyard of 29 Hanbury Street. On the morning of Saturday 8 September 1888 the body of Annie Chapman was found near the steps, lying parallel to the fence. She was, we believe, the second victim of Montague Druitt (Stewart P. Evans)

Above left: Blind Man's Bluff. This *Punch* cartoon of 22 September 1888 mocked the police and their perceived incompetence in solving the Whitechapel murders. (Stewart P. Evans)

Above right: The Old Bailey. The murders came to a halt for three weeks in September 1888 while Montague Druitt was defending Christopher Power on an attempted murder charge, here, at the Central Criminal Court. (© Sarah Agius)

Below: The discovery of Elizabeth Stride's body by cabman Louis Diemschutz on August 30 1888. (Stewart P. Evans)

THE WHITECHAPEL MONSTER SEEN BY TWO MEN.

A young, fair-featured man wearing a salt and pepper jacket was seen talking to Catherine Eddowes just before a bobby found her mutilated corpse in Mitre Square, on 30 August 1888. (Stewart P. Evans)

Above left: A sketch of Catherine Eddowes' horrific post mortem wounds, drawn at the crime scene by Frederick Foster, the city surveyor.

Above right: The scene at 13 Miller's Court where Mary Jane Kelly was a tenant in a ground floor room. The mutilated body of Mary Jane Kelly was seen by John Bower through a window when he was sent to collect her overdue rent. (Stewart P. Evans)

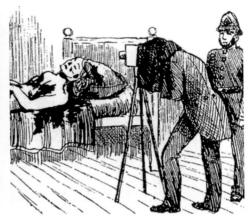

Above left: The mutilated remains of Mary Kelly lie on her bed in her room in Miller's Court. Constable Walter Dew, an eye witness to the scene described it as 'a sight I shall never forget to my dying day'. (Stewart P. Evans)

Above right: An illustrator's version of the Miller's Court crime scene. In reality police photographed not only Kelly's remains but also the retinas of her eyes hoping they had captured the image of her murderer – without success.

Below: The unfinished Eiffel Tower, as it stood in 1888 when we believe Montague was spirited away from England to take refuge in a private asylum near Paris.

Above left: St Nicholas's Church, in Church Street, Chiswick. This shows the street Montague would have walked down (towards the front of picture) on Tuesday 4 December 1888 as he headed to the Thames. The Lamb Brewery sat next to the Lamb Tap Pub and the brewery tower can be seen in the distance. Tuke's Manor House Asylum sat roughly behind this, about a 5-minute walk away. (© Sarah Agius)

Above right: A view of the Thames at the bottom of Church Street. Montague Druitt's body was found by a waterman based at the nearby Thorneycroft's wharf. The corpse surfaced almost a month after the suicide. (© Sarah Agius)

Below left: The Lamb and Tap as it stands today. This establishment was a public house in 1888 and hosted the coronial inquest into Montague's suicide. Dr Thomas Diplock wound up proceedings quickly because Montie's brother William Druitt was the only witness called who actually knew the deceased. William appears to have given false testimony. (© Sarah Agius)

Below right: Montague John Druitt's grave as it stands today in the cemetery of Wimborne Minster in Dorset. The date of death is recorded as 'Dec 4 1888' which attests to William Druitt's knowledge of the final days of his brother's life.

Above: James Ludovic Lindsay (1847–1913) wrote the mysterious 'Crawford Letter' about an unnamed relative of the 'Ripper'. (Image by Leslie Matthew Ward 'Spy' Courtesy of Wellcome Collection CC)

Above right: 8 Strathmore Gardens, Kensington, was the upmarket home of Dr Robert and Isabella Druitt. Montague was a regular visitor. (© Sarah Agius)

Right: Dr Robert Anderson, Assistant Commissioner of the CID from 1888 to 1901, the loathed superior of Sir Melville Macnaghten. The 'Crawford letter' was addressed to him.

Below: Winchester College, Du Boulay House, 1882. The Revd J. T. H. du Boulay, seated fourth from left, knew Montague as a student. Henry Grylls Majendie, seated first left, was the son of Sir Vivian Majendie and lived with the du Boulay family. (Courtesy of the Warden and Scholars of Winchester College)

Above left: A young Arthur du Boulay Hill, pictured at Winchester College in 1869 with his uncle the Reverend J. T. H. du Boulay, would later become an assistant master at the College and know Montague Druitt. Later his sister Isabel Majendie would marry Montague's cousin Reverend Charles Druitt. (Courtesy of the Warden and Scholars of Winchester College)

Above right: Arthur du Boulay Hill in his later years. A confidante of the Reverend Charles Druitt, he is likely to have been the 'North Country Vicar' who wrote a letter to the *Daily Mail* claiming to know the identity of the 'Ripper'. (Courtesy of the Warden and Scholars of Winchester College)

Below left: The 1911 short story version of *The Lodger* was expanded by the author Marie Belloc Lowndes into a novel in 1913. It is a fictional variation on the Druitt solution to the 'Jack the Ripper' case.

Below right: Christabel, Lady Aberconway (1890–1974), Sir Melville Macnaghten's favourite child who had copied a vital document by her father which named Montague Druitt as the 'Ripper'. (Christopher McLaren)

The Lodger
by
Mrs Belloc
Lowndes
Author of
"The Decree
Made Absolute"

Illustrations *by* Henry Raleigh

The English Patient

In early November 1888, Paris was all abuzz with preparations to host the World's Fair (*Exposition Universelle*) the following year. Locals and visitors marvelled at Gustave Eiffel's magnificent tower, even though it was only half finished.[1] Yet Parisians, like everybody else, also had their heads buried in their daily newspapers. They were learning what they could about the latest and most horrific atrocity across the Channel by 'Jack the Ripper' ('*Jack l'Eventreur*'), this time against a young voluptuary who had reportedly lived in France for a while and who styled herself as *Marie Jeanette* Kelly. Though the details were kept sketchy on the orders of Scotland Yard, the elusive maniac had literally torn his latest female victim limb from limb. This knife-wielding lunatic, apparently as cunning as he was repulsive, had turned a humble, one-room abode into a cramped corner of Hell. Witnesses who had actually seen this gory spectacle had been left shattered; they said they would never be able to forget such a sight as long as they lived.

A day or so after the atrocity in London, an English 'lawyer' under 40 years of age, was driven in a Parisian carriage accompanied by a Church of England 'clergyman' of about the same age. They were headed for a private and delicate rendezvous at a Paris hotel. The pair may have seen Eiffel's incomplete masterwork of modern architecture from their window – but the anxious men were hardly in much of a mood to enjoy it. The third passenger, whom they were escorting, was a slightly younger Englishman, sedated but not so dopey that he could not with assistance from his friend and his cousin manage to ascend a flight of stairs.

The two Englishmen were engaged in an elaborate cover-up of the third man's crimes; they were accessories before and after the fact for 'Jack the Ripper' – and knew it. This Continental escapade was high risk, but the stark alternative – the third man arrested, charged, convicted, then hanged or publicly institutionalised – drove them on. A lawyer and a clergyman, hitherto pillars of the Victorian bourgeoisie, were knowingly breaking the law, several laws in fact. Maybe if the whole affair blew up in their faces they might have to abscond abroad too. The lawyer and the clergyman travelled with a letter of introduction by an English doctor who was in on the ruse – as a precaution written by another's hand. In previous correspondence this doctor had already alerted the French physician about the serious mental condition of the English Patient.

This French doctor was the director of an exclusive asylum for mentally ill patients who themselves had, or their families had, access to enough money to pay for his discreet but expensive treatment. This type of sanatorium catered for prominent families who were desperate that the shame of insanity was kept out of sight of high society and the vulture press. If that meant locking up a family member who had become an embarrassment, so be it. The asylum was committed to humane and progressive methods of caring for the sick; in comparison with other such institutions of the day on both sides of the Channel that were infamous for systemic abuse and the mistreatment of their charges, this French hospital was practically a hotel. This particular asile privé *was located about 20 miles from Paris in the secluded countryside and named after the director. It was practically invisible from the main public thoroughfares. A converted mansion as well as the doctor's plush home, it only accommodated about twenty-five patients at any one time, as well as a small staff of nurses and attendants. The French medical man in question was a leading expert in 'homicidal mania'; a Victorian-era concept of insanity that meant sufferers of the malady were in a state in which they were not responsible for their atrocities. To hastily shoehorn the younger Englishman into this asylum abroad would cost the family a small fortune – yet worth every penny if it kept the wolf of social ruin from their door. The lawyer and the clergyman had used false names, and the ill man was also going to be committed under a pseudonym – whether he was* compos mentis *or not.*

The English doctor provided the drugs they would need to keep the English patient subdued and manageable, and then he wished them all a safe journey. The letter sent from London gave assurances about the extortionate fees; the patient's 'friends' were prepared to pay liberally for his treatment and accommodation. According to the London doctor, with classic English understatement, the patient was said to be suffering from 'slight homicidal mania'.

In his reply to the London physician, the French director of this small, exclusive hospital made it crystal clear that money alone would not suffice: appropriate certificates, the Frenchman advised, would need to be furnished by two more English doctors and, upon arrival in France; the patient must be prepared to submit to an examination by two other French doctors. A reply from England came quickly affirming that these conditions would be met. The lawyer and the clergyman had letters sent from other English doctors – but they were nothing more than forgeries. The latest correspondence announced that within a few days, the English patient would be escorted by 'close friends' to Paris. At short notice the French director was informed by telegram that the day had arrived. The English party would arrive tomorrow and meet him at a discreet hotel in Paris.

In his carriage the French director travelled the following morning with two other French doctors, well known to him, who would examine the English patient immediately upon arrival. This was done at the insistence of the patient's concerned friends; that their business be conducted and completed on the same day so that they could make sure their ill friend was safe and comfortable in the sanatorium, while they returned at once to England.

In fact, the Englishmen were so anxious to conclude their business without delay that in their second letter they had enclosed a powerful incentive to expedite this affair with all speed: the equivalent of a blank cheque which would defray the costs of the other French physicians and any other extraneous fees, payable at a French bank. The lawyer and the clergyman had decided that this was a calculated financial risk they had to take, as time was short and their options limited.

Promptly at 10 a.m. the trio of French doctors, all experts in lunacy, flanked by two burly attendants, arrived at the hotel and were ushered into a room containing the three English visitors. The lawyer introduced himself under a false name and claimed to be only the dear 'friend' of the patient. The English patient, with a new name, lay on a couch fully dressed and dozing. The clergyman remained mostly pensive and quiet after introductions (both spoke fluent French). He introduced himself by his true vocation: an Anglican clergyman (though he was not wearing a clerical collar) and then he added something else: he revealed he was a 'cousin' of the patient. This jarring bit of candour by the priest caused the lawyer to quickly add that the patient had no other relatives, whatsoever, and was quite independently wealthy. He also proffered the introduction written by the English doctor.

Aware that strangers were in the room the man on the couch began to stir but could not speak coherently, alternating between mumbling and raving. The lawyer lamented that his poor friend's brain had been deteriorating for about six months but that the worst symptoms had only developed within the last six weeks.

Whether the French doctors grasped that this timeline coincided with the commencement of the mutilation murders in London's infamous Whitechapel is unclear. They certainly had no trouble pronouncing the patient clinically insane following the most cursory examination. They just as hastily countersigned the English doctors' certificate and departed.

As for the problem of communication, the lawyer assured the French director that his unfortunate friend was a French scholar, and therefore once lucid they would have no trouble understanding each other. After several hours' journey back to the remote though palatial retreat the lawyer and the clergyman stayed only long enough to see their friend and cousin settled into his private apartment and to pay, in advance, three months' worth of fees. The lawyer also warned the director that his friend had been diagnosed with 'spasmodic homicidal mania' and thus was prone to the most fantastic and grotesque delusions.

'What form do they take,' queried the Frenchman?

'He will probably confess', replied the lawyer, 'to atrocious crimes that he has, of course, not really committed.'

Did the French physician at this point wonder, 'Am I about to host 'Jack l'Éventreur'?

If the director was harbouring any suspicions in that regard, the pair of English gentlemen were quick to cough up yet another 'ample sum' to defray any other costs the new patient might incur. The Anglican cleric asked if a weekly letter could be forwarded to the London physician, briefly outlining the young man's progress and response to treatment, or lack thereof. Flush with cash, the French director happily agreed.

Then the lawyer introduced a tragic element; if his friend should expire while being treated he asked if the director could please notify him immediately. The shocked French physician judged such an outcome to be highly unlikely and quite alarmist; the young man looked to be in excellent physical *health, what with his slight but athletic figure (and robustly tanned face).*

Nonetheless, the Frenchman affirmed that he would telegraph the lawyer if the worst came to the worst (he repressed his irritation – of course he would have done so without being asked).

The moment the lawyer and the clergyman felt that they had completed their distasteful business they departed to Paris then caught the ferry. The director had placed the English patient in a corner of his mansion-hospital wherein he could enjoy the comforts of a sitting room and bedroom – and be securely sealed off from the other inmates. Almost at once his behaviour oscillated between extreme violence and an almost comatose lethargy. The director gave the young Englishman a heavy opiate to sedate him; it knocked him out for nearly thirty-six hours. One of the larger male nurses was put in charge of him. But there was something that the French physician did not know about this member of his nursing staff: although the attendant had lived in France for many years – and everyone took him to be a native – he was, in fact, English. This unforeseen element would soon prove disastrous for all the elaborate arrangements made by the pair of English gentleman.

Shortly thereafter the French/English attendant discovered that the new patient was conscious and lucid. Not having a clue that he was in France, he asked, in English, 'Where am I?' The nurse was evasive. Perhaps mistaking him for a dullard, the patient rattled off the names of four London hospitals and politely asked if he was in the care of one of them. Making no answer, the attendant summoned the director. After the exchange of only a few words in French, the English patient relapsed into a state of incoherence.

Another dose of opiates was administered and the patient again fell into a deep, untroubled sleep. As he departed, the director briefed the attendant; the English patient, he assured him, might accuse himself of all sorts of crimes but that they must all ignore such ravings; they are no more than a symptom of a disordered mind. That's why, the director assured him, the English patient is in our care.

By the next day the Englishman was again conscious but unaware of his surroundings; he was in the grip of a troubled conscience and was speaking in his native language again. He found himself reliving every one of his crimes, accompanied by an incessant need to act them out in his hospital room. He 'conversed' with Polly Nichols, and Catherine Eddowes and Mary Jane Kelly before striking them down, all over again. The English patient described in sickening detail how he tore and dismembered their bodies, how he absconded with some of their organs. He worked himself into such frenzy that he had to be forcibly restrained by three attendants; they bound him to his bed, hand and foot. He then relapsed into a heavy slumber. Several times the English-born attendant witnessed this homicidal pantomime – and alone among the staff he understood every word that was spoken. This did not mean the nurse was familiar with every detail of the hideous crimes currently plaguing London, but he understood that the patient was naming men, women and places that seemed important to the patient.

The one aspect of the Whitechapel saga with which the attendant was certainly familiar was the generous reward that the British government had offered for any information that would lead to the identification of the perpetrator. The following day the Chief of the Detective Department in the Rue Jerusalem District of Paris listened carefully as the asylum attendant breathlessly informed him – as a matter of 'public duty' – that his workplace was the current location of 'Jack the Ripper'.

The Chief faced a most uncomfortable dilemma: on the one hand he knew that this English swine standing before him was motivated by money, and perhaps was exaggerating the symptoms of this poor patient to get his hands on that big, fat reward. On the other hand, the police chief also knew that if he did not act – and act quickly – and this patient really was 'Jack' and he escaped, and mayhem ensued, he, the police chief, would be held responsible.

First he made a trip to the sanatorium and, predictably, his arrival caused consternation. Though the director was angry at the appalling betrayal by his staff member, he was far more fearful that his palatial sanctuary for the 'best families' could soon be under siege from the gendarmes of not one but two countries. The physician blustered and bluffed trying to persuade the police chief that the English patient was merely hallucinating; that in other parts of his establishment he could introduce the chief to 'Joan of Arc', to the 'Emperor Napoleon' and even to 'Our Lord and Saviour'. The police chief was sympathetic. He felt duty bound to point out, however, that this new arrival was not known to the physician – he might not be 'Jack the Ripper', which meant a great deal of fuss and embarrassment for all concerned, but such a benign determination would have to be made by British authorities. As it turned out the couple of days that elapsed between the director having been tipped off, and the arrival of English detectives from the Metropolitan Police, was enough for the latter to find that 'the bird had flown'. From what the crestfallen detectives learned of

*the patient's ravings and admissions, they were convinced that the
missing patient had indeed been 'a participant in the fearful crimes
that had for so long terrorised a large section of the inhabitants of
the East End of London'. Who was he, they wondered?*

Subsequent enquiries by the English detectives reached a quick and
frustrating dead-end because the names given for the lawyer, the
clergyman, the patient and the two English doctors who had signed
the certificates, were all fake. Even the personal linen left behind by the
patient, the detectives noted, contained neither his name nor initials.
The police did locate the English physician who had initiated the
correspondence, as he was real, but he flatly denied having done any
such thing and proved that the handwriting in the letters was not his
own, nor was the address used his registered mailing address. The police
accepted – perhaps too credulously – that some unknown imposter had
exploited the doctor's good name without his knowledge or consent.

The story of the mysterious English patient in a French asylum who
was probably 'Jack the Ripper' only leaked to a single English-speaking
newspaper, *The Philadelphia Times* on 13 January 1889 (a source only
found a few years ago by the American writer and researcher, Roger J.
Palmer – *see* Appendix II). Though the correspondent for *The Philadelphia
Times* in Paris covered the scoop at great length, he published not a single
name because, according to his own account, the English ones would have
been bogus anyhow. We believe that the English patient was Montague
Druitt, the lawyer and friend was his brother William, and the clerical
cousin was the Reverend Charles Druitt.

For that to be true we are relying on the article's timeline – a
timeline bereft of any *specific* dates – being inaccurate by a week or so
as it claims to be referring to events that took place in mid-December
when Montague Druitt was deceased (the article is a tangle of 'a few
days before' and 'about ten days before' and 'three weeks before that'
and therefore we think it is reasonable to postulate that with such
looseness the timing could easily include an extra week).

It is also unclear who the reporter's source was. Presumably since the
American journalist was based in Paris – and there are no known examples
of the story appearing in British media – his source was French. It is likely
it was leaked by the local police chief to reassure fellow citizens that
their police were on the ball, whereas the English constabulary had been
outsmarted by the maniac and his confederates. Since the article heavily
implies, quite improbably, that the patient remains in the French asylum –
yet Scotland Yard's detectives are still baffled and impotent –perhaps those

English cops were trying a long-shot bluff to flush out the 'confederates' which failed. This was the article's eye-catching if cluttered headline:

WHITECHAPEL FIENDS
A Most Remarkable Story That Comes From Paris.
POSSIBLY THIS IS A CLUE
One of the Supposed Murderers, Sent to an Asylum Tells Much
That is Startling.
From a *Times* Correspondent.

If the reporter was simply fed the entire tale by a single, self-serving informant then its details in terms of timing and location could easily be vague and a little distorted so he could not follow up with a sequel to embarrass any other VIP patients at that exclusive institution. We were unable to find a private, French asylum that *exactly* fits the limited data provided in the American article, but we found one which does match very well if the information has been slightly altered for the purposes already suggested. This hospital was a humane and progressive asylum in Vanves, a few miles from Paris. It was a converted mansion, relatively secluded from the main thoroughfares, surrounded by picturesque trees and shrubbery near a small village. The director in 1888 was Dr Jules Falret, the son of the famous and accomplished Dr Jean Pierre Falret (1794–1870) who had founded the asylum in 1822 (with another doctor, Félix Voisin). The asylum was not *named* after Falret, but it was certainly inseparable from it.

Falret Snr had done everything he could to make the residence appear and feel more like a gentleman's country estate than a lunatic asylum. Each resident had their own garden to tend and enjoy. It hosted both 'maniacal' and 'tranquil' patients, each with their own private room decorated to be 'agreeable and cheerful' (males and females were strictly segregated into different wings) while violent, noisy patients were removed to rooms located far from the rest. The asylum at Vanves could accommodate up to seventy patients, but that number fluctuated over the years – at one point falling to as low as forty-six. For those with the money, their mentally distressed relative could have a dignified and even active life as they tried to recover; the non-violent patients could go on chaperoned excursions, enjoy horseback riding and convivially mingle with staff at parties.[2]

We found an undated pamphlet about the Vanves asylum in the Wellcome Collection titled: *Retreat at Vanves, near Paris, for Reception and Recovery of Ladies and Gentlemen afflicted with*

Disorders of the Mind: under the immediate direction of Drs Voisin and Falret. In this advertisement, the line that would have been pertinent to the Druitts is the assertion that 'Drs Voisin & Falret having spent some time in England, and *having had several English patients in their establishment, understand the peculiar management they require.*' (Our italics)

There is also a strange, almost comical episode that brought the idyllic establishment at Vanves to the attention of the world, certainly to people such as the Druitts who regularly read daily newspapers. *The Daily News* in London on 21 July 1887 published an article headlined 'The Lunacy Case in France' which has remarkable parallels with the *Philadelphia Times* article of a little over a year later.

The Paris-based British journalist told of how a French aristocrat, Baron Raymond Seilliere, had been lured into a trap by scheming members of his own family; they had him committed to the Vanves asylum as being mentally impaired. According to the Baron, however, he was the innocent victim of a common nightmare: what if you found yourself in an asylum and could not convince anybody you were sane? The motive was money, as the Baron was a multi-millionaire. His avaricious and cash-poor sister the Princess de Sagan exploited a weakness in the Baron's rather bohemian private affairs – he was devoted to his 'wife' but their union was not recognised by the State and his children by her were loved but were technically illegitimate. The Princess, knowing she had the legal authority to have him committed, cooked up an audacious scheme. Her brother had recently returned from a tour of the United States. Encouraging him to talk about his adventures (supposedly fantastical) would prove that his mind was unbalanced – at least it did to an eavesdropping physician who had been hidden behind a screen in her drawing room. The sister pressed their spineless cousin to lure her brother to the asylum (which of course did not look like one) where the startled noble would be detained indefinitely:

> They came up to the asylum; a double door swung open, and was shut behind them. As the carriage rattled into a courtyard, such an expression came over the cousin's face that the Baron remembered warnings he had of a plot to lock him up. Keepers [attendants] closed around the carriage, 'I am done for' said the captive to himself; 'the cage is shut behind me. There is no hope except in playing a double game.' The Baron therefore pretended not to perceive he was in a madhouse.

The Baron could hardly be accused of paranoia. A draconian 1838 law meant that a person so sectioned by a member of their family could remain imprisoned – in this case at least it was to be an elegant and luxurious confinement – for the rest of their lives, and without means of appeal. Fortunately, the Baron had friends who included politicians, members of the American Legation and, unusually for an aristocrat, a pack of admiring journalists. They began to mount a counter-coup on behalf of him and his common law spouse and children. The key to the success of this campaign to liberate the unfortunate Baron was that his family and friends had won the support of the Prefect of the Police, a M. Graguon. He confronted the asylum staff and its director and insisted on interviewing the patient alone: 'When the conversation was ended the Prefect of Police was taken to Dr Falret, and said to him, "You have odd ideas about lunacy. I have tested the Baron in every possible way, and if he is out of his mind I, too, must be a madman, because he is just the same as I am".'

The police chief demanded that the Baron be forthwith released into his custody. An affronted Dr Falret refused point blank to comply. He warned the policeman the latter would be held responsible for 'any evil consequences, or for any injury the lunatic might, in one of his fits, inflict on anyone when at large'. The doctor further huffed that the State required another doctor's certificate to free an already certified patient. Returning to Paris empty-handed, Graguon conferred with the doctor who worked for the Prefecture of Police, a Dr Garnier, who was sent to the asylum to make his own assessment. He confirmed that the Baron was perfectly sane and well. Under this concerted pressure the Princess buckled and her brother was released. According to the reporter, Baron Raymond Seilliere did not seem visibly shaken by his ordeal but quoted him as vowing that, after this close call, he would take steps 'to prevent his wife and children ever being trampled upon again by his relatives'.

Consider how much the American article about the 'The Ripper' being put into an exclusive French asylum in late 1888 mirrors the story of the Baron in mid-1887. At great expense and under false pretences, an affluent respectable family place an inconvenient member in a French sanatorium near Paris. Quickly their scam unravels due to a police chief being informed that the patient is not what he seems to be. The chief goes, in person, to find out the truth and his intervention causes the patient to soon depart. It may be that because it was an American reporter they did not want the Vanves asylum, host to all sorts of patients from prominent families, to have to endure further humiliating exposure. Hence the names were withheld and the details fudged a little (for example, a few miles outside the capitol became 20, and so on). It may in fact be the same police chief involved in both stories, with his rank altered, as it would make sense that the English-born attendant would go to the cop who had so dramatically visited the asylum and so effectively thrown his weight around the year before.

Our circumstantial case for the true identity of the English patient also rests on the broad contents of *The Philadelphia Times* article matching other known sources on Montague Druitt, which just seem too coincidental for it not to be him. For example, it has always puzzled researchers as to why Montague Druitt's sporting club ended his membership on 21 December 1888 for 'having gone abroad'. The cryptic wording of the sporting club's minutes does make sense if his fellow gentleman had been informed he had travelled to a foreign sanatorium for urgent treatment (and for an indefinite period). They could hardly expect Montie to provide a letter of resignation, nor could they bother the unfortunate man to supply one, nor would they place in their club's minutes the specific reason for his absence abroad.

On 23 September 1913 the retired and highly regarded head of the Special Branch from 1888, Jack Littlechild, wrote to George R. Sims. His letter is quite fawning, as he knew that Sims was a celebrity and from the upper classes, though the ex-chief was delivering what he presumed to be unwelcome news. In his various columns, interviews and articles, Sims had frequently described the Whitechapel assassin as undoubtedly a mad English surgeon who had committed suicide in the Thames (and just once, in 1907, he claimed that Scotland Yard's second-best suspect was a young, American medical student – which we argue is yet another fictitious variation of Montie Druitt). Expressing his dissent as politely as possible, Littlechild replies that this 'likely' suspect had in fact been an American quack doctor, Dr Francis Tumblety. This flimflam man, an affluent eccentric, was a genuine police suspect in 1888: 'Tumblety was arrested at the time of the murders in connection with unnatural offences and charged at Marlborough Street, remanded on bail, jumped his bail, and got away to Boulogne.'[3] The ex-police chief's memory is perfectly accurate in recalling that Dr Tumblety had been arrested as, possibly, the Whitechapel murderer but then had been charged for homosexual offences. After receiving bail, he had promptly fled to France, his first stop on his way to hightailing it back to the jurisdictional safety of New York City.

The allegation that Dr Tumblety as a 'Ripper' suspect on the run was recounted in splashy headlines in a plethora of American newspapers. Whereas Littlechild's memory of Tumblety's final destination, puzzlingly, breaks down completely in the very next line of his letter: 'He shortly left Boulogne and was *never heard of afterwards*. It was *believed he committed suicide* but certain it is that *from that time* the 'Ripper' murders came to an end.' (Our italics)

Littlechild thought that Tumblety had vanished and his exact fate still remained a mystery, when, in fact, he died of natural causes in a St Louis nursing home in 1903. Bizarrely the ex-police chief muses that the suspect may have committed suicide, presumably in France. His memory has probably been contaminated by George Sims fictitiously describing the unnamed Druitt as a middle-aged, wealthy doctor. Littlechild's memory has conflated two suspects. He correctly recalls aspects of Tumblety; in 1888 he was 56, self-made and styled himself as a medical man. The element of suicide, however, is hopelessly mistaken.

Unless, of course, Sims' by then iconic profile of the murderer has inadvertently dislodged an authentic recollection in Littlechild's jumbled mind about somebody else. Is he, at that moment, recalling the English patient whom the CID was pursuing in France and who was found, much later, to have committed suicide? If so, that can only be a reference to Montague Druitt, and Littlechild's letter to Sims, albeit written twenty-five years after the crimes, arguably, if tenuously, links the drowned barrister to France. It is also worth noting that at the time the 'Ripper' murders in the East End were perceived as occurring with protracted infrequency over several years. The official judgment that they ceased with the Mary Jane Kelly atrocity is the revised 'autumn of terror' timeline created by police chief Melville Macnaghten and propagated to the public from 1898 – created, in other words, to suit Druitt; the murderer of five of the eleven Whitechapel victims between 1888 and 1891. Subsequent prostitute murders in the East End cleared Dr Tumblety, at the time, as he had remained in the United States. Once more, Littlechild's memory is sliding across to the semi-fictionalised account of the young English barrister.

In 1894, CID Chief Constable Melville Macnaghten, unbeknownst to his department, would compose two versions of an internal report that declared 'Mr M. J. Druitt' to be possibly or probably, depending on which version you read, 'Jack the Ripper'. In both versions Macnaghten writes that Druitt 'disappeared at the time' of the murder of Mary Jane Kelly. This, we argue, is a cryptic reference to Druitt's temporary sojourn abroad. It is something Macnaghten would not want to spell out in any detail whatsoever because it ended so unsatisfyingly for Scotland Yard. On the other hand, if the whole truth was about to come out, in 1894, then Macnaghten wanted it acknowledged that the police did – eventually – know that Mr Druitt was not where he was supposed to be; he had vanished. Also in both copies of the memorandum the then Chief Constable adds another two suspects deemed worthy of mention alongside the drowned Englishman, one of whom is a Russian compulsive thief named Michael Ostrog (a hapless criminal who used a multitude of aliases). Macnaghten wrote that Michael Ostrog's whereabouts at the time of the murders were a mystery. The following is from the so-called draft version of his report:

> No: 3. Michael Ostrog. *A mad Russian doctor* & a convict & unquestionably a homicidal maniac. This man was said to have been *habitually cruel to women*, & for a long time was known to have carried out with him surgical knives & other instruments; his antecedents were of the very worst & his whereabouts at the time of the Whitechapel murders could never be satisfactory accounted for. *He is still alive.* (Our italics)

And this is how he wrote about the same suspect in the official, filed, version of the same report:

> (3) Michael Ostrog, *a Russian doctor*, and a convict, who was subsequently *detained in a lunatic asylum as a homicidal maniac*. This man's antecedents were of the worst possible type, and his whereabouts at the time of the murders could never be ascertained. (Our italics)

It can be shown that Melville Macnaghten knew about this criminal in some detail as he kept personal tabs on his comings and goings. On 7 May 1891, the police chief wrote to the Medical Superintendent at Barnstead Asylum where Ostrog had been committed as a wandering lunatic, yet Macnaghten suggested he was faking his illness: 'I shall feel obliged if you will cause immediate information to be sent to this office in the event of his discharge ... if it is found that he is feigning insanity.'[4]

The significance of Michael Ostrog is twofold. First of all he was not a qualified doctor; at best he had been a medical student in his native Russia but had never graduated (perhaps he had only *dabbled* in science). Macnaghten, who disparages the Russian as a dangerous confidence man, knew this – yet twice he blithely describes Ostrog as a 'doctor' just as he does M. J. Druitt. This proves, again, how broadly – and generously – this definition of a medical man could be thrown around in the Victorian era. Something else Macnaghten may have learned about Michael Ostrog by the time he composed his reports is that the professional liar claimed to have an iron-clad alibi for the Whitechapel murders of 1888: he was locked up in a French asylum. This was the primary reason to include Ostrog, in case the failed hunt for the English patient was uncovered by the press. Macnaghten could leak that the actual suspect was not English but Russian, and was probably being deceitful, as usual, about the episode.

To the astonishment of Scotland Yard – and no doubt Macnaghten who could only, conversely, have been pleased by this development – later in the same year of 1894 the Russian's alibi was proven to be true by the French authorities. Quite rightly, Ostrog's latest English conviction was voided (for theft, which he could also not have committed due to the same alibi) and he was paid substantial compensation. Though cleared of the Whitechapel murders of 1888, for personal reasons of revenge and public relations, Melville Macnaghten stubbornly hung onto this Russian reprobate as an alleged suspect. A few years later Macnaghten would disseminate this idea to the public, albeit without naming the man. Mac was investing in a useful excuse for why British police were hunting a lunatic 'Ripper' suspect in a French, private asylum (when it turned out, Macnaghten could later argue if he needed to, that it was this Russian deadbeat Ostrog and he had been in some crummy State institution – with an iron-clad alibi – rather than the cushy private retreat replete with horseback riding, cocktail parties and private gardens).

There is further textual evidence pointing to the identity of the troubled Englishman abroad being Montague Druitt. In the American article from 1889 the 'lawyer' deploys exactly the same deflective lie as William Druitt would at the inquest into his brother's suicide, as recorded by the *Acton, Chiswick & Turnham Green Gazette* of 5 January 1889. William reportedly committed perjury by claiming, under oath, that apart from himself and their ailing mother, his deceased sibling 'had no other relative'. On this aspect of William possibly pretending to be a mere friend, the true crime writers Major Arthur Griffiths and George Sims – both briefed by Macnaghten – in their accounts disguised William Druitt as a 'friend' of the unnamed

Montague. In his regular widely read column in *The Referee,* Sims went a step further. For example, this report of William Druitt's testimony in the same Chiswick daily informs us:

> Witness [William Druitt] heard from a *friend* on the 11th of December that deceased had not been heard of at his chambers for more than a week. *Witness then went to London to make enquiries...* That was on the 30th of December... Witness had deceased's things searched where he resided... (Our italics)

The 16 February 1902 issue of Sims' regular 'Mustard and Cress' column slightly fictionalises William's frantic search for his missing brother as that of a quest by concerned 'friends'. Sims adds what William would never have volunteered at the inquest; these un-identified people *already* fear the missing Englishman is 'The Ripper' due to his having been a voluntary patient in a private asylum:

> The homicidal maniac who SHOCKED THE WORLD as Jack the Ripper had been once – I am not sure that it was not *twice – in a lunatic asylum.* At the time his body was found in the Thames, *his friends,* who *were terrified at his disappearance* from their midst, were *endeavouring to have him found* and placed *under restraint again.* (Our italics)

France is not mentioned, but Sims will persistently claim to his readers from 1902 to 1917 that the real killer had been a voluntary patient in a private asylum and, during his stay, had been diagnosed as a 'homicidal maniac'. According to Sims the periodically deranged Englishman had confessed to his physicians of his bestial need to savage East End prostitutes (the patient's treatment is also fictionally backdated to *before* the commencement of the homicides) which is close to the account of the 1889 American article. Sims also writes about a super-efficient police dragnet rapidly closing on the 'mad doctor', but he was found to have already committed suicide in the river (the fictional element is that the police were hunting a suspect whose name they knew when they did not – *see* next chapter).

Nonetheless, the brief stay in a French asylum under an assumed name may have further confirmation from the same source – from George R. Sims. His writings are a vital window, albeit made from wavy glass, into what Melville Macnaghten knew concerning the truth about Montague Druitt and had told his friend the famous writer. And

Sims had no qualms about exploiting that truth in his work. He wrote several short stories between 1892 and 1897, which we argue are veiled variations on the Druitt solution (*see* Chapter XVII).

One of them strongly points to the English patient in a French asylum having been Montie Druitt. *Dr Swainson's Secret*, by George R. Sims, debuted in the Saturday edition of *The Cardiff Times* on 22 February 1896 and was republished into the late-Victorian and early-Edwardian years. In this compact little thriller, Sims dramatises a private crisis that had devastated an ultra-respectable English upper-crust family to whom reputation was virtually synonymous with oxygen. The news that caused their distress was that one of their own suffered from homicidal mania.

The story opens with Harold Frederick D'Alroy Temple, 10th Earl of Templeton, pacing up and down in the lush grounds of his ancestral estate. So tormented is the Earl that he finds 'the beauty of the scene mocked him. The very sunshine which flooded the land mocked him... putting his face in his hands [he] sobbed like a child.'

Into the garden strides Dr Swainson, aged 60, a physician and family friend, who runs a private asylum for members of the English aristocracy. Seeing the nobleman acting so histrionically, the medical man counsels that since he is slumped over in full view of the tourists who can visit parts of the estate, he needs to be more circumspect:

> 'Come, come,' he said kindly, 'this won't do. If anyone could see you it would be sure to lead to gossip, and you know how important it is that there should not be the slightest suspicion anywhere of what has happened.'

The doctor confers with the Earl about the serious matter that has required his services. A young girl in the village was attacked the previous night by an unknown assailant; she was stabbed in the chest, ran home covered in blood and, miraculously, survived due to a metal stay deflecting most of the blow. Though she cannot identify her attacker, the victim recalls with a chill a sound: 'Her assailant gave a peculiar laugh – a laugh that the girl herself describes as "unhuman" [sic] – and disappeared in the darkness.'

In his son's bedroom, the Earl discovers a bloodstained cuff on the slumbering young man's shirt. The mortified father also digs up a bloodstained knife buried in the garden under his son's window. Confronted with the incriminating evidence the young man laments he sincerely cannot remember committing an act of near-murder on a poor girl he has never met. Dr Swainson confirms to the dumbfounded Earl that people who are afflicted by this type of mania do temporarily suffer amnesia. The nobleman is incredulous:

'Possible! – that he could have attacked the girl overnight and woke up the next morning his mind a perfect blank as to what had occurred?'

'Yes, I have known several cases of homicidal mania, in which the attack, having passed away, there has been no recollection of anything that occurred when it was at its height.'

The doctor counsels that the Earl has a public, moral and lawful responsibility to turn his son over to the authorities. His lordship does not disagree, but pleads that loyalty to a member of his family, whom he both loves and is his heir, trumps society's demands on his conscience. The doctor quickly concedes that the young man is ill and needs expert help, not jail. He suggests the safest course is for him to be sent to a *private, French* asylum until he is cured. The doctor advises:

'Very well. Then it must be understood that he is going to travel abroad. You will leave quietly with him this evening... I will... take your son with me to a friend of mine in Paris, a young doctor attached to one of the great French asylums, and who is skilled at dealing with cases of this sort. He will receive him *into his house* as a guest, but *under another name*, and by that name he will be known to the doctor's family and *everyone connected* with his establishment.' (Our italics)

The desperate Earl agrees and asks Dr Swainson if there is any chance his son can recover. The latter is non-committal, pointing out that – as with the Druitt family – this noble family has a history of severe mental illness: the young man's maternal grandmother died while under care in an asylum, and his maternal uncle is also being secretly treated by the doctor for bouts of insanity. The son's seclusion abroad will not come cheap – the Earl will have to fork out more than £1,000 a year, while high society is to be misinformed that the Earl's heir is on an extended tour of some remote part of India.

During the year that the young nobleman is in France, his family at home falls apart. His mother the Countess goes to visit her father and does not return. The estate is closed to visitors and its master becomes a miserable recluse. Just when the violent assault is on its way to being forgotten by the local community, the shattering news spreads in the village and across the whole country that the Earl has been found strangled in his garden.

Scotland Yard investigates and suspicion quickly falls on a likely suspect: a poacher nabbed by the Earl who had finished his sentence the day before the murder. On the other hand, there were no witnesses to the presumed return of this jailbird. A young man accompanied by an older man were seen catching a train on the fateful day, but they remain unidentified (like Tom Sadler in the case of the 1891 'Ripper' murder of Frances Coles, this poacher with a grudge is the perfect circumstantial suspect – who never ends up being charged). The family solicitor wants to send an immediate telegram to the new Earl, who has 'gone abroad' to inform him of the tragic news and of his own accession.

The Countess successfully stalls while calling for the help of the family's reliable crony, Dr Swainson. The good news for the widow is that her son is much improved and his physicians confidently believe a relapse to be unlikely. The bad news is that one of the male attendants, Pierre, has been in close proximity to the young Earl in the French asylum and that Pierre, knowing he is soon to die of an illness, has left a confession for the English doctor.

This letter contains the worst possible news. It reveals how he, Pierre, followed the young English patient when the latter, again in the grip of his mania, slipped away from the sanatorium. He tried to head off the young man at his aristocratic estate but arrived too late to prevent him from strangling his own father. (So Pierre and the young man were the pair of strangers seen fleeing on a train).

Unfortunately it is the young Earl who reads the dying attendant's testimonial first, and discovers the terrible truth about his dual personality. Upon subsequently reading it, a horrified Dr Swainson asks a pertinent question of the placid young man, commendably resigned as he is to turning himself in to the nearest police station:

'Pierre...! But he did not know who you were. You were never known by your right name when you lived in Paris!'

'Yes, *I knew who I was, and I had told them often* – but I never knew I was mad... God knows what crimes I have committed in the past! If I could have committed this awful deed without knowing it, what may I have not done before?' (Our italics)

The plot now takes a notably diabolical swerve as Dr Swainson persuades the young Earl that it is the soon-to-expire asylum attendant, Pierre, who is the real murderer and madman, which the physician knows to be a despicable lie. To make sure that this cover-up takes immediate effect, Dr Swainson wastes no time heading upstairs to the dying Frenchman's bedroom and tells him that the Earl has also read his confession. Pierre drops dead from shock.

We interpret this macabre scene as an in-joke; revenge on the *English* attendant at the French asylum who had caused the Druitts so much grief. In Sims' story, the English doctor throws the letter into the nearest fireplace and manipulates the French doctor into believing that his attendant, whose body is barely cold, was quite mad and homicidal. As for the Earl, whose dark passions could still erupt at any time, all's well that ends well, as he has got away with serious assault and patricide.

> Dr Swainson kept his secret to the end. Lord Templecombe was safe, of that he felt sure. He lived ten years, and saw no relapse at any time. And today Lord Templecombe looks back upon that ghastly chapter in his life and wonders how he could have ever believed such a thing. He has taken his seat in the House of Lords, is a model landowner, and beloved by all his people.
>
> But he has never married. He had always told Dr Swainson that he should live and die a bachelor. Perhaps it was his firm belief that the Earl would keep his word that induced the doctor to keep his secret.

More likely what would really have induced the pragmatic Dr Swainson to keep the Earl's secret is that in Victorian England class and title were all-consuming concerns; far more important than pesky inconveniences such as the rule of law and due process. Such rules were just to keep the peasants in line. This is an otherwise trifling and contrived story by George Sims but one with a decided sting in the tail; we leave the Earl as a beloved model landowner yet also the maniacal murderer of his predecessor, who cannot risk marriage. The story arguably provides insight into the hypocritical, extra-legal attitude of the Druitts. The unseemly haste with which Dr Swainson sheds his bourgeoisie/Christian values when the crunch comes demonstrates, we think, how the real clan covered up for their mad Montague without the slightest qualm. (The exception is the glum clergyman who in the American article insists on revealing he is the patient's cousin, not 'friend').

Part of that expensive and risky effort by the Druitt family to keep their maniacal relative out of the clutches of the law and thus protect their reputations was, probably, to place Montie in the pleasant and progressive French asylum at Vanves run by Dr Jules Faret – whom they knew would provide confidentiality as part of the deal. However, the elaborate arrangements backfired almost at once, as the earlier one had with the Baron, and the Druitt family had to retreat to a fall-back option; this time placing 'Jack the Ripper' in a private, English sanatorium.

Before that, his police pursuers would have to be thrown off the scent if they connected Dr Druitt's nephew, arrested and quickly released on the night of the double murder, with the description of the patient who was using a false name. A lucid Montague would have to be chaperoned while he fulfilled some of his public duties in order to prove he was normal, *compos mentis* and thus above suspicion.

XIII

The Police Net Closes

Following the French close call and with Scotland Yard on their heels, the solicitor and the clergyman were forced to place their mad family member in an English asylum; Manor House in Chiswick, run by the progressive doctor brothers Thomas Seymour Tuke and Charles Molesworth Tuke. These physicians were well known to the Dr Robert Druitt wing of the family, and the doctors' sister Caroline, who resided in the asylum's family quarters, would holiday with Charles and his wife Isabel Majendie, as a companion, in Switzerland the following year.[1] Their institution was not quite the Vanves resort but nor was it a Bedlam-type horror either.

Before he could be quietly placed in care Montie Druitt argued the biggest case of his brief career, before the Chief Justice, Lord Coleridge no less. Previously on 19 November 1888, he had attended his sporting club meeting – we believe he was accompanied by William who quietly informed the other committee members that his brother was soon to be 'going abroad' for his health.[2]

Eight days later Montague was in court arguing perfectly lucidly that his client should enjoy the same franchise rights as an owner of a dwelling: Within a few days the sources show that the same lucid Montie Druitt headed for his rendezvous with the Thames to drown himself. Why? We argue it was for the usual reason that criminals kill themselves; he felt cornered and out of options. A police net was fast closing on him. The constabulary were pursuing an English patient who had given them the slip and, presumably, returned to England with the assistance of his people. What the police did not know was his real name.

An 1888 newspaper article reveals the police had been systematically trawling all *private* English asylums for 'The Ripper'. *The Aberdeen Evening Express* of 28 December 1888 claims that this family, affluent enough to place their relative in a private institution, is apparently shielding him to avoid social ruin (it is repeating a scoop by the London correspondent for the *Dublin Express*):

> ... Stated nakedly, the idea of those [the police] who have been so patiently watching for the murderer, is that *he has fallen under the strong suspicion of his nearest relatives, who, to advert a terrible family disgrace, may have placed him out of harm's way in safe keeping.* ... detectives have recently visited all the registered *private* asylums, and made full enquiries as to *inmates recently admitted.* It is needless to say that the various county asylums, particularly those *in the neighbourhood of London*, have been similarly visited. (Our italics)

The police of 1888 would not have been crashing through private asylums – inevitably causing alarm and consternation among wealthier people with embarrassing family secrets – to pursue a whim. For that matter, what would the recent admission of anybody to such an institution actually prove? Scotland Yard must have been onto a strong lead to risk such a backlash from potentially influential people.

Another primary source that hints at the search for the English patient and the family who were protecting him is this cryptic, yet menacing statement made in the Commons by the Home Secretary Henry Matthews (who had rejected the Poole petitioners to save Henry Young). As reported in the *Nottingham Evening Post* of 26 November 1888:

> Those who continue interested in the chase for the capture of the Whitechapel murderer have been struck with a statement incidentally made by Mr Matthews, in reply to a question on Friday. Asked why he had not offered a pardon for any accomplice concerned in the earlier crimes, the Home Secretary said that in the case of Mary Kelly, the latest victim, there were certain circumstances, wanting in the earlier instances, which made it more probable *that other persons, at any rate after the crime, had assisted the murderer.* This hint of *the existence of accessories after*

the fact is quite new to the London public, for nothing in the very
full reports published at the time indicated anything of the kind;
and although the police authorities—perhaps rightly—refuse to say
upon what grounds the Home Secretary's statement was based, it
affords a *hope that something more than a visionary clue has been
obtained.* (Our italics)

*Either Montague read about this line of inquiry in the newspapers or
heard from the Tuke brothers that police were soon to arrive. Either
way he knew that the dragnet was tightening every day, perhaps
becoming an almost hour-by-hour proposition. Montague was under
no illusion about the possibilities which stood before him now. He
had witnessed the hopeless distress of a man such as Henry Young
whose life would soon be extinguished by a hangman's noose. He had
also cringed as Christopher Power was led away from the dock in
the Old Bailey, grateful to Montague that he would not be returned
to Holloway Prison yet blissfully unaware that a life caged in a state
institution for the insane might make Henry Young's scaffold appear
to be the more humane finale. These options were for Montague not
options at all. If 'Jack the Ripper' was ever captured, he would either
hang or be certified insane and used by the State as a case study in
evil, a curiosity.*

*Montague decided that his end would come about on his own
terms. He was a gentleman and would opt for a gentleman's exit.
A winter chill heralded Tuesday December the fourth 1888. Before
the police had a chance to arrive, Druitt dressed in his gentleman's
attire as if leaving for work, quietly left his room and entered the
grounds of the asylum. Moving closer to the boundary his form
dissolved into the shadows cast by the stand of mature trees. He
easily scaled the wall beside them and unflinching began his final
race. The walk from Manor House Asylum to the water's edge
was downhill and quite straight and even in the dark of night or
in the hours before dawn, easy to navigate. Church Street at this
hour was deserted. Montie hurried, careful not to stumble or to
alert another soul to his presence. He passed to his left The Lamb
Tap public house alongside its own brewery. Unlike the night-long
ruckus of Whitechapel, at this hour the pub and its surrounds
stood silent. To his right Montague passed St Nicholas' Church and
burial ground. Panicked yet in control and barely able to breathe,
the sight of the Holy Cross, even in the gloom must have brought
comfort to one who, by confession, hoped to still meet his maker.*

The boundary of the raised graveyard scattered with sarcophagus and burial monuments led him now to the vast expanse of water gently lapping at the street's end. Amongst the assortment of debris washed in by the Thames, Montie methodically gathered stones, filling all of his pockets with their cumulative weight. Once done, and with a glance at his pocket watch, shoulders back, he walked defiantly into the Thames. Cold water filled his shoes, his pockets, his mouth, his lungs. Such a blessed relief.

One of the first reports of the recovery of the body a month later is from the *County of Middlesex Independent* on 2 January 1889 – with William Druitt mistakenly called 'friends', plural, while Montague is aged by a decade.

FOUND IN THE RIVER

The body of a well-dressed man was discovered on Monday in the river off Thorneycroft's torpedo works, by a waterman named Winslow. The police were communicated with and the deceased was conveyed to the mortuary. The body, which is that of *a man about 40 years of age*, has been in the water about a month. From certain papers found on the body *friends in Bournemouth* have been telegraphed to. An inquest will be held today (Wednesday). (Our italics)

Once more, George R. Sims' Edwardian articles on the case in *The Referee* are essentially accurate. In that later era, Sims writes frequently of a police dragnet fast closing on Jack but just missing him. In this safely sanitised version, the herculean, super-efficient police are about to arrest the 'mad doctor' while the maniac's 'friends' are trying to find him so he can be placed – again – in a private asylum. In his *Referee* column of 13 July 1902, Dagonet wrote:

...[the] process of exhaustion which enabled them at last to know the real name and address of Jack the Ripper. In that case [the police] had reduced the only possible Jacks to seven, then by a further exhaustive inquiry to three, and *were about to fit these three people's movements in with the dates of the various murders when the one and only genuine Jack saved further trouble by being found drowned in the Thames*, into which he had flung himself, a *raving* lunatic, after the last and most appalling mutilation of the whole series.

But prior to this discovery the name of the man found drowned was bracketed with two others as a Possible Jack and *the police were in search of him alive when they found him dead.* (Our italics)

Apart from Sims disguising William Druitt as the concerned 'friends', the only surviving account of William testifying, in some detail, to his efforts to find his missing brother Montie are recorded as mentioned in the previous chapter in the *Acton, Chiswick and Turnham Green Gazette* of 5 January 1889. It shows that William committed perjury in a number of instances, surely as a result of his desperation. He must have felt he might just get away with such gross dissembling because he knew something the jury and the reporters did not.

XIV

Cover-up at Chiswick

On 3 January 1889, the Lamb and Tap public house in Church Street in the outer London suburb of Chiswick was selected as a convenient location to hold a coroner's inquest. The proprietors suffered little inconvenience as the entire procedure lasted just a few hours. A handful of reporters from local newspapers attended, but none were present from the major dailies in the city. The brevity of the inquiry and lack of major media interest did not indicate the gravity of the event being decided upon by the experienced coroner Dr Thomas Diplock, aged 58, and a jury of all-male local worthies. The subject of the inquest was the once handsome and athletic English gentleman, Montague John Druitt, who had drowned himself in the Thames, just down the road. His earthly remains would be soon interred in a grave in his home town of Wimborne, Dorset.

Dr Diplock conducted a professional, even brusque inquiry. Police Constable George Moulson, who had been alerted by a local waterman Henry Winslade to the grisly discovery of a corpse bobbing up in the polluted river, testified about what had been found in the deceased's pockets: some coins and two uncashed cheques from the London & Provisional Bank for considerable sums (£60 and £16). Also found were transport tickets: an expensive first-class season rail pass from Blackheath to London (Southwestern Railway) and a second-half of a return from Hammersmith to Charing Cross, dated 1 December 1888. As might be expected, the well-dressed corpse yielded some gentleman's accoutrements: a silver watch, a gold chain with a spade guinea attached, a pair of kid gloves and a white handkerchief. In each of his pockets were four large stones. The bobby further testified that he could see no signs of foul play, such as external injuries on the head or torso.[1] Ironically, it would have been easier for all concerned if Mr Druitt had been coshed, robbed and his body hurled over a bridge into the drink because if he was found to have committed suicide with his mental faculties intact, there would probably be unease from the Church of England about his being buried in consecrated ground. On the other hand, this distasteful finale for a family of the so-called 'better classes' would be immediately nullified if the jury, under the direction of the coroner, ruled that the dead man had obviously been in a deranged state and was thus not responsible for the mortal sin of self-destruction.

For any Victorian in that room, particularly if they were consumers of the liquid produced at the Lamb Brewery next door, the name 'Druitt' would have made them inevitably think of the celebrated Dr Robert Druitt, M.R.C.P.S., who had passed away five years before. In 1865, Dr Druitt had published *Report on Cheap Wines, Their Quality and Wholesomeness with a Short Lecture to Ladies on Wine*. It was dedicated to Prime Minster William Gladstone whose Liberal government had campaigned for the improvement of public health via the consumption of lighter beverages. For his era, Dr Druitt was considered progressive; he recommended in the same report that ladies who worked for a living – maids, governesses and nurses – should indulge in a light wine; 'a glass or two at mid-morning as healthful, strengthening and enlivening'. Was this Montague Druitt, a sad suicide, something of a stain on the family of such a famous and accomplished man? That would be a terrific angle for a newspaper story, especially as it would scoop Fleet Street. However, it seemed the answer was no, for the deceased man's older brother, William H. Druitt, a Bournemouth solicitor, testified that apart from himself and their mother, the dead man 'had no other relative'.

This was accepted without question by Dr Diplock, as was William's explanation for his sibling's otherwise inexplicable act of suicide – their mother, Ann, William revealed with bracing candour, had been institutionalised this past July suffering from a progressive mental disease. On 11 December 1888, William said, he had been informed by an unidentified 'friend' that his barrister brother had not been at his inner-city chambers during the previous week. Alerted to potential trouble, William went to the school in Blackheath where Montague was not only a part-time schoolmaster but also a lodger. Sure enough, said William, he had found a note there among his brother's belongings 'alluding' to suicide. This was read aloud and summed up by Dr Diplock to the jury as: 'Since Friday, I felt like I was going to be like mother, and the best thing was for me to die.'

In the Victorian era it was a crushing social stigma to have to publicly admit that a member of your family was so mentally ill they had to be placed in care. With his frank admission about his poor mother, William Druitt – himself a coroner of some experience – would have seemed honest to a fault. If anybody in the room, either a reporter or a member of the jury, had thought that William's brother's suicide was a rather extreme, even implausible over-reaction to one parent's illness, it was, again, not queried by Dr Diplock. The coroner accepted all of William's testimony without question, including that he had last seen his brother for a single night in October 1888.

Only one reporter for a local Chiswick daily subtly signalled in his article that William's account was, well, a bit odd. This newspaper article from the *Acton, Chiswick and Turnham Green Gazette* of 5 January 1889 is the only surviving document that mentions the timing of when William claimed to have learned of his brother's disappearance: 11 December 1888, followed by the date of when he arrived at the school frantically searching for him – 30 December 1888. By his own account, it took William Druitt nearly three weeks to show up at Montague's lodgings. Had nobody else at the school thought to check his belongings, if he really was unaccountably missing? Within 24 hours of arriving at the Blackheath school, and supposedly finding the allusive note, his brother's corpse resurfaced in the Thames. Reportedly, Montague's pockets revealed no form of identification (it was likely that the cheques first identified William as they must have been payments to his sibling from the former's legal firm). Diplock showed no interest in the lucrative payments, who had made them, or for what specific service Montague had been renumerated.

Another discordant note sounded when William Druitt reported that he had learned at the school that his brother had been summarily fired for 'serious trouble'. Again Dr Diplock showed a remarked lack of curiosity as to the details of this potentially significant episode. Was Montague fired because he was absent without explanation, or because he had exhibited such insane behaviour they could not provide a long-standing employee with even the dignity of a face-saving resignation? This detail was apparently so hurriedly dealt with that other reporters did not even bother to mention it in their sympathetic accounts of the painful loss of this promising barrister and sportsman (and for that matter why was the coroner so coy about asking for the name of the 'friend' who allegedly tipped off William that his brother was missing from his legal chambers?)

A basic question was apparently not addressed at all – what was the late Mr M. J. Druitt doing in Chiswick? Did work or social commitments bring him to this particular suburb? His headstone would assert that he committed suicide on 4 December 1888, yet his train ticket was bought three days earlier – and not reused. Where was he for those few days? Where did he stay at night? Was he there, in Chiswick, perhaps with friends or acquaintances, or at a hotel? Should any such people have been called to testify as to his state of mind on the eve of his suicide? In fact, nobody who must have interacted with Montague between 11 October and 4 December 1888 bore witness to his movements or state of mind, a gap of nearly two months.

The inquest was entirely reliant on the testimony of the older brother. Very near where the body surfaced was located an expensive, private asylum run by two progressive physician brothers, Thomas and Charles Tuke. Was the deceased going to see them due to feeling distressed or overwhelmed, but changed his mind and diverted to the river? Or was he already their patient and at some opportune moment had slipped away and drowned himself in the Thames? Perhaps he could not face the shame of life in a 'madhouse', however comfortable. Is that what his allusive suicide note meant: Montague could not face the same fate as his mother? Dr Thomas Diplock pursued no enquiries in any of these directions. He wrapped up proceedings quickly and tidily. Since Montague had an apparent family history of mental infirmity the jury found that the deceased had killed himself while the balance of his mind was in a temporarily disordered state. Case closed. Dr Diplock's findings left no obstacle to the burial of Mr Druitt's remains in consecrated ground.

What nobody at the inquest could possibly have known was that Dr Thomas Diplock and William Druitt knew each other, or at least knew of each other. On 21 June 1884, Diplock had been the coroner at an inquiry into another suicide of a middle-class English gentleman: William Hopkinson, aged 23, who had histrionically shot himself after his proposal of marriage to a Miss May Warren was rejected. As he would do again with the tragedy of Montague Druitt four years later, Dr Diplock returned a verdict of 'suicide while of unsound mind'. The late William Hopkinson was a nephew of Isabella Druitt (née Hopkinson) who was by then the widow of Dr Robert Druitt. Dr Druitt had been Uncle Robert to Montague and William Druitt. And Diplock contributed pieces to the *Medical Gazette* which was edited by Dr Robert Druitt.[2] Therefore when William testified in 1889 that he and his ailing mother were the only surviving members of Montague's family, it was a brazen lie – and Diplock must have known it. In fact, Montague had three surviving brothers, three sisters, uncles, aunts and a number of cousins.

Yet if Dr Diplock was chummily covering for a prominent clan, with whom he was already familiar, he likely did not know to what desperate lengths William Druitt had taken to deceive *him* as well. We know from another source that Montague was probably not fired from his school at all – instead it was from one of his gentleman's sporting clubs: the Blackheath Cricket, Football and Lawn Tennis Company. That club's minutes of 21 December 1888 record: 'The Honourary Secretary and Treasurer, Mr M. J. Druitt, *having gone abroad*, it was resolved that he be and he is hereby removed from the post of Honourary Secretary and Treasurer.' (Our italics) It is quite a macabre statement to read, as the prominent gentlemen at that club meeting had no idea that they were sacking a waterlogged corpse, which was beginning its slow ascent back to the air-breathing world. Why dismiss Druitt simply because he was out of the country? Why not allow him to resign from overseas, or before he departed, or upon his return? This strange little mystery does make perfect sense, however, if the club members had been informed that poor Montague had been *taken* abroad by family to be treated at a private asylum for a mental illness. In that case nobody would expect him to be able to fulfil his duties, not in the foreseeable future – not even to be able to write a letter of resignation. What seems at first harsh and heartless about the Blackheath Club's minutes, may have been the very opposite; they discreetly shy away from any references to Mr Druitt's incapacity due to illness.

William Druitt's tainted testimony at the 1889 inquest in Chiswick exposed a nervous need to deflect Montague's dismissal away from his sporting club (whose members believed he had at some point gone abroad and knew he was, by implication, incommunicado, to the school instead). The same school wherein Montague's room and belongings, according to William's own contradictory account under oath, had remained undisturbed. Furthermore, the headmaster of the school, George Valentine, had a brother on that same sporting club's board (William Valentine) who on 21 December 1888 must have known that Montague had not got into 'serious trouble' (unless mental illness is so defined) but had apparently ventured abroad and was not expected to return, at least for the coming semester.

We think that after his brother vanished from the Tukes' asylum, William Druitt had been to the Blackheath School much earlier. He knew Montie was not there. But as the weeks, and Christmas passed with no word from his missing sibling, he may have feared it looked odd if he, William, did not again investigate his brother's place of residence – so William went back. Fortuitously his brother's corpse was found in the Thames the very next day. We think this gave the wily solicitor the idea of having supposedly found a letter in Montie's room explaining his impending act of self-destruction. Nobody attended the inquiry to contradict William's account. George R. Sims has the timing of the conjunction of the school visit and the resurfacing of the body virtually to the day, as we see in his *Referee* column of 16 February 1902: '*At the time* his body was found in the Thames, *his friends*, who were terrified at his disappearance from their midst, *were endeavouring to have him found* and placed under restraint again.' (Our italics) Other regional newspapers had no desire to further defame a deceased young man who had obviously been temporarily demented and, consequently, left out the part about his peculiar-sounding dismissal from the school. By contrast they paid tribute to this talented young man who had so tragically thrown it all away. *The Southern Guardian* of January 5 1889 repeated the lament of another newspaper:

SAD DEATH OF A LOCAL BARRISTER.

The Echo of Thursday night says: — An inquiry was on Wednesday held by Dr Diplock, at Chiswick, respecting the death of Montague John Druitt, 31 years of age, who was found drowned in the Thames. The deceased was identified by his brother, Mr William Harvey Druitt, a solicitor residing at Bournemouth, who stated that the deceased was a barrister-at-law, but had lately been an assistant at a school at Blackheath. The deceased had left a letter, addressed to Mr Valentine, of the school, in which he alluded to suicide.

Evidence having been given as to discovering deceased in the Thames — upon his body were found a cheque for £60 and £16 in gold — the Jury returned a verdict of 'Suicide whilst of unsound mind.' The deceased gentleman was well known and much respected in this neighbourhood. *He was a barrister of bright talent, he had a promising future before him, and his untimely end is deeply deplored.*

The funeral took place in Wimborne cemetery on Thursday afternoon, and the body was followed to the grave by the deceased's relatives and a few friends, including *Mr W. H. Druitt*, Mr Arthur Druitt, *Rev. C. H. Druitt*, Mr J. Druitt, sen., Mr J. Druitt, jun., Mr J. T. Homer, and Mr Wyke-Smith. The funeral service was read by the vicar of die Minster, Wimborne, the Rev. F. J. Huyshe, assisted by the Rev. Plater. (A possibly estranged brother, Edward Druitt, did not attend. Our italics)

The Reverend Charles Druitt attended the funeral of the man he knew to be 'Jack the Ripper', a secret known to only a few others. With Montague deceased and officially a suicide due to a hereditary mental weakness, the family could breathe easier. The police hunt of the asylums in France and England had nearly caught him, but they remained – and would remain – empty-handed. The words of the Home Secretary about seeking 'accessories after the fact' must have rung in their ears as they watched Montague's coffin lowered into the ground (they paid for an extra deep grave, as if fearing he might flee again). This excruciating nightmare – for them, for the poor victims of the East End and for the harried authorities – was now, thankfully, behind them. The family could go on with their lives and pretend it never happened.

What the Druitts who knew the truth about Montague did not count on was the possibility of other copycat killers also attacking or slitting the throats of defenceless Whitechapel 'unfortunates' and the potential arrest, conviction and execution of the wrong man, or men, for the heinous crimes of their maniacal relative. As the events of 1889 to 1891 would prove, the clan's ordeal was far from over.

XV

Veiled Correspondence

By 1889 Mrs Isabella Druitt well understood the aftermath of tragedy. Like so many women of her time, she had experienced the grief of loss. By the age of 66, she had lost siblings and her parents and had been for six years a widow. She was seen as the matriarch of the Druitt clan, beloved and relied upon for advice and approval by its members scattered all around the country. The death of her husband Doctor Robert Druitt was, as ever, stoically borne by Isabella. She needed to be strong, supporting their beloved children to achieve success in both profession and marriage spheres. This she would do, Isabella had assured her beloved husband during his final illness. Like her sister-in-law Ann Druitt of Wimborne, she understood how the death of the head of the household could cause a family to falter. Unlike Ann however, Isabella's fortitude had grown from the understanding that she could survive even the cruellest of tragedies, the deaths of two of her children, Cuthbert and later Katherine. This had taught her that although overwhelming, grief could be worked through and life could continue.[1]

In 1889 and residing at an expensive private asylum in Brighton, Ann Druitt, trapped in her own mental twilight, was perhaps oblivious to the death of her son Montague – if she even remembered him. Not so for Isabella Druitt. The aftermath of her nephew Montie's wicked actions and subsequent suicide had an impact on her family's world. Isabella knew that something would have to be done to protect her family and possessing greater resilience than any of her children, she felt she would be the one best suited to deal with it.

We believe her second son Charles, the 'Pope', had been drawn into Montie's disgraceful decline. Taking his cousin's confession, Charles was sure that Montie – the previously learned barrister, schoolmaster and talented sportsman – must have been suffering from 'epileptic mania'. This was the condition the family members had settled on as the explanation for the horrors – a Victorianism for a physical illness in which the patient has homicidal fits he or she sometimes cannot even recall (despite the fact Montie had confessed)[2]. How could any member of this clan demonstrate such evil without an uncontrollable mental affliction being the cause?

Mrs Druitt was, apart from her heartbreak over the actions of her nephew, also very sorry for Charles. Newly married to the much loved Isabel (née Majendie Hill), he had been dragged into this whole sorry story simply by doing his duty as a vicar. Montie's brother William, as Isabella could acknowledge, had probably suffered the most. It was he, apart from the five victims of Montague's madness, who bore the brunt of his brother's actions. William, however, was now content to leave everything in the past. He did not want to discuss the matter with anyone and had made it clear to Reverend Charles and his Aunt Isabella that he expected them to now behave as if nothing had happened.

By September 1889, it was clear to everyone close to Charles that his health was precarious. His anxiety was such that he had developed digestive problems that impacted on his ability to minister to his parish. It was decided that Charles should speak to Dr William Cholmeley who had been a great friend of his father Dr Robert Druitt (he wrote the family approved biography of Dr Druitt of 1883).[3] After their meeting at 63 Grosvenor Street, London, Dr Cholmeley came to the conclusion that Charles' state of health had become grave enough that Charles must escape his environs to renew his body and spirit. A part-time position was found with a Mr Sankey, an expert on church music, who ministered in the Veytaux Chillon Vaud region of Switzerland. Mr Sankey appeared to be very pleased to receive the newly married couple and was happy to have two fellow musicians in Charles and Isabel, to share his love of music.[4] Charles was terribly anxious about his state of affairs but finally gained approval for leave and a replacement was found for the Harnham parish. Charles later confided to his mother that if he had known the upset and work it would cause to go away 'for rest' he would never have agreed to it.[5]

Correspondence from that time also suggests that Charles was promised a meeting with someone who, unusually, is never named, about a matter that was of great concern to him – which is also never explicitly spelled out. The clergyman is guarded in his communication to his mother and it is clear that the matter has been discussed by the two of them and it is extremely sensitive.[6] Charles wants his mother to have the letter but only forwards it when, as he makes clear, he is certain that his mother is back at Strathmore Gardens to receive it personally with a second, enclosed, communication (avoiding the potential for perhaps a servant or a friend seeing it). He tells Isabella that because a certain person 'never came' to collect the letter that Charles had written, he would abandon that plan and send it direct to her.

Charles and Isabel stayed with Mrs Druitt at 8 Strathmore Gardens in Kensington in early October 1889. Mrs Druitt was pleased to hear that Miss Caroline Tuke, a young friend of Charles' and Isabel's, with whom she too was well acquainted, would join her son and daughter-in-law in Switzerland. Miss Tuke was the sister of the physicians Thomas Seymour and Charles Molesworth Tuke of the Manor House Asylum at Chiswick, from where Montague Druitt absented himself before committing suicide – and where his mother Ann Druitt would spend her last days and expire in 1890. Caroline lived in the family quarters of the progressive asylum with her mother, brothers and their families. Caroline was a Deaconess in the Church of England and a great friend and confidante of both Charles and Isabel. Charles had worked closely with Caroline on matters pertaining to the women and children of the church, particularly parish schools. All of their concerns about Charles' 'worries and poor health' were further discussed during their stay and by the time Charles and Isabel set off on their journey, Mrs Isabella Druitt has concluded that something must be put in place to set her son's mind at ease.

The Druitts who knew the truth about Montie must have been especially fearful about the possibility of another man being wrongfully charged with the crimes. What could they do to forestall such a miscarriage of justice? If they went to speak to someone in authority to explain what they knew, could they be arrested and charged for withholding information? And if it came to light that Montie's brother William and the Reverend Charles had spirited the real villain away to France to cure his 'epileptic mania' or 'slight homicidal mania' rather than hand him over to the police, wouldn't they be charged as the 'Ripper's' confederates? All of them could become fodder for the gossip-hungry tabloids. Mayor of Christchurch James Druitt Snr seems to have understood this dilemma all too well. Around the time of Montague's funeral, James abandoned his family memoirs for six years. When he returned to the task, he never mentioned his drowned nephew nor that wing of the family.

On 17 July 1889 a police constable on his East End beat found a woman in Castle Alley who was very recently murdered. Almost nothing is known about Alice McKenzie except that she was about 40 years of age and enjoyed smoking a pipe – hence her nickname 'Clay Pipe Alice' – and that she escorted a blind boy to a music hall on the night of her death. She had been stabbed to death, in the throat, and there was some half-hearted attempt at mutilating her body. As with Liz Stride, it was thought that the fiend was interrupted before he could fulfil his more grotesque post-mortem desires. The newspapers, one coroner (Dr Thomas Bond) and the Police Commissioner James Monro were in no doubt – 'The Ripper' had returned after an extended hiatus. A typical headline from the *Amberley and Wilmslow Advertiser* of 19 July 1889 outlined the crime and the general belief as to who was responsible:

ANOTHER EAST END TRAGEDY.
'JACK THE RIPPER' AGAIN AT WORK.

There seems to be little doubt that the murder which took place in Castle Alley, Whitechapel, early yesterday morning was the work of the miscreant who last year perpetuated the series of horrible crimes which made the district so notorious.

The case was extensively covered across the Atlantic, including in the *Trenton Times* (New Jersey) of 17 July 1889:

JACK THE RIPPER AGAIN
A Fresh Victim Discharged at Whitechapel

ONE MORE DISSOLUTE WOMAN
Found Horribly Mutilated in Castle Alley, a Short Distance from Where the Other Murders Were Committed

The body was horribly mutilated and bears undoubted evidence of the fiend whose atrocities in Whitechapel have terrorized the whole district repeatedly. The police are as far as ever from a clue to the identity of the murderer and seem perfectly paralysed.

Several newspapers simply listed every Whitechapel murder of a 'fallen woman' from Emma Smith in April 1888 through to Mary Jane Kelly in November 1888, and sweepingly asserted every atrocity was by the same madman. One can only imagine the trepidation of certain Druitts to this hideous development. They knew that whoever had so cowardly assaulted and killed Alice McKenzie, it was not the same man as had done five of the seven earlier homicides. The dilemma was how to communicate this certainty to somebody in authority – and prove it – without revealing their identities.

With Charles and Isabel abroad, Mrs Isabella Druitt advised her daughter Emily that she has taken steps to ease Charles 'feelings of guilt and angst'. Of late, Mrs Isabella Druitt had become particularly drawn to reports about murders in Whitechapel and elsewhere, however unlike other residents within the London area who felt the need to lock up lest 'Jack the Ripper' came calling, Mrs Druitt in November 1889 was sleeping, as she tells her daughter Emily, with the window wide open.[7] Isabella was however distressed at the newspaper's unrelenting alarmist headlines. She laments, to Emily that 'The howlers are shouting out "another Whitechapel Murder".' Mrs Druitt appears to know that the press claims are spurious and exploitative. Is this merely a commonly expressed observation about tabloid-driven hysteria or is it because she knew her nephew was the deceased maniac? In November of 1889, Mrs Druitt had been following newspaper reports of the trial of a John Watson Laurie for the murder of a Mr Edwin Rose in Edinburgh. Although different to the Whitechapel murders, the reality of capital punishment weighed heavy on her mind. Upon reading of Laurie's conviction she expressed the reality of a guilty verdict for murder, 'I see that man Laurie is condemned.'[8]

At this time, Charles' plan for 'rest and rejuvenation' was not proving to be straightforward. His wife Isabel wrote to his sister Gertrude that Charles had passed out while out walking with a group of men. He had to be picked up and carried back to Mr Sankey's residence. In light of the family's diagnosis that Montie's murderous actions were the result of 'epileptic mania', Isabel urged Gertrude to convince Mrs Druitt that the doctor had stressed that Charles' medical event had nothing to do with 'epileptic fainting'.[9] Charles was annoyed to learn that Mr Sankey had, behind his back, written a letter to Dr Cholmeley demanding to know the true reason for Charles taking up the position in Switzerland. In response, Charles' mother conferred with Dr Cholmeley and a reply was sent to Sankey, the contents of which by all accounts must have dampened his curiosity. However, this meddling may have caused Charles and Isabel to cut short their Swiss sojourn, as by the spring of 1890 they had returned to Harnham and resumed their parish duties.

Mrs Druitt found another article of interest to her that November 1889. A report was written, again concerning Whitechapel, of an American gentleman, Mr R. Harding Davis, a journeyman journalist who, with the aid of a letter of reference was able to call on Dr Robert Anderson the head of the Criminal Investigation Department. Harding Davis requested a police escort, which would act as his guide around the murder scenes of Whitechapel. Anderson must have considered the American's referee to be of suitable standing as he promptly passed the tourist on to Inspector Moore to show him around. In the article, Anderson is quoted as defensively observing; 'After a stranger has gone over it he takes a much more lenient view of our failure to find Jack the Ripper as they call him, than he did before'.[10]

We think Mrs Druitt seized upon the idea of visiting Dr Anderson to privately inform the Assistant Commissioner that they were worried that some other man might be arrested and tried for the five murders her relative had committed. Further details could, in theory, be withheld because, as the murderer was almost a year in his Dorset grave, there could be no trial. A further attraction for Mrs Druitt to personally visit Anderson is that her home in Strathmore Gardens was less than a 10-minute walk to his house in Linden Gardens. The dilemma was that Dr Anderson would, of course, ask both for her identity and her proof. How could he not? This would, however, sacrifice their anonymity forever.

She wanted what might be impossible – for the Assistant Commissioner to agree to see her, listen to her story, but refrain from asking her name or the name of the alleged killer. There was only one card that Mrs Druitt could play to gain such an encounter with law enforcement on her terms; as expected in Victorian high society, her ace was class. Never one to step back from a job which needed to be done, Mrs Druitt set off in a carriage to Cavendish Square to call upon a man reliable in both his social rank and his discretion, a gentleman who was known to her late husband through the various committees and hearings they had attended together. This gentleman coincidently had also become distantly connected to her own family upon the marriage of Charles and Isabel Majendie Hill. He would understand the gravity of the situation and know just the right way to discreetly help Mrs Druitt.

James Ludovic Lindsay the 26th Earl of Crawford and the 9th Earl of Balcarres (1847–1913) was known for his devotion to the study of astronomy. A Conservative Member of Parliament and a Freemason, he was a devoted philatelist, ornithologist and bibliophile. His younger sister Lady Margaret Majendie was also a minor celebrity; her domestic melodramas such as *Precautions – a novel* were popular with discerning female readers. George R. Sims often sought out Lady Margaret to include her tales in various compendiums he edited.[11] By 1889, Lady Margaret had been a widow for almost four years. Her late husband Lewis Ashurst Majendie had been a Conservative politician. They had lived at Castle Hedingham in Essex, with their daughter the Hon. Aline Majendie, who was later a lady in waiting to Queen Victoria. Lewis was a cousin to Colonel Majendie and to Isabel Majendie Hill's mother Maria.

The surviving 'Crawford letter', was found by the writer and editor of the internet blog, *Casebook: Jack the Ripper*, Stephen P. Ryder. It was among a collection of Sir Robert Anderson's correspondence held at Duke University (North Carolina) and the brief letter arguably provides evidence of such an intervention, probably by one of the Druitts. Surely the familial connection with Crawford is too big a coincidence for the contact not to be one of Montie's clan? It is undated and addressed to Dr Robert Anderson by the Earl of Crawford. We think that the Earl, in an act of self-protection, misled Anderson because he *did* know the identity of the woman in question: she was Dr Robert Druitt's respectable widow:

2 CAVENDISH SQUARE
W.

My dear Anderson,

I send you this line to ask you to see & hear the bearer, *whose name is unknown to me.* She has or thinks she has a *knowledge of the author of the Whitechapel murders.* The author is supposed to be *nearly related to her, & she is in great fear lest any suspicions should attach to her & place her & her family in peril.*

I have advised her to place the whole story before you *without giving you any names,* so that you may form an opinion as to its being worthwhile to investigate.

Very sincerely yours,
Crawford (Our italics)

This tension between the need to reveal the broad identity of 'Jack the Ripper' as a deceased, English gentleman and yet simultaneously to conceal his singular features – in order to protect his respectable relations – would persistently reoccur in the Late Victorian and Edwardian eras. This may have been the first attempt by certain

Druitts to have their cake and eat it too. If so, it failed. Dr Robert Anderson never annotated the letter with, for example, the name of the woman who had met him on the recommendation of the Earl because, presumably, he never learned it. We think that Anderson was probably quite solicitous in order to please her aristocratic patron. He made it clear to the lady, nevertheless, that she was quite mistaken. The recent murder of Alice McKenzie had proved, Anderson likely countered, that unquestionably the same maniac was still at large killing poor women in the East End, albeit less frequently. The police chief probably thought he was doing this obviously refined and affluent matron a favour by refuting her vague claims about a man 'nearly related to her'.

In an angst-filled November letter, however, Mrs Isabella Druitt informs Emily that she has visited 'Cavendish Square', which matches the Earl's address. Uncharacteristically, no details are provided, yet her daughter must understand the implications of that location without further elaboration. Mrs Druitt then laments that she feels she may never be rid of this 'encumbrance' – again, no clarifying details.

Mrs Isabella Druitt's small book containing names of people within her social circle or of her acquaintance has survived.[12] As to be expected it lists relatives, friends and colleagues of her late and esteemed husband. The authors also discovered in this small, long-forgotten book a name that connects Mrs Druitt once more to the 'Ripper' case: Farquharson

We believe this to be Henry Richard Farquharson, the Tory Member of Parliament representing West Dorset between 1885 until his untimely death in 1895. Born the same year as Montague, 1857, and an enthusiastic breeder of Newfoundland dogs, he does not come across as a particularly likeable or attractive figure. He reacted to an honest mistake by some of his younger dog handlers, one which had led to the expensive loss of a number of dogs, by beating the boys within an inch of their lives. Far from an important political figure – a country squire backbencher with little to say in the Commons – Farquharson seems to have had a penchant for not keeping his mouth shut. Though he was not Mrs Druitt's representative, as she lived in Kensington, London, he was well known to the Wimborne Druitts as his extensive estate was a few miles from their home town. The MP and Montie, and their respective families, were part of the local elite who mixed at balls, royal visits and other social events. Reverend Charles Druitt would certainly have known Henry Farquharson as his local Member of Parliament because, by 1891 with the Bishop of Salisbury as his patron, Charles was appointed Vicar of Whitechurch Canonicorum. (The couple would live in the Vicarage with their firstborn child Isabel Mary Carola born 1890 and later followed by a son Charles Edward Hobart in 1892. Charles would minister at the historic Church of St Candida and Holy Cross until his death in 1900).

In early 1891 this same Farquharson would be telling his friends in London that he knew, as an indisputable fact, the identity of 'Jack the Ripper': the murderer had been a surgeon's son who had taken his own life. This is the very first time that Montie Druitt, albeit unnamed, enters the extant record as the solution to some of the Whitechapel murders. How on earth did the Dorset MP learn of the Druitts' crippling secret and why did he feel free to tell other people?

Was it simply the proximity of living a few miles from their family home and from the cousin who had likely taken Montague's confession before he drowned himself in the Thames? Was it gossip along the Conservative party's constituent grapevine; perhaps from Tory mayor James Druitt Snr to the national politician? Or, as the name in the little book suggests, was it because after the outreach to Dr Robert Anderson had failed, Mrs Druitt tried again, this time with her tormented son's representative in London. We think that Isabella Druitt might have thought that a politician, who was also an upper class gentleman, an Old Etonian, a Tory, and an officer of the State, would have the authority with Scotland Yard to let them know the 'Ripper' was no more – without revealing the name of his deceased constituent who had been the killer. If she approached Farquharson perhaps she told him that her son, Reverend Charles, was going to reveal something of the truth on the tenth anniversary of Montie's drowning, but that it would be an impenetrable mix of fact and fiction. If this is what happened, then these Druitts had once more miscalculated – Henry Farquharson was enthusiastically indiscreet.

This West of England MP must have been dazzled that he was being handed the solution to the Whitechapel mystery. Of all people, he must have mused, it was a nephew of *the* Dr Robert Druitt. Perhaps Farquharson got a kick out of bragging that the foul murderer (Montie having been a Conservative Party member) had voted for him. In early 1891, Farquharson began telling people that *he* had solved the case. To be fair, the MP did stick to the cover story; Montie's identity must be clothed in a bit of misdirection. Below is one of the earliest references to this devastating leak. It can only be imagined the consternation and dismay this article must have caused to the Druitts who knew: William, Charles and his mother, Isabella and most probably her two youngest daughters, Emily and Gertrude. From the 11 February 1891 edition of *The Bristol Times and Mirror*:

> I give a curious story for what it is worth. There is a West of England member who in private declares that *he has solved* the mystery of 'Jack the Ripper'. *His theory* – and he repeats it with so much emphasis that it might almost be called *his doctrine* – is that 'Jack the Ripper' committed suicide on the night of his last murder. I can't give details, for *fear of a libel action*; but the story is so circumstantial that a good many people believe it. He states that *a man with blood-stained clothes committed suicide on the night of the last murder*, and he asserts that the man was the *son of a surgeon*, who suffered from homicidal mania. I do not know what the police think of the story, but I believe that *before long a clean breast will be made*, and that the accusation will be sifted thoroughly.

Henry Farquharson would not be named until the following year (*see* Chapter XVII) and only once, but his impact on the whole saga was considerable. Some of his fictitious data was never used again: for example, a surgeon's son, by implication a young gentleman from a well-to-do family with access to medical knowledge and training, who was found with bloodstained clothes (in reality, Montie's clothes were soggy from the polluted Thames). As we only have a glimpse of Farquharson's 'doctrine' it is unclear whether the bloodstained surgeon's son was encountered by a witness. The MP seems, nonetheless, to have skirted around the confession to a priest and the drowning in the Thames. By contrast, the detail about 'Jack' instantly taking his own life in the wake of murder – in effect his confessing to his guilt by a melodramatic act of remorseful self-destruction – would have a very long shelf life. In a stroke, the MP's compression of the three weeks between the Miller's Court horror on 9 November 1888 and Druitt's suicide on 4 December 1888 caused the entire French detour to neatly vanish. This revealing and concealing of Montague Druitt's identity must have been small comfort to the family. Within two days of this article appearing in the regional press, and being republished in London newspapers, an unexpected event took place that once more seemed to rescue the family from the threat of exposure and humiliation and is covered in the next chapter.

To go back in time for a moment; on 13 June 1887, Gertrude Druitt had written to her mother, Mrs Isabella Druitt about the poor mental health of Montague's mother, Ann: 'Aunt William is to go to Linden Gardens.' There is a Linden Gardens in Chiswick near the Tukes' asylum and it was rumoured they held houses there for affluent patients to discreetly recuperate. Now let us fast forward to 4 July 1892, when Reverend Charles writes to his mother Isabella from his Whitechurch parish: 'We are eagerly expecting your visit and shall be ready to receive you and Rose on Tuesday 2 August for as long as you like to stay. We are glad to know the *Linden affairs* look brighter again now.' (Our italics) Since Ann Druitt had been deceased for two years by then, we wonder if 'Linden affairs' is family code for the 'Ripper' crisis; combining as it might the Tukes at Chiswick and Dr Robert Anderson's address (39 Linden Gardens, London).

By 1892, as subsequent chapters will show, various Whitechapel storms buffeting the family had momentarily calmed, whereas a year before the family faced exposure.

Saved by an 'honourable schoolboy'

No doubt every policeman, from the humblest bobby on his beat all the way up to the Police Commissioner in his lofty office, daydreamed about arresting 'Jack the Ripper' – of getting their hands on that madman before he could savage another 'fallen woman' and foully desecrate her remains. Any policeman who pulled off such a coup would be a hero to a grateful nation and, furthermore, would probably be thanked by Her Majesty in person. The flipside of such a satisfying fantasy, however, would be the nightmare of *not* catching 'The Fiend' when you had the chance – of the maniac humiliating Scotland Yard yet again maybe thanks to your lack of courage or intelligence.

We must pity poor Ernest Thompson, a new young bobby on his maiden beat. On 13 February 1891, close to 2 o'clock in the morning, PC Thompson entered the arch of Mint Street, an area called Swallow Gardens. He saw a woman lying on her back in the middle of the narrow roadway. At first he thought it was just another sad drunk in his way until he ventured closer and flashed his bullseye lamp towards the human form. Immediately he saw that her throat was severely slashed (right to the spinal cord the autopsy would later determine) and a river of blood flowed horribly from the fatal wound. As the stunned Thompson moved closer, the victim's eyes fluttered open – or at least appeared to. According to the *Western Gazette* of 20 February 1891, he stayed with the victim and found that her 'pulse had not ceased beating when he bent over and grasped her wrist' and afterwards he 'quickly gained assistance, the streets of the neighbourhood were searched by constables, and a doctor was summoned'.

Did Thompson read this crushing description in the London *Times* of the following day describing his honest misjudgement?

It was at this moment Constable Thompson distinctly heard the sounds of retreating footsteps. Evidently the murderer had a very narrow escape. Had the officer at once and speedily taken up pursuit he would, in all probability, have effected the capture of the man who had committed this crime: or, at least, he might have had a good view of him, and so have been able to furnish particulars which might have led to his ultimate capture. The constable, it should be mentioned, is a young man of little experience in police work, having been in the force only six weeks ... A more experienced officer would, probably, have taken up the chase, with the result that the author of the deed would doubtless have been caught, and so have put an end to these series of crimes in Whitechapel.

Ernest Thompson was painfully embarrassed, but a young woman named Frances Coles had lost her life (in 1900 PC Ernest Thompson would also be tragically killed in the line of duty).[1] At 32 years of age and known by the Dickensian nickname 'Carrotty Nell', she had endured a life blighted by squalor and limited opportunities. She was by no means destitute; Frances Coles had a job at a factory stoppering bottles of medicine, but it was poorly paid and tedious. As did so many others, she slipped into casual prostitution and full-time alcoholism. Heartbreakingly at the time of her murder, 'Carrotty Nell' had stubbornly clung to the last vestiges of bourgeoisie respectability; she had successfully concealed her double life from her family and friends. The first time her bootmaker father learned that his daughter had become a 'fallen woman' was the same moment he discovered she was deceased – and had passed into posterity as the latest atrocity committed by 'The Ripper'. In his 1934 memoirs Detective-Sergeant B. Leeson captures well the chill that ran down the collective spine of England at the news of Frances Coles' untimely death: 'Another Jack the Ripper murder! Only those who were living at the time and who were old enough to appreciate it can imagine what that meant. When that dreaded news flashed round, not merely all of London, but all of England was terrified.'[2]

There was however, one English family who were just as terrified, but not for the same reason as the rest of the populace. As the keepers of the terrible secret about their deceased relative Montague, their fear was that an innocent person might be swept by an angry mob and a complacent State to the gallows. Newspapers proclaimed the return of the fiend almost gleefully. To take but one example, here is *The Eastern Post & City Chronicle* of 14 February 1891:

THE RIPPER AGAIN
ANOTHER HORRIBLE TRAGEDY IN WHITECHAPEL

Another of the series of terrible crimes which have been connected with East London during late years was committed at an early hour this (Friday) morning. The revolting features which have characterised most of these murders hitherto were happily absent: but the circumstances of the crime, the character of the victim, and the mysterious feature by which the deed is environed, undoubtedly place it in the same category. The time chosen by the murderer, the locality, and the precautions taken to escape detection are in all respects similar to those followed on previous occasions.

Scotland Yard mobilised a small army to search tenements, streets, doss houses, ships and the docks.[3] Within a day of the murder of Frances Coles, this sweep seemed to pay off – an arrest was made. PC Thompson's mistake in providing useless comfort to a warm corpse did not seem to matter. Not only was this suspect culpable for the Coles' murder, his movements looked likely to match the previous crimes of 'Jack the Ripper'. For a few days the Whitechapel Murders had a happy and satisfying ending for all concerned, apart from the latest victim on the slab and those who had preceded her. This time the killer had been caught and prevented from launching another reign of terror. He was a burly, hard-living gentile, a sailor and an Englishman named James Thomas Sadler, whom everybody called Tom. The evidence against him, at least for the Coles' murder, was he had been seen drinking excessively with her on the night Frances was stabbed to death. They had quarrelled; he had later sold an allegedly bloodstained knife at a Sailors' Home, and he was seen to be drenched in blood by a number of witnesses. His own wife, neglected and betrayed by Tom, gave an interview in which she accused him of having exactly the bad character required to be a multiple murderer. Tom Sadler was a sailor, a ship's fireman, and the best Whitechapel witness had described a man who at least appeared to be attired like a seaman. Despite his fervent denials, Sadler was arrested for Frances Coles' murder. CID detectives carefully checked out his exact known whereabouts for the previous crimes. An angry mob bayed for Sadler's blood when he was escorted to court.

On 18 February 1891 a reporter for *The York Herald* had somehow managed to track down the identity of the 'West of England' MP. He promptly confronted Henry Farquharson and asked him to explain the contradiction between the killer supposedly being a deceased surgeon's son, as the politician had been persuading his London cronies, and yet here was another victim presumably killed by the same criminal maniac. Knowing the anxiety his big mouth had already caused for the Druitts, this was an opportunity for the wildly indiscreet politician to row back on the leaking of 'his doctrine'. He could have replied that he thought he must have been mistaken, or that he had no further comment to make as the matter was *sub judice*. Instead, narrow-minded vanity won out:

> The Member of Parliament, who recently declared that 'Jack the Ripper' had killed himself on the evening of the last murder, *adheres to his opinion*. Even assuming that the man Saddler [sic] is able to prove his innocence of the murder of Frances Coles, *he maintains that the latest crime cannot be the work of the author of the previous series of atrocities*, and this view of the matter is steadily growing among those *who do not see that there is any good reason to suppose that 'Jack the Ripper' is dead* …. (Our italics)

For a politician, Farquharson was being honest and, since the Druitts could not be identified, he probably believed he was being fair. After all, this sailor Sadler, whether he killed Frances Coles, or not, was not 'Jack' – and this MP knew it for a fact. We believe that this public comment by the Tory politician, albeit still not named, left the Druitts forever embittered against Farquharson; from their point of view he was the quintessential loose cannon poised to sink their ship. Soon others would share this same negative opinion and do something about this pest.

George R. Sims sensed a rush to judgment on the part of his fellow pressmen and the Tory Home Secretary Henry Matthews, whom he so openly despised. Dagonet in *The Referee* of 22 February 1891 raised the prospect that Sadler's wife had been coached by agents of the government. He was also scathing about the constabulary's effort to catch 'Jack', an attitude that would soon be dropped – in fact totally reversed within eight years – allowing us to discern the approximate date when the famous writer must have learned the truth about Montie Druitt: 'Never, surely, was there a more outrageous attempt to prejudice a case *sub judice* than that made by the newspapers which published the statement of Sadler's wife. The statement was really nothing less than the case for the prosecution, put together with all the trained skill of an expert.'

By then the case against Tom Sadler as either Frances Coles' murderer or as 'The Ripper' proved to have all the tensile strength of a wet noodle. The Seamen's Union paid for a decent lawyer to mount a vigorous defence of one of its members (which proved as nimble and effective as that by the deceased barrister, Montague J. Druitt). On or about 18 February 1891 the Mitre Square witness, which has to be Joseph Lawende, was 'confronted' with suspect Sadler and stated categorically – and unsurprisingly – that this was not the same man he had seen chatting with the Mitre Square victim Catherine Eddowes.[4] On closer inspection, the knife in question was almost too blunt to even cut cheese. Sadler had improbably claimed that the copious bloodstains found on his clothes were due to being assaulted three times on the relevant night by three different gangs of toughs, the first of which had robbed him. Yet this turned out to be true and, ironically, one of the witnesses to the sailor's plight was a beat cop who further observed that Sadler was too inebriated – he could barely walk – to be a danger to anybody but himself. In early March 1891 all charges were dropped and Tom Sadler left the courthouse, this time to be met by a crowd cheering in triumph for a man who had been wrongly accused. He successfully sued newspapers who had openly called him 'Jack the Ripper'.[5]

During the Sadler fiasco we believe Isabella Druitt, with or without her tormented clergyman son, approached Colonel Vivian Majendie for help. In hindsight, perhaps they should have approached him from the very start. At that moment, knowing the full story, the Chief of Explosives naturally turned to his close friend and confidant who was also the police chief at Scotland Yard's CID. Under normal circumstances this would surely signal the end of the road for the clan's cover-up and the beginning of the exposure of crimes committed by certain Druitts, as accessories after the fact. Even with the murderer dead and gone, Scotland Yard could now blame and shame a family of the 'better classes' for not being more co-operative with law enforcement – for not putting the safety of the realm first. Certain members of the family must have stoically braced themselves for the knock on the door by some senior police official whose no doubt fierce, judgmental expression would epitomise the Druitts' overdue reckoning. By a remarkable stroke of luck the Druitt family's cover-up held, because instead they were confronted by a very tall, very handsome, smartly dressed gentleman beaming a big smile and offering a firm handshake – and who arrived alone. With his magnetic affability and evident prosperity, this man reminded people of a businessman or a stockbroker, one flush from a recent success in the City and only too happy to crack open the champagne.[6] This unusually upper-class police chief would prove to be the Druitts' salvation from disgrace and opprobrium.

The then 37-year-old Chief Constable of the CID, Melville Leslie Macnaghten, must have seemed even younger to the astonished Druitts due to his boyish demeanour. During the Edwardian sunset before the Great War, Macnaghten, by then Assistant Commissioner of the CID, was a seamless fit for this jauntier, more relaxed era following the stiff Victorian straightjacket, as so fulsomely noted by his friend George R. Sims in his *Referee* column of 30 June 1907 (the same year the police chief was knighted by the equally relaxed and charming sovereign Edward VII, whom Sims so remarkably resembled):

Hearty congratulations to Sir Melville Leslie Macnaghten the amiable Assistant Commissioner of Police and Chief of the C.I.D. Sir Melville has done splendid work at the Yard, and done it with that dignified discretion which makes the ideal 'policeman'. His charm of manner is responsible for the statement that a well-known murderer once declared that it was a real pleasure to be found out by 'such a nice kind gentleman'.

In the British Library we found this short letter to Macnaghten by a renowned actor and theatre manager who also praises Macnaghten for his affability [MS 57485]:

> June 17 1905
> His Maj. Theatre
>
> My dear Macnaghten,
>
> I wish you many happy returns for your birthday and that you may continue to hunt down crime with that amiability which never forsakes you. I shall look forward to seeing you on Thursday. Perhaps you can take a little supper with me after?
>
> Believe me always,
> Herbert Beerbohm Tree

Macnaghten's eventual successor as head of CID, Sir Basil Thomson, paid tribute to him on pages 2 and 3 of his book *Queer People* in a chapter titled: 'The Detective in Real Life' (Hodder & Stoughton, 1922):

He had an astonishing memory both for faces and for names: he could tell you every detail about a ten-year old crime, the names of the victim, the perpetrator, and every important witness, and, what was more useful, the official career of every one of his seven hundred men and his qualifications and ability.

The fifteenth of fifteen children from a mixed Scottish-Irish clan, Mac's father, Elliot Macnaghten, had been the third-to-last chairman of the once hegemonic East India Company. Elliot's last child was a graduate of the exclusive Eton College, but had not gone on to study anything at university. Many reformers, progressives and socialists derided the Eton of the late nineteenth century as perpetuating the unrepresentative ruling elite of well-groomed, well-caned boring snobs who would, in the name of Queen and Empire, keep all non-white subjects firmly in their lowly place (a school in which physical abuse was practically integral to the curriculum).

To the emotionally arrested Melville 'Mac' Macnaghten, by contrast, his days at Eton were the happiest of his entire life and, what is more, he claimed to appreciate this joy while he was living them. His memoirs lovingly, if pathetically, recount his school days as one long, fun afternoon of games, sports and amateur theatricals. So wonderful was his time as a border at Eton that despite a successful career, public acclaim, a knighthood, a happy marriage (to a dark-eyed beauty and Canon's daughter named Dora Sanderson) and four children, for Mac those marvellous days at Eton condemned the rest of his life to anti-climax. In that same memoir from 1914 he would write gushingly about a fellow Etonian who would go on to be one of cricket's greatest batsmen:

> The cricket-field and the playhouse have given me more pleasure than anything else in life ... C. I. Thornton, the most wonderful boy hitter ... I can see his loose figure now coming down the pavilion steps, cool as an iceberg, firm as a rock ... Perhaps no human being has ever given me quite the same amount of pure delight as did 'Buns' Thornton, by his mammoth hitting in those days.

Craving a life of adventure and derring-do – and knowing he was never going to be a scholar, a statesman or a soldier – once graduating from Eton, to which he would use any excuse to return for visits as an Old Boy, Mac eventually decided to be an overseer on the family plantations in India. This was after his apoplectic father talked him out of his desire to become an actor, though Mac later joined the Garrick Club for actors and writers, and there happily struck up a friendship with George R. Sims. Young Macnaghten's hopes that the exotic locale and the responsibilities of bringing civilization to the locals ('excellent fellows') was something of a busted flush. He stuck it out for twelve years, miserably cut off from everything he adored: Eton College, Lord's Cricket Ground and West End theatres.

A traumatic event in India, however, propelled Mac towards his ultimate vocation. In 1883, while riding out to investigate why some Indians were behind in their rent, Macnaghten was ambushed and assaulted by disaffected rebels. Fortunately he was rescued by loyal locals and would go on to make a complete recovery. In the subsequent inquiry into the violent incident, Macnaghten greatly impressed the Chief Inspector of Bengal – a gruff, honest Scot named James Monro – with his calm and objective approach to the investigation; his total lack of rancour or need for retribution struck Monro as mature and judicious. So, four years after becoming Assistant Commissioner of CID in 1884, Monro offered Mac a job. Returning to England for good with his young family, Macnaghten could hardly wait to take up his position at the Yard: Assistant Chief Constable (Crime). The Police Commissioner, General Sir Charles Warren, had agreed to the appointment and the Home Office had confirmed it in writing to Monro on 29 March 1888. Macnaghten's elation would, nonetheless, prove to be short-lived as the job offer was abruptly withdrawn.[7] Warren suddenly had cold feet, which acutely embarrassed Monro as he had already offered the position to Macnaghten. After much acrimony between Warren and Monro over this issue, their professional relationship irretrievably broke down and the Assistant Commissioner resigned a few weeks later (though Monro probably retained a parallel position as head of Special Branch hunting Irish terrorists).

The shock to Macnaghten cut very deep. His celebrated likability was like an irresistible force that could always be relied upon to overcome resistance from Eton masters, Raj colonials, even from some criminals. In Sir Charles Warren, however, Mac found to his dismay he had collided with an immovable object. Consequently he was left without a job and with his reputation as a 'sound man' tarnished (his 'sacking' before he had even started had, mortifyingly, reached the press too). In his memoirs of 1914, Macnaghten could not bring himself to admit that he had been so humiliatingly 'blackballed', claiming *he* had turned down the offer due to other pressing commitments. Not only did this reversal of fortune leave him embittered for the rest of his life, it would also affect how he conducted his private 'Ripper' investigation into the Druitts.

But why had this debacle in the highest echelons of the law enforcement of the State happened at all? In the same memoir may lie a clue; the retired Macnaghten mercilessly pummels Warren, albeit unnamed, as an authoritarian bully whose harsh methods in quelling rioters had undermined faith among common people in British democracy.[8] It is quite a charge, and an atypical one for Mac, as it was the sort of damning interpretation usually made by the Left of the political spectrum (some Conservatives had complained Warren was not brutal enough at muzzling the scum). This may be a glimpse into a serious difference of opinion between the two men that caused the rift in 1888. Did Sir Charles Warren, an educated and experienced administrator, an admired officer, accomplished archaeologist, and a robust liberal who sided with the working classes, learn of Macnaghten's adverse opinion of his handling of 'Bloody Sunday'? Did it cause him to take a second look at this Old Etonian's rather thin credentials to join the force?

To Warren, Macnaghten may have seemed to be the worst kind of Tory twerp; nothing but a yes-man for his infuriating subordinate, Monro, who pompously acted as if he and the general were administrative equals. He, Sir Charles Warren, looked in the mirror and saw a real man staring back at him; whatever one's sympathy for the unwashed, grown-ups like him had to make made hard and painful decisions to prevent London from falling to the mob. If Macnaghten was indiscreet about critiquing the Commissioner's riot control methods, then – apart from the insult – 'Good Old Mac' may have struck Warren as unreliable, as too naïve; a Sherlock Holmes wannabe so incompetent he had had his rear end handed to him by usually dutiful 'Hindoos'.

Warren is often portrayed as a divisive autocrat whose own lack of even temperament made him a poor fit for the job of police supremo, and there is undoubtedly a measure of justice in this negative appraisal. The way he brought such debilitating turmoil to Scotland Yard in order to thwart Macnaghten's appointment does exhibit a manic quality. He sensed something so off-putting about Melville Macnaghten that he fought tooth and nail to prevent the recruitment of this Etonian smoothie. We think Sir Charles rejected Macnaghten because he saw with belated clarity a 'rogue elephant' lumbering towards Scotland Yard; a born-to-rule elitist – however amiable in personality – who would do as he pleased once handed power. Due to social class he would 'out-rank' everybody on the force, and would not feel constrained by anything as trivial as the law. For any man to become unashamedly teary-eyed at singing his alma mater's boating ballad signalled, to Warren at least, that such a man's first loyalty would always be to his pals inside the Old Boy network.

If that were the case, then General Sir Charles Warren was prescient. Macnaghten would be a much more successful and popular police chief than his martial nemesis, but when it came to the way the Chief Constable (later Assistant Commissioner) handled the Druitt solution to the 'Jack the Ripper' case he would, indeed, put loyalty to friends, and the dissemination of favourable propaganda for the Yard, ahead of any legal niceties involving the murderer's family and their cover-up. In fact, he joined in, and led the obscuring of the truth, from inside Scotland Yard. To borrow the title of John le Carré's espionage classic from 1977, Melville Leslie Macnaghten was an 'honourable schoolboy'; he broke the rules but always from a benign and compassionate motive.[9]

The long-anticipated resignation of General Sir Charles Warren on 10 November 1888 thrust his rival, James Monro, into the position of the new Police Commissioner. With Macnaghten's patron back in the saddle it was only a matter of a decent interval before the Old Etonian made his comeback and, at last, started his distinguished career at Scotland Yard as Assistant Chief Constable on 1 June 1889. If it was hoped among his superiors that Mac would keep his head down and deferentially blur into the woodwork as a dependable paper-pusher, they were to be disappointed. Macnaghten fled his desk any and every opportunity to be among the detectives and bobbies in the mean streets of London – and loved every minute of it.

Well not quite *every* minute. The new Commissioner, James Monro, was also a Protestant fundamentalist. Sharing this sectarian, apocalyptic ideology was a prominent Irish lawyer who had experience gathering covert intelligence against home-grown terrorists – Dr Robert Anderson. Monro appointed Anderson to be Assistant Commissioner (Crime) and thus Macnaghten's immediate superior. He would prove to be the second bane of Mac's professional life during the final decade of Victoria's reign. On one side you had a charming, public school graduate, and a true crime enthusiast since childhood, and on the other was a humourless, conceited and prudish recluse who never conceded error. It is an understatement to say the two chiefs did not get along – hatred is not too strong a word to describe the subordinate's uncharacteristic contempt for his boss, and the latter returned the ill-feeling by despising his deputy as an immature embarrassment with weak nerves.[10]

In his memoirs, Mac would simply airbrush Anderson out of existence as thoroughly as Stalin would do to Trotsky (Macnaghten names many police colleagues towards whom he feels affection and respect, but of the man he worked with, cheek by jowl, for twelve years there is not a single word). As will be shown in the next chapter Mac played a characteristic, schoolboyish prank on Anderson, using no less than the Whitechapel case as the instrument of an exquisite revenge. Otherwise, Macnaghten's preferred method of avoiding Dr Anderson was to be as far away from the office and the tedious paperwork as possible. The more sensational the case – usually a juicy murder, though sometimes he had to settle for a mere kidnapping or burglary – the more likely that Mac would be hurtling to the scene of the crime. Macnaghten won over his working and middle-class colleagues with his disarming lack of upper crust reserve; he was fun, sympathetic and respectful of their hands-on experience. This manly affection was reciprocated – the police who worked closely with Mac adored their boss. They felt privileged and valued as he regularly invited them to his plush home in Pimlico to review clues and evidence, lubricated by a seemingly limitless supply of brandy and cigars.[11]

For Macnaghten, his new life as a police boss was not Eton – nothing ever could be – but it was the next best thing: he was an official sleuth serving Her Majesty having jolly adventures with other manly men, together solving true crime mysteries and bringing the villains to justice. And one case fascinated this self-styled Super-Mac above all others, to the point of obsession – 'Jack the Ripper'. In an epic history of British policing Major Arthur Griffiths would describe Macnaghten in 1898 as a 'man of action' who kept near him the

> ... gruesome pictures, always under lock and key, photographs, for instance, of the victims of Jack the Ripper ... reproducing with horrible fidelity the mutilated remains of a human body but which might belong to a charnel-house or abattoir. It is Mr Macnaghten's duty, no less than his earnest desire, to be first on the scene of any such sinister catastrophe. He is therefore more intimately acquainted perhaps with the details of the most celebrated crimes than anyone in Scotland Yard.[12]

As soon as Macnaghten arrived at Scotland Yard in the middle of 1889 he buried himself in the files of the Whitechapel case. He read through every single letter from the public, most of which were entirely spurious. Unflinchingly he pored over the hideous autopsy photos (apart from keeping his own copies, he had some others made for George Sims). He was on the scene of the Alice McKenzie and Frances

Coles murders – with the latter's homicide he personally led the search of the taverns, docks and ships for her killer.[13] Although it took him a year, Macnaghten doggedly tracked down the journalist who had hoaxed the 'Dear Boss' letter that spawned the killer's catchy moniker. Macnaghten spent many a 'dreary' and 'disappointing' night in the East End slums trying to nab the maniac. Candidly, he found the 'acrid smell' pervading the lodging houses of Whitechapel and Spitalfields to be 'peculiarly abominable'.

> I remember being down in Whitechapel one night in September 1889, in connection with what was known as the Pinchin Street murder, and being in a doss house, entered the large common room where the inmates were allowed to do their cooking. The code of immorality in the East End is, or was, unwashed in its depths of degradation. A woman was content to live with a man so long as he was in work, it being an understood thing that, if he lost his job, she would support him by the only means open to her. On this occasion the unemployed man was toasting bloaters, and, when his lady returned, asked her, 'if she had any luck'. She replied with an adjective negative, and went on to say in effect that she had thought her lucky star was in the ascendant when she inveigled a 'bloke' down a dark alley, but that suddenly a detective, with India rubber soles to his shoes, had sprung up from behind a wagon, and the bloke had taken fright and flight.

Macnaghten shows himself to be clear-eyed about poverty being the cause of people sliding into degradation: the toasted bloater cook is living off the woman's immoral earnings. There is also a telling reference to 'The Ripper' in this vignette:

> With additional adjectives the lady expressed her determination to go out again after supper, and when her man reminded her of the dangers of the streets if 'he' (meaning the murderer) was out and about, the poor woman replied (with no adjectives this time), 'Well, let him come the sooner the better for such as I.' A sordid picture my readers, but what infinite pathos is therein portrayed.[14]

The police chief in 1889 could not assure this poor woman that she did not have to fear 'Jack' anymore, as he did not yet know that the murderer was in fact off the street and in his grave. As he conceded for the first time in his fun and vivid memoirs of 1914, the Yard was fruitlessly chasing a 'ghost' until 'certain facts' were received by Mac that led to a 'conclusion' about his identity. Did Macnaghten actually meet the Druitts, or at least a Druitt? It is impossible to conceive that such an obsessed, hands-on and discreet figure could have been held back from making a thorough investigation of a 'Ripper' solution, one that had come his way from such a close friend as Colonel Vivian Majendie. In his book he pays tribute to Majendie as 'one of the most delightful personalities I ever came across and a very loyal friend.'[15]

In his memoirs of 1917, George Sims fondly reminisces about the close friendship between the three men and their wonderful dinners every Monday night at the police chief's home.[16] Yet again it is in *The Referee* articles of Sims that we see a glimpse of this putative contact between Macnaghten and certain Druitts. Though the encounter is partially disguised – and backdated from 1891 to 1888 – it is confirmation that Macnaghten (and perhaps Majendie) conferred with William, Charles and Isabella Druitt. At the time this article was published in *The Referee* of 5 April 1903, Sims was engaged in a public spat with the retired chief detective, Frederick Abberline, over the latter's assertion that a convicted wife poisoner from Poland, alias George Chapman, was the real 'Jack' (*see* Chapter XIX). Somewhat exasperated at being challenged yet unable to name Macnaghten as his unimpeachable source, Sims felt he needed to play an ace – and he played it only this once – in his 'Mustard and Cress' column:

A little more than a month later the body of *the man suspected by the chiefs* at the Yard, and by *his own friends, who were in communication with the Yard*, was found in the Thames. The body had been in the water about a month. (Our italics)

With his much-celebrated encyclopaedic powers of recall Macnaghten could have easily put this together with what the Druitts divulged; the arrest of Dr Robert Druitt's nephew on the night of the double murder and the failed hunt for an elusive, never-identified English lunatic in France and England was the same man. We think Macnaghten was both thrilled to know the identity of 'The Ripper' but he also had to cope with the dual bureaucratic and political headache of knowing. The police had arrested the murderer and let him go too easily, they had managed to miss catching him near Paris and again when he returned to London. Though in no way personally responsible, Mac could not be indifferent to this potential 'cluster bomb', as the late Dr Druitt's clan was connected to his friend Majendie. If it all came out, the Druitts subsequent sinking would inevitably drag the colonel's squeaky clean name down into the muck with them. Increasing Macnaghten's strain, in 1891 he was told that the Reverend Charles Druitt, who had taken the maniac's confession, was decidedly wobbly about honouring Montague's wish that he wait ten years before revealing the truth (albeit to be clothed in fiction, as the 'West of England' MP had already covertly attempted by telescoping the timeline of Druitt's final murder and subsequent suicide).

The arrest of Tom Sadler for Frances Coles' murder – and the almost hysterical media speculation that he was 'Jack' too – had caused much agonising for Charles Druitt. The clergyman told the police chief he felt compelled to come forward, despite the unsatisfactory outcomes of the approaches to Dr Robert Anderson and Henry Farquharson, respectively. We theorise that Macnaghten, Majendie and Sims were disgusted at the MP's imbecilic and tin ear betrayal of Isabella Druitt, albeit Farquharson thought he was only sharing what he had been told with close cronies – and had done so with the details sufficiently disguised. The Macnaghten/Sims/Majendie troika decided, nonetheless, that, despite his status as an Old Etonian, Farquharson would have to be cut loose; to use private school jargon for expulsion he would have to be 'sent down' in order to protect the Druitts and the Majendies. As General Warren may have feared, Macnaghten moved to manage the people involved and to manipulate the media without informing, let alone warning, his colleagues at Scotland Yard. There is no evidence, whatsoever; that any one of them knew the whole truth of the Druitt solution (they would be fobbed off with bits of prankish misdirection).

What is more, the Chief Constable saw nothing wrong or inappropriate about strategising with a famous writer and a colonel seconded to the Home Office. Frankly, Mac did not trust his colleagues to keep the secret; especially not the egocentric Dr Anderson (even Farquharson had acted so oafishly and *he* was a fellow Old Boy). Confirmation that George R. Sims was briefed about Montague John Druitt being the Whitechapel killer – and by inference his source has to be Macnaghten and Majendie – comes from a previously unknown 'Dagonet' column only recently unearthed by the authors. Once and for all, as we will see, this 'Mustard and Cress' piece from 1 November 1891 proves that Melville Macnaghten – much maligned in modern books on this subject as hopelessly ill-informed about his chosen suspect – knew the accurate details about Druitt: a suicide who died young, slightly built yet very strong, of respectable appearance with a fair moustache who had never graduated as a surgeon. Furthermore, and again this is vital, he knew that the timing of Druitt's suicide did not explain the cessation of the Whitechapel murders – if all were supposedly committed by a single killer – because East End homicides continued *after* his death.

In Germany, Sims wrote in this definitive column, a serial murderer and mutilator of women driven into prostitution had been recently seen by witnesses during his latest attempt at mayhem. George Sims/ Dagonet uses this foreign case as the springboard for informing his readers about the unnamed Druitt as a conceptual profile for their own yet-to-be-identified maniac: 'If Jack the Ripper should resume operations in London this winter, the police will do well to take a hint from the Berlin affair of the other day, which seems to run on all fours with our Whitechapel murders.' The German murderer was reportedly young, blond, with a fair moustache and slightly built. Sims 'speculates' about the likely profile of 'Jack' as if it had just occurred to him, the bon vivant and amateur criminologist, after learning about this Continental counterpart in violent mania:

> I think it extremely likely that the Whitechapel murderer was or is an individual of the type now wanted by the Berlin police – *not necessarily blond, but young and slight*, and possibly *refined in appearance* – and my reason is this: The insane motive is most probably a desire to see death, to look upon the actual palpitating heart, to feel the warm blood of the victim, and this would be more likely to occur to *a student, a dabbler in science*, an inquirer into the mysteries of existence, than to a rough, vulgar, or drunken corner man or bully. (Our italics)

Accurate regarding Druitt having brown hair, the writer denies 'Jack' is blond – but does not deny the feature of the fair moustache – while at the same time he goes on to allude to the unnamed Druitt's athletic prowess. He also implies that Montie *was* arrested and somehow managed to outwit the constabulary:

> Not only the reckless hacking of the victim's body, but *the cleverness of the murderer in escaping detection and eluding pursuit*, is to my mind an evidence of insanity. The reputed *strength and cunning* of the madman are perfectly true; the very superabundance of his nerve energy may be the cause of his insanity, and his nervous force may

not only enable him to put forth *abnormal muscular strength*, but also *to think acutely*. If the madman's faculties were levelled up all round he would be *possessed of marvellous genius...* (Our italics)

Proving that it is not a coincidental congruence of Druitt-like particulars with this Berlin suspect, Sims now moves closer to the depressive illness and ultimate fate of the drowned barrister. He even hints at the amoral murderer feeling some kind of histrionic guilt for his heinous actions:

> ... but for every exaltation of faculty there is a *corresponding depression somewhere*, and in the case of *the homicidal maniac* the regions of the brain concerned in conscience, which is essentially a perception of good and evil effects based upon experience and memory, are torpid. The homicidal maniac has no more conscience than a block of wood. And little boys have less conscience than grown-up people, as witness the case of the youngsters who tried for fun to wreck the Eastbourne express by putting railway chairs on the line. *Conscience itself*, however, *may be exalted* in the maniac, and then we get *various forms of melancholia*. (Our italics)

Sims further speculates that the English murderer should be a patient in an asylum, rather than hanging from a scaffold or rotting in a jail, an allusion to Druitt's abortive attempts to gain treatment in two separate asylums. Sims concludes, however, that it is probably too late, anyway, because 'Jack' in his manic-depressive mental state has already committed suicide:

> The discovery of the Whitechapel maniac, to my thinking, is more *a question for medical experts* than for detectives. It is very possible that, *if still alive*, he may change his tactics, and for this reason the recent mysterious case of poisoning in Lambeth, where a wretched woman was induced by a 'young dark man' to drink poison out of a bottle, ought to be very closely and assiduously investigated. But *possibly the Whitechapel murderer is dead*. The homicidal maniac often *turns his hand against himself*. (Our italics)

Why were Macnaghten and Majendie, two such discreet officers of the State, preparing the public through Sims for 'The Ripper' to turn out to be a young, college-educated gentleman and suicide (and therefore a miscreant who could never be brought to earthly justice)? Why were they edging closer to admitting that the murderer would turn out to be Montague John Druitt? There can be only one explanation for the troika to have begun this propaganda campaign. Macnaghten, Majendie and Sims had glumly accepted that the Druitt solution was on the verge of spilling out of Dorset due to the Reverend Charles' tiresomely troubled conscience. The troika were scrambling to regain control of a narrative that was slipping from their grasp.

There are further textual indications for our interpretation of this column's significance. Sims' excuse for writing this speculative profile; a German 'Jack' who has killed a prostitute by slashing her throat and has, at last, been recently seen by witnesses, is contrived. The crimes were committed between 18 March 1890 and 21 February 1891. Six prostitutes in succession had had their abdomens slashed by the same, knife-wielding client though only one – a woman named Nitche – had died of her wounds. Furthermore a description of the assailant had been circulating across Europe for months, as can be seen in the *East London Advertiser* of 7 March 1891, a series of crimes that had stopped the month before (the British newspaper has confused the names of two of the victims):

A GERMAN 'JACK THE RIPPER'

The Public Prosecutor at Küstrin, near Frankfurt, has offered a reward for the capture of a German who, since September last, is believed to have made five attempts to murder five different women, after the fashion attributed in England to 'Jack the Ripper'. His last victim, a woman named Wilden [sic], who was attacked on February 21, and received a wound measuring about 8 in. across the stomach, died on Saturday. The assailant is described as *a man about 30 years of age, with a blonde moustache. He wore sailor's clothes.* (Our italics)

No wonder Sims, presumably with Macnaghten and Majendie, took special note of the German 'Ripper'; the latter's description – a 30-year-old man with a blond moustache and dressed like a sailor – matches Montague Druitt quite uncannily. Consequently, Sims dropped 'Jack's' age by a decade (just as in a memo in 1894 Mac would up Druitt's age by the same amount, *see* Chapter XVII). As Sims writes, truthfully: 'the Berlin affair ... seems to run on all-fours with our Whitechapel murders' (the only fatal assault had taken place in Berlin). Sims changing the suspect's age may, again, be a glimpse into how much Macnaghten talked openly with Sims about Scotland Yard's operations regarding its most high-profile crimes. The leading German suspect really was a man in his early 20s, just as Sims had written, named Fritz Sturzebecher (never charged). But Herr Sturzebecher was not a university student – he was a house painter. Where did this inside information about the German suspect's true age come from? The Berlin press claimed that Scotland Yard were in touch with the German authorities. Apparently both country's senior police had noticed the similarity between the sets of crimes, albeit only one victim had succumbed to her injuries in the Continental case – and even those wounds had not involved the same post-mortem 'hacking' as Sims had written in his article. In the *Berliner Gerichts-Zeitung* of 29 October 1891 is this tantalising titbit: 'the suggestion has therefore been followed by the London Police Department to bring files [regarding] the Whitechapel murderer "Jack the Ripper", to determine from them the possible motive to the similar crimes, which are so similar to the one in Holzmarktgasse.'

In his 1891 column, George Sims outlines some accurate data about the unnamed Druitt, yet still without rendering him recognisable to his neighbours and colleagues (a student rather than working barrister). This meant shying away from admitting the speculative 'profile' was of a professional man. Being a barrister was not relevant to the murders, anyhow, but having once been a medical student most certainly was – and so Sims pretended the German maniac was also studying at some college. He was not. The promotion of Montague Druitt from a mere 'dabbler in science' into a fully qualified and middle-aged surgeon was still several years in the future. Nonetheless, below the radar, this impending crisis seems to have dissipated. Again Reverend Charles must have held off. There is no sequel in the extant literature we could find. Possibly because Macnaghten or Majendie convinced Charles that he must stick to his cousin's practically death-bed wish. Reveal the truth, if you must, but do so a decade after the crimes to give everybody involved – the Druitts, the Majendies, and Scotland Yard – enough clear air far above this black cloud. Thus any future revelations would cause only minimal reputational damage, if any.

The evidence for this shift, of the real story dissolving back into the shadows like the grin of the Cheshire Cat is that Sims will never again write so candidly about the unnamed Druitt's true details (in 1907 he will even go so far as to completely mislead his readers by claiming that there had, indeed, been a young, medical student suspect. According to the writer this man was allegedly the *second* best suspect the Yard ever had, but he was an American who remained, as of writing, in rude good health).[17]

The years immediately after the family was saved by the 'honourable schoolboy' would prove a mixture of normality disrupted by sudden, nerve-wracking moments when the Whitechapel case threatened their tranquillity. Evidence that the gentlemanly cover-up could be breached would come in 1908 with the works of a minor writer named Frank Richardson.

A member of the Garrick Club with Melville Macnaghten and George R. Sims, somehow he became the only person, at least published, who discovered the whole truth of the Druitt solution (for a fuller treatment of this source's impact *see* Appendix I). In one of his books the Whitechapel case is alluded to and he changes Druitt into 'Dr Bluitt', which must have caused acute dyspepsia in some quarters. In another book by the same author from the same year there are even more extraordinary examples of how thoroughly briefed Richardson must have been.

In *The Other Man's Wife* (Eveleigh Nash) he plays with the Druitt/Ripper particulars like a cat toying with a mouse. The main characters in the text have the names Montague, Ethel and William which match the names of Montague Druitt, his brother William Druitt and their youngest sister Ethel. (The other main character Richard is a variation of the author's surname). Sims is jocularly referred to by a passing remark about 'Tatcho'. There is also reference to a photographed encounter between Edward VII and Montague – arguably a dual reference to Sims' claim about resembling, when young and ill, M. J. Druitt in a single photo, whilst also himself being frequently mistaken for the king. Richardson throws in the question, 'Is Montague mad?' It is the protagonists' surname however, that points in the direction of the author's insider knowledge. He calls them 'Mayville', just two letters removed from Macnaghten's first name. The vocation of Montague Mayville is that of actor and he is linked, albeit in a throwaway remark, to the concept of homicide: 'I believe Montague that you would consider it a good advertisement to be tried for murder.' Nicknamed Montie, he is a mixture of altruistic and narcissistic impulses: he gives to the Lord Mayor's Fund whilst also being obsessed with seeing his name in the press.

Strikingly, Richardson even knows what Montague Druitt looked like. With pinpoint accuracy, he describes *his* Montie as strongly resembling the real actor Herbert Beerbohm Tree when he was young (the same actor who was friends with Macnaghten). Finally there is a quote, which makes no sense in the narrative, but which certainly would have, to those who knew the whole story of the Druitts and Whitechapel – it refers, cryptically if somewhat menacingly, to the murder trial in Poole which may have set the promising barrister on his homicidal path, and to Sir Vivian Majendie whose familial link to the family drove Macnaghten and Sims to join the cover-up: 'By art the actor reveals himself; but he can't do it unless the dramatist helps him. If I want a coat I go to *Poole* and I say 'Poole my boy, here am I, *Vivian Marradyne.* You know me – I know you!' (Our italics) The cheek of Frank Richardson was seventeen years in the future, whereas those in charge of the cover-up would have to dodge all sorts of obstacles in the immediate aftermath of what was learned in 1891.

Memos of Misdirection

In early 1892, we believe that Melville Macnaghten decided to anonymously brief a credulous, Conservative-owned newspaper with the latest inside information regarding the police hunt for 'Jack the Ripper'. This alleged hot scoop's real purpose was to reveal Henry Farquharson as the West of England MP – and to prove him wrong. Whether the MP would be fooled was quite another matter, and largely irrelevant. It was a pre-emptive strike, an attempt to publicly discredit Farquharson and also, perhaps, to convince him that anything divulged by Dr. Druitt's widow was mistaken or should be kept firmly under his hat.

According to a *Western Mail* article, a London correspondent had conferred with a 'Scotland Yard Detective' who claimed that the most comprehensive surveillance operation had been following the killer. With bracing candour, the unidentified police official reveals that the prime suspect *knows* he is under surveillance. Even if the 'final link in the chain of evidence' remains just out of reach, the senior cop airily concedes, oh well, the police are still protecting the public from any more horrors – and will continue to do so indefinitely if that's what it takes.

This unlikely tale is almost certainly fictitious, as no such elaborate budget-busting CID operation is recorded in any other extant sources. It certainly sounds like Mac, with its 'Buns' Thornton-style enthusiasms and juvenile exaggerations. Then comes the article's real purpose: to debunk Henry Farquharson and his 'doctrine' while simultaneously reassuring Isabella and Charles Druitt that Super Mac was in full and effective 'damage control' mode:

> Mr Farquharson, M.P. for West Dorset, was credited, I believe, some
> time since with having evolved a remarkable theory of his own in

the matter. He *believed that the author of the outrages destroyed himself*. But if the police have been on the right track *this theory is naturally exploded*. [Our italics]

Not two months later, George Sims published a short story titled *The Priest's Secret*, which we argue is a fictional rendering of Montague's confession to Charles, written to convince the conscience-stricken clergyman not to divulge what he knew – at least not yet.[1]

The story takes place in a palatial estate in England as its owner, Mr. John Arcwright, a successful entrepreneur, lies dying upstairs in the master bedroom. He is attended by his devoted second wife and a few friends. One of those preparing for the end is the young Anglican reverend John Wannop, who strikes many of the locals in the village as a haunted man. But the soon-to-be-widow, the trusted doctor, and the clergyman know and conceal a terrible secret: when young in the wilds of California, Arcwright, gripped by what he believed was a fatal mania, murdered his family with a knife rather than let them suffer a worse fate from marauding robbers. Afterwards he tried to kill himself with the same bloody knife but only fainted.

Upon waking, Arcwright discovered that he had been rescued by other settlers, who naturally presumed that his family had been butchered by the robbers. He has spent the rest of his charmed life making a fortune and salving his conscience by being a generous and adored philanthropist. When ill in Rome, however, Arcwright had confessed the truth to the young clergyman, who had become like an adopted son. That same reverend has been conflicted for years over this revelation, as he confides in the physician, who also now knows the truth from his patient's ravings. This dialogue is, we think, a fictional version of the moral struggle that Charles Druitt expressed in the wake of Montague's confession:

'You agree with me that it is absolutely necessary to keep silence on the subject. You consider that I have done right in holding my peace all these years.'

'Most certainly. I can quite understand that as a clergyman you may have had some scruples as to your duty, but looking at all the circumstances I think you are fully justified.'

'And you, now that you also know the truth, will keep silence too?'

'Absolutely. If the circumstances under which the story reached me – from the mouth of a delirious patient – did not justify me I should only have to think of that brave devoted wife upstairs, and that would decide me. Besides, even presuming that the poor fellow [was] alone in the world, what good would come of betraying him now?'

'None, none,' replied the curate, the tears coming into his eyes.

'But I sometimes wish that he himself had had the moral courage to confess the truth – to tell his horrible story and risk everything.'

As with Reverend John Wannop, we think that the Reverend Charles Druitt had to live with knowing the homicidal secret of the outwardly respectable gentleman to whom he was related, and which he had covered up while Montie was still alive. If keeping the secret was debilitating for the fictional Wannop, we argue that the real Dorset vicar's physical health was comparably precarious as a result of the mental conflict he had to endure – and which continued for many years after his cousin had died.

The year 1892 saw a national election, won by the Liberals. Though the party fell short in the popular vote, a shaky governing coalition was formed with smaller parties. The following year, the handily re-elected Henry Richard Farquharson was sued for slander by his defeated liberal opponent, C. T. Gatty. With strong echoes of his 'son of a surgeon' indiscretion, the incumbent had unwisely repeated a story he was told by a constituent: Gatty had been expelled from a private boys' school for a homosexual act. Yet in court before the Lord Chief Justice, himself a Liberal grandee, the Conservative party member's barristers devastatingly established that the story was almost correct. Gatty had, in fact, been sexually abused by a master – and the school had covered up the crime by encouraging the student to leave. The future Liberal candidate was not, however, expelled, so Farquharson was found guilty of libel. He was ordered to pay £5,000 in compensation (reduced by half on appeal).[2]

The Liberal and tabloid press were thrilled to crucify this upper-class politician and none more so than the progressive George R. Sims – but he was the only journalist to mention the MP's brief and mostly unidentified connection to the Whitechapel crimes. In *The Referee* of June 25, 1893, Dagonet offers a typical denunciation in humorous verse:

It ought to be allowable to cover him with shame,
To *hint he's Jack the Ripper*, or *at least deserves the name*;
No words should be too slanderous at anyone to aim,
If spoken in the heat of an election. [Our italics]

Yet again, this was a pre-emptive strike by a member of the trio of friends on a fellow gentleman (and for Macnaghten, a fellow Conservative and, most painfully, an Old Etonian) who had shamefully blotted his copybook by putting Colonel Majendie's spotless reputation at risk, as well as antagonising the clan of the late Dr. Robert Druitt. The libel verdict was excellent insurance in case Farquharson was ever again to mention what he knew about the Druitt solution. Sims's poem is a ruthless and hypocritical demolition of the luckless MP when you consider that the famous writer is a secret adherent of Farquharson's 'doctrine' regarding the true identity of 'Jack the Ripper'.

From learning the ghastly truth in early 1891 to quashing Farquharson in 1892 and 1893, the trio must have felt that normality had been achieved. Yet in early 1894, they were quite unexpectedly again plunged into crisis. A popular tabloid claimed to be the recipient of a major leak: senior police were covering up the true identity of 'Jack' in order to protect their own reputations and that of a solid bourgeoisie family. One can only imagine the ripples of fear such claims inspired in certain Druitts. Incredibly, the newspaper was both right and completely mistaken: they had the wrong madman, the wrong respectable family, and the wrong senior policeman committed to concealment. '*The Sun*' of February 13, 1894, trumpeted the news that 'Jack' was long dead.

According to the newspaper, the Whitechapel assassin had become, by 1891, a stabber (or 'jobber,' as it was called) of young women, but only in the buttocks through their clothes and without causing a fatal injury. Though he was not named in 1894, *The Sun* was referencing a mentally ill young man from a middle-class family named Thomas Hayne Cutbush. That year, 1891, he had been committed without a trial to life in Broadmoor, an institution for the criminally insane. Very inappropriately, the reporters had weaseled their way into the asylum and observed the mute, nearly immobile Cutbush, who was by then forever lost in an imbecilic dusk.

The instigator of this massive red herring was an embittered Scotland Yard inspector, William Nixon Race, who had been involved in the jobber case and who leaked to the press in 1893 that his superiors 'knew' Cutbush was also responsible for the Whitechapel murders (and thus had, by implication, denied Race the kudos of having nabbed 'Jack', too). For all its outlandish and unproven claims – no more than unsubstantiated gossip – *The Sun* was sensitive to criticism that it was about to undermine a respectable family:

> We have been implored not to reveal names, for the very obvious reason that, even remotely, people shrink from possible and almost certain annoyance of being associated in even the remotest degree with his hideous crime.

Colonel Vivian Majendie could only have said 'Amen' if he ever read those words. The following day, *The Sun* reiterated its commitment to be discreet about the respectable relations of the unnamed Cutbush, knowing that such pillars of the Victorian community would be unfairly tarnished, even socially destroyed, if their identities were known. It professed to be sympathetic to their dilemma; if those family members suspected his guilt, well, what were they supposed to do? (The efforts to hide a mad, homicidal relation in an expensive French asylum might have engendered much less sympathy.) Although the Druitts were in the clear, the following words' accuracy in describing their private shame must still have caused palpitations:

> But at this moment our readers must be satisfied with less information than is at our disposal. 'Jack the Ripper' has relatives; they are some of them in positions which would make them a target for the natural curiosity – *for the unreasoning reprobation which would pursue any person even remotely connected with so hideous a monstrosity, and we must abstain, therefore, from giving his name in the interest of these unfortunate, innocent, and respectable connections....*They have tended him, nursed him, watched for him, borne with him with a patience that never tired, with a love that never waned... in imagination picturing this tiger who marched from crime to crime as some innocent, harmless, and helpless child in need of protection.... [Our italics]

Macnaghten, Sims, and Majendie worried that this false accusation of a locked-up lunatic who, for all his violence, had never killed would force the tremulous hand of the Dorset vicar – would he feel the need to spill the beans four years ahead of schedule to prevent another innocent from being falsely accused?

Macnaghten felt he had to tell the public what he had known for three years: Frances Coles in 1891, Alice McKenzie in 1889, and Rose Mylett at the end of 1888 (another murdered 'unfortunate,' who may have died of hunger rather than strangulation) were killed by other unknown killers and not by the single madman who had slaughtered Polly Nichols, Annie Chapman, Liz Stride, Kate Eddowes, and Mary Jane Kelly. (Separate murderers, probably gangs, had earlier dispatched Emma Smith and Martha Tabram.) As usual, George Sims was wheeled out to pretend that everybody had always known this to be true. He wrote in *The Referee* of January 14, 1894:

... there is every probability that some of the Whitechapel murders which were universally credited to 'Jack the Ripper' *were not the work of the genuine Jack at all, but of miscreants impelled to similar deeds by the sensational newspaper reports* of the first performances of the original artist. [Our italics]

The Sun was relentless; its solution to the Whitechapel murders dominated each succeeding issue of that newspaper for a whole week. Under the most excruciating pressure since he had been fired by General Warren, Melville Macnaghten, probably in the privacy and safety of his office at his home, considered his options later that same month. Surely this story, about which everyone seemed to be talking, would have to be addressed by the new government in the House of Commons. The Conservative Party, now in Opposition, would hardly want to touch such a story, but the new administration of the Liberal lion, William Gladstone, had men who hated anything remotely Conservative, and they knew the top men at Scotland Yard were all Conservative holdovers. One or more might recall Henry Farquharson and his 'son of a surgeon' solution (the MP's conviction for slander helped here, as he had already been discredited as a scurrilous gossip).

Nevertheless, the whole truth about 'Jack the Ripper' might emerge from Dorset through Reverend Charles. What then? Just when Mac needed the wise counsel and support of his mentor, James Monro, he was bereft of it. As intractable as Warren, Monro had resigned in 1890 over an honourable dispute with the previous government regarding conditions and pay for his men. Although Edward Bradford, the new commissioner of the Metropolitan Police, was an army officer like Warren, he was an easygoing, backslapping chap with experience of colonial India – a perfect fit for the manly, affable Mac. After learning of the truth about Montague Druitt in 1891, the Chief Constable knowingly concealed this revelation from his colleagues at the Yard. It was a gamble, motivated by loyalty to his friend Majendie and to members of his class – a calculated risk that might now be about to backfire. If the Druitt solution became publicly known, including, God forbid, the French asylum misadventure, Macnaghten's role in the whole affair would cost him his job – for the second time. He could expect the worldly Bradford to be sympathetic, but Mac would still have to fall on his sword for such a breach of professional etiquette (no doubt accompanied by a pompous sermon from Dr. Anderson, along the lines that he knew Macnaghten would never last).

Keeping as 'cool as an iceberg' and 'firm as a rock,' Macnaghten decided he would have to take steps to save his professional skin and yet also try to reassure the Druitts that they would be protected even if Montie's identity – minus the name – was debated in the Commons. The Home Secretary, Herbert Henry Asquith, would help there; Macnaghten knew he could handle this Liberal up-and-comer. Asquith was a talented, articulate, but low-born snob; he was keen to ingratiate himself with the men of the ruling elite (and even more so with their wives).[3]

What if, Macnaghten thought, he bypassed Bradford and Anderson and wrote directly to Asquith? Certainly the home secretary would be flattered by a briefing document to provide the minister with 'talking points' if awkward questions were raised in the Commons in response to the tabloid exposé. In such a memorandum, Macnaghten could obscure both his personal contact with the Druitts and that their Montague had been briefly arrested and prematurely released. He could point to Druitt as a notable police suspect, certainly more promising than 'the jobber,' but show that there was a lack of hard evidence to vigorously pursue him as the solution. This would bury the embarrassment of how and why they did not know he was the English patient absconding from France – whom they were tracking but had never identified while he was alive. Mac, who had bluffed an Eton schoolmaster when caught smoking by the most brazen stonewalling, could now see some daylight peeking through the gathering storm clouds.[4] What if he blended the two streams of intelligence about Montie, which had come to the police years apart, as if they were a single river – to, in effect, backdate what he had learned in 1891 to 1888? In this rewrite, a bungle could thus become a near triumph. The chief constable knew that torturing the data would not stand up to much scrutiny; the information about this Mr. Druitt would, inevitably, be a hopeless paradox. On the other hand, he might just get away with it, especially if at the same time he opened a second front by leaking the document – or a libel-proofed version of it – to reliable allies in the press, such as George R. Sims. Macnaghten knew all too well that even basic data released to the public – 'young,' 'barrister,' and 'Thames suicide' – would fatally expose the Druitts to their neighbours and colleagues. The age and vocation of the murderer would have to be obscured, even altered, which risked making the police look incompetent if the correct data became widely known.

Choosing to neither date nor address this first document to anyone, Macnaghten composed a draft copy that he could utilize for public dissemination should it become necessary. The first section of the memorandum explained that the non-murderer Thomas Cutbush was obviously not 'Jack' and that Inspector William Race was an embittered fool – and a thief too, for keeping a knife that Cutbush may have used to jab, or job, his victims. Macnaghten inserted a bold fib that perfectly reflects his arrested adolescence. Exploiting the coincidence that there was a retired police superintendent named Charles Cutbush, and again gambling that Asquith would not check, he portrayed the Broadmoor lunatic as *the nephew* of the ex-cop (practically his *de facto* son, since Macnaghten also lied by writing that the young man's father was deceased). In reality, ex-superintendent Cutbush and Thomas Cutbush were not even distantly related, and Macnaghten had to have known this and yet went ahead with the deception.

We theorize that Macnaghten's falsely linking the two Cutbush men was meant to provide a benign motive for any police cover-up. Unlike the attention-seeking Race, Mac implied, senior men were sensitive that this lunatic had a kindly uncle who was once on the force and who would be embarrassed by the association. It was nothing whatsoever to do with 'Jack the Ripper'.

In this document intended for the public, Macnaghten mentioned all of the Whitechapel murders, from Smith to Coles, but he again misled any reader by claiming the police knew that whoever massacred Mary Jane Kelly could not function for long in the aftermath of such horror. The real killer, with his mind obliterated by his own ghastliness, would either be sectioned into an asylum by his family or would quickly take his own life – or maybe both. Thomas Cutbush was still alive; ergo, he could not have killed Kelly and, ergo, he could not have been the Whitechapel assassin. Beginning with Sims's column of a few days earlier in February 1894, Macnaghten gave the misleading impression that the police knew *at the time* that Kelly was the final victim of this singular maniac and thus knew *at the time* that all subsequent Whitechapel murders had to be by copycats. In fact, this was only learned by the same police chief 'some years after.' It was not until Macnaghten wrote his own memoir twenty years later that he would try to correct the record he had himself distorted.

Mentioning Druitt as the only alternative solution to Cutbush would give the game away, so Macnaghten added two other men who had been on suspect lists but had been rejected as unlikely. One of these spurious suspects was the Russian thief Michael Ostrog, who had claimed – truthfully, as it turned out later in 1894 – to be in a *French* asylum during the murders. The other minor suspect roped in from some file was Aaron Kosminski, a Polish-Jewish immigrant who had been permanently institutionalized in early 1891 (he had threatened a female relation with a knife and was eating from gutters).[5] To make him plausible as somebody driven to dysfunction in the immediate aftermath of the Kelly murder, Macnaghten backdated his incarceration to early 1889. For the coming leak to the press to be successful, Macnaghten would have to make it clear that he, the chief constable, believed Druitt was the probable killer. The gentleman's arrest by PC Spicer, however, was completely rewritten as merely a police sighting of the *Polish* suspect:

> No one ever saw the Whitechapel murderer (unless possibly it was *the City P.C. who was on a beat near Mitre Square*) and no proof could in any way ever be brought against anyone, although very many homicidal maniacs were *at one time, or another*, suspected. I enumerate the cases of 3 men against whom Police held very reasonable suspicion. [Our italics]

The takedown of PC Spicer had been accomplished by removing the Polish-Jewish witness, Joseph Lawende, and replacing him with a bobby. In effect, the witness and the murderer have swapped their ethnicities and roles. Macnaghten then upped the ante by inserting his expert opinion into the mix:

> *Personally*, after much careful & deliberate consideration, I am inclined to exonerate the last 2 but *I have always held strong opinions regarding no 1.*, and the more I think the matter over, *the stronger do these opinions become.* The truth, however, will never be known, and did indeed, at one time lie at the bottom of the Thames, if my conjections [*sic*] be correct. [Our italics]

By the 'truth' lying 'at the bottom of the Thames' he presumably means that while the body resurfaced, the killer's incriminating knife did not, and thus the one that the inspector claimed to be 'Jack's' weapon was nothing of the kind. Macnaghten suggested that the Druitt family was not connected to the famous Dr. Robert Druitt by denigrating the family as only 'fairly good' whilst also exonerating them; they only 'suspected' their member's guilt, because his sexual mania was only an allegation. Though referring to him as 'Mr.' and not 'Dr.,' he recreates Druitt for public consumption as a middle-aged medical man. The interregnum in France is hidden as a question mark regarding the mad doctor's immediate movements and whereabouts after the murder of Mary Jane Kelly. Mac was careful to give the impression that he only learned of the dark suspicions against this man from some unnamed intermediary, not that he had ever met the family himself. Here is the 'No. 1' suspect whom Macnaghten, as an expert sleuth, supposedly believed more strongly to be guilty than did the dead man's own family:

> No. 1 Mr M. J. Druitt *a doctor of about 41 years of age & of fairly good family*, who *disappeared at the time of the Miller's Court murder*, and whose body was found floating in the Thames on 31st Dec: i.e. 7 weeks after the said murder. The body was said to have been in the water for a month, or more – on it was found a season ticket between Blackheath & London. *From private information* I have little doubt but that his own family *suspected* this man of being the Whitechapel murderer; it was *alleged* that he was sexually insane.[6] [Our italics]

The obvious question is, since this now middle-aged 'Dr. Druitt' sounds so promising – with his surgical experience, maybe gaining sexual excitement from violence, concerned relations, and a suicide which would explain the cessation of the murders – why was this prime suspect not taken into custody? Macnaghten had tried to deflect attention from the fatal blunder of Druitt's arrest and release by writing 'no proof could be brought against' him or anybody else – but why not? The answer is left open-ended. Once finished, on February 23, 1894, Melville Macnaghten quickly handwrote a second version of the same memorandum. This time he dated the document and headed it 'Confidential.' He would place this memo on the official file and, if necessary, send to Home Secretary Asquith. The main difference is that the chief constable dropped any reference to the bobby who saw the Polish suspect in Mitre Square (if that detail was mentioned by Asquith, ex-PC Spicer might realize he was being grossly misrepresented).

In this filed version of the memo, Macnaghten also swaps places with the Druitt family; they now 'believe' in their member's culpability while the chief constable is supposedly agnostic about who is the more probable suspect of the trio – except that all three are more likely to have been 'the fiend' than the once violent and now docile Thomas Cutbush. Yet with Montague Druitt, Macnaghten massaged the data once more to render him almost wholly accurate yet deliberately incomplete. The incorrect age by a single digit is not repeated. His medical qualifications are, at best, hearsay – maybe he was not even a registered doctor, as in an 'occasional' medical student. Remarkably, Macnaghten places on the official file that Mr. Druitt was most definitely erotically fulfilled by ultraviolence (so no wonder his own family 'believed' he was 'Jack the Ripper').

In reality, Mac and the family knew Montague was the 'Ripper' as he had confessed to his clerical cousin and to his brother, and the crime scene details of that confession had been posthumously verified by the chief constable. The family had hushed up what they knew, but it had spilled briefly into the public sphere several years later. That and much else had to be veiled with a very thick curtain, though Macnaghten now implied that this deceased M. J. Druitt was a relative of the famous doctor with that name.

(1) A Mr M. J. Druitt, *said to be a doctor & of good family* – who disappeared at the time of the Miller's Court murder, & whose body (which was said to have been upwards of a month in the water) was found in the Thames on 31st December – or about 7 weeks after that murder. He *was sexually insane* and from private information I have little doubt but that *his own family believed* him to have been the murderer.[7] [Our italics]

As it turned out, the crisis over Cutbush never seems to have metastasized as Macnaghten and Sims had feared. The home secretary did not answer questions in the House of Commons, as none were asked. Scotland Yard was not troubled by any internal review of the matter. The 'Jack the Ripper' murders had already retreated into recent history – there were plenty of other issues, crises, and cases with which to grapple. Macnaghten, Sims, and Majendie could breathe easier, and the chief constable now had the security of M. J. Druitt's name on file – apart from his 1888 arrest record – as a significant suspect.

If Asquith, or his successors, read out the details of this drowned man, he would be described as a doctor and not a lawyer, and propriety would take care of the names being withheld, what with the 'mad doctor's' being beyond the reach of due process. Macnaghten kept the draft at his home, while the official version was filed at Scotland Yard – it was never sent to the Home Office. Nobody at Scotland Yard even knew these non-identical memos existed (at least not in their true form and import).

Nevertheless, by the end of 1894, Macnaghten must have felt it was prudent to inform the masses that the Whitechapel assassin was definitely and safely dead. The version of his memo for public consumption was not yet to be deployed. Instead, Macnaghten seems to have leaked to trusted reporters glimpses of the truth that the gentleman-murderer had died whilst under care. One of the earliest examples of Mac's propaganda campaign is found in the *Evening*

Star (New Zealand) of January 1, 1895, in an account its London correspondent had reported on December 14, 1894.

The linchpin of the article is the murder of a young woman named Augusta Dawes, who was fatally stabbed by a stranger on Holland Park Road in Kensington. She was swiftly slashed to death by a young lunatic, Reginald Saunderson, who for three years had been an inmate at a private asylum that is quite reminiscent of Vanves in France. Saunderson was not under guard; he just slipped away, and the weapon he used to butcher an innocent woman was the one he used for gardening. Before he was identified as a mere twenty-two-year-old, there was idle speculation that the Ripper might have returned. The real assailant fled to Ireland and was captured within a few days. The conundrum for the state was whether Saunderson suffered from blackouts when he committed atrocities and therefore, as a mental incompetent, could not be tried for Dawes's murder. We think Macnaghten exploited this sensational case to inject some data into the public realm about Druitt that both revealed some of the truth whilst also misdirecting press and public:

THE REAL RIPPER

The Kensington murder having in a small way revived the 'Jack the Ripper' scare, the authorities have thought it well to acknowledge what many have long suspected – viz. that the mysterious hero [*sic*] of the Whitechapel horrors is dead.

For 'authorities,' read 'Macnaghten,' entirely alone and charming a reporter with an inside scoop that was not for attribution.

The Sun you will recollect, made a rare to-do over the supposed discovery of this assassin some months back, but the police quietly pooh-poohed its wonderful yarn.

For 'police,' again read 'Macnaghten'; behind his calm 'pooh poohing' had been his frantic composing months earlier of two versions of the same memo, aimed at different audiences, in case the cover-up he had commandeered was about to unravel.

The police, however, pointed out that there were self-confessed Rippers in every asylum in Great Britain....The real 'Jack', it seems, belonged, as many suspected all along, to the medical profession – *or rather was a student*. His *friends* at last discovered the horrible truth and had him *confined in an asylum*. When he *died a year ago the evidence in their possession* was submitted to Scotland Yard, and convinced them they had at last found the genuine Ripper. [Our italics]

It is the same kind of sly mix of fact and fiction in which Macnaghten and Sims will engage for years to come about the Druitt solution. How exactly can friends bundle a person to whom they are not related into a private asylum? This unlikely aspect matches the *Philadelphia Times* article of 1889; a clergyman cousin and a lawyer who is supposedly only a 'friend' of the English patient helps escort and pay for his confinement. Druitt had expired six years before; therefore Macnaghten was throwing off the reporter about when 'the genuine Ripper' had died ('a year ago' is about when Mac wrote his memos of misdirection). The 'friends' reportedly possess damning evidence they promptly provide to the police, when in reality the family only very reluctantly, we argue, briefed Macnaghten in the wake of the Farquharson betrayal over two years later.

Remarkably, when *The Referee* commented on the new semi-official 'Ripper' revelations in its Sunday issue of December 9, 1894, more of the truth was revealed than ever would be again, at least until the 1960s. The columnist was not George Sims – though he must have been his source – but a Scot named John Ferguson Nisbet. An experienced journalist, sometime playwright, and a dramatic critic for *The Times*, J. F. Nisbet also wrote for *The Referee* at a time when Sims was a co-owner of the newspaper. Most suggestively, Nisbet also 'dabbled in science,' publishing in 1891 *The Insanity of Genius and the General Inequality of Human Faculty: Physiologically Considered* (London: Ward & Downey). We theorize that it was this positively received treatise on the supposed biological origins of great men's talents that drew Macnaghten and Sims to Nisbet. For example, these words on page 29 of Nisbet's work may have enlightened the pair on the enigma of Montague Druitt:

The word *genius* is susceptible of many interpretations. For the purposes of this inquiry I give it the widest, applying it not merely to the creative gift in literature and art, but to that inherent ability *which enables its possessor to excel in any given sphere of human activity*, literary, artistic, scientific, administrative, military, commercial, religious, philanthropic or *even criminal*. [Our italics]

And from the same page:

Some of the forms of insanity may be due to an impairment of these connecting fibres, especially when the patient has insane impulses which his reason seems to hold in check. Not infrequently *patients feel a desire to murder somebody*, but have sense enough to control it, and even to *place themselves voluntarily under restraint* lest the impulse should overpower them. [Our italics]

This book came out in March 1891, and Sims as Dagonet wrote about the unnamed Druitt on November 1 of the same year with opinions that strikingly indicate he (and Macnaghten) had read J. F. Nisbet's book. To repeat a few words from that critical source already quoted in the previous chapter:

The *very superabundance* of [the Ripper's] *nerve energy* may be the cause of his insanity, and his nervous force may not only enable him to put forth abnormal muscular strength, but also to think acutely. If the madman's faculties were levelled up all round he would be *possessed of marvellous genius…*

An 1894 issue of *The Referee* makes it clear that Nisbet had been briefed about Montague Druitt by his employer, George R. Sims, and in his column 'Our Notebook' Nisbet connects elements of the young Kensington murderer with the Whitechapel assassin:

For a key to the Whitechapel mystery, in fact, we have only to turn to the Kensington murder. There we see the man, the mode, the opportunity, and *the escape*.
   The story that the Whitechapel murderer was eventually shut-up in a lunatic asylum by his friends, and that he has since died there, I can well believe. But for Saunderson's confession the Kensington case might have had a similar sequel. The young man escaped from a home for eccentrics, conducted by Dr Langdon Down at Hampton Wick, *and turned up some little time afterwards among his friends in Ireland.*

Nisbet is alluding, we believe, to what he has been told about the Vanves misadventure, and to an unguarded Montague's returning in haste back to London, then later slipping out under the noses of the Tukes at Chiswick into a handy watery grave.

When a homicidal lunatic is at large it is scarcely likely that he will not go on with his misdeeds until caught red-handed; *but if recaptured by his friends (from whose custody he may have escaped) before his connection with a particular crime or series of crimes is known*, the probability is that his guilt will never be brought to light. [Our italics]

Then Nisbet succinctly sums up what is our interpretation of the veiled Second Act of this complex story of multiple homicides and gentlemanly misdirection and deflection. This thumbnail passage is confirmation of our entire book's revisionist thesis:

I understand that *the relatives of Jack the Ripper* did at last *know or suspect* the truth about their charge, though, for reasons that can be well understood, *they preferred to hush up the affair*. [Our italics]

That Nisbet here oscillates between whether the family knew or merely suspected the truth about the unnamed Montie means he may have read, or perhaps been orally briefed about, the contents of Macnaghten's twin yet non-identical memos. The dramatic critic and amateur scientist then alludes to the Henry Farquharson intervention of 1891, recalling that the maniac suffered from a form of epileptic mania (or at least so the Druitt family wanted to believe) and perhaps providing a glimpse of Montague's outward personality – charming but opaque – and finishing with a backhanded criticism of the Tukes' establishment's lack of security:

From a description given some two or three years ago of the lunatic supposed to be Jack the Ripper, I gathered that the wretched being had *lost consciousness of his crimes,* if, indeed, he ever had it. When 'on the job' however, this monster was probably a plausible, *affable gentleman,* with nothing to attract attention beyond a strange gleam at times in the depth of his eye, or a little secretiveness and reserve in his habits.

Saunderson, for his part, was so little suspected of being dangerous that he seems to have been allowed to come and go at the Hampton Wick institution pretty much as he pleased. *Whether the supervision exercised at private asylums or 'homes,' as they are very often called, is all that could be desired is a point upon which the public will be glad of information.* [Our italics]

In 1894, hardly anybody noticed this bombshell. The clock was, however, still ticking towards the ten-year milestone in 1898 or 1899, when the Reverend Charles Druitt was committed to revealing the truth in some form to fulfil Montague's next-to-last wishes.

Knight Takes Bishop

Consider the shock Joseph Lawende, a dignified commercial traveller and immigrant success story, must have felt when the police knocked at his door in early 1895. It was more than seven years before, on 30 September 1888, when Lawende had seen what appeared to be a young sailor and a middle-aged prostitute amiably chatting. When it was discovered the former had killed the latter and brutally carved up her corpse in the dark, this prime eyewitness had told the Acting City Police Chief Henry Smith that he doubted he could recognise the man again, as he had only caught the barest glimpse of him. This was discounted by a faction at the Yard, including Melville Macnaghten, who reasoned that Lawende was being evasive because he was afraid of reprisals from the assassin. Once the Chief Constable had privately learned of the Druitt solution, he knew that the Polish immigrant had described the barrister with impressive accuracy: a gentile-featured, silver-tongued Englishman of medium size, sporting a fair moustache.

Now it was February 1895 and Lawende was again contacted by Scotland Yard; he opened his door to CID detectives who asked if he could accompany them, to be of assistance in their enquiries. There was only one possible reason – they had caught 'Jack the Ripper', or at least thought they had. It must have felt like deja vu *for Lawende as he rode in a carriage to some forbidding structure where they were detaining the latest candidate to be 'Jack'. Four years before, almost to the day, they had escorted him not to the expected line-up, but just into a room where he found a burly, squat Englishman with a straggly beard – the sort of volatile low-life who still seems punch-drunk even when he has not touched a drop. Were the police serious? Could they not read his witness statement from 1888?*

Lawende pretended to take a long, thoughtful look at the suspect in the murder of Frances Coles before pronouncing: 'no, not him'. Of course it was a 'no'. This human mollusc was hardly the lithe charmer Lawende had seen with that poor woman in Mitre Square.

The CID detectives barely concealed their disappointment. Only one of the men in attendance, easily the tallest and who looked and sounded nothing like a copper – for one thing, he spoke with a posh accent – approached him and apologised for the inconvenience. He also extended his hand and thanked him with a warm smile and a firm handshake (disconcertingly this police chief acted as if they were old friends).

Lawende learned from the newspapers that the suspect was a sailor named Tom Sadler. When the bucolic proletarian was freed, after all charges were dropped, Lawende felt vindicated.

Four years later Joseph Lawende expected a replay of the events of 1891; a waste of his time, though he was too polite to say so. He guessed that this was the suspect who had been arrested with much media fanfare, on 20 February 1895, for the attempted murder of prostitute Alice Graham.

Despite her assailant inserting a knife into her private parts, Alice Graham had survived and was able to identify William Grant (a.k.a. Grainger) as the man who had attacked her. Grant was a ship's stoker from Cork, Ireland, though he was also reputed to have some medical training – the press called him a 'surgeon'. A gentile sailor caught in the act of assaulting an East End prostitute with a knife. Maybe ... he was 'Jack the Ripper'? Certainly sections of the press were trumpeting the return of The Fiend after a long sabbatical. Here is a typical example from the *Hawaiian Gazette* of 8 March 1895, repeating a London story from 21 February 1895:

IS IT JACK THE RIPPER?

An attempted murder, surrounded by many circumstances similar to the Jack the Ripper crimes, was perpetrated this evening at Spitalfields, one of the eastern suburbs of London. The screams of a woman attracted a crowd to a lonely thoroughfare, and the people arriving first upon the scene caught a man red handed in the act of butchering a woman of the unfortunate class. The unfortunate victim was not dead when help arrived, but she had been injured in a terrible manner. The man was bending over her prostrate body, and with a long bladed knife was hacking his victim's body in a manner which characterised the shocking crimes attributed to 'Jack the Ripper'. The man was at once taken into custody and gave the name of Grant. He further said that he was a ship's fireman. The police have made inquiries, with the result that certain clues they have obtained suggest that the prisoner may be Jack the Ripper.

Again Lawende was escorted into a dank room and found a surly prisoner. He was taken aback, for it really was the same man – at least that is what his memory told him. The suspect before him was not yet 40, had many tattoos – which he did not recall seeing on the skin of the 'sailor' in Mitre Square – and had a dark rather than a fair moustache. Everything else seemed to be identical: a wiry frame, a domed forehead, straight hair plastered against the sleek skull, the V-shaped face dominated by a large nose and punctuated by a small chin and the piercing eyes with hooded lids. The long passage of time intersected all too easily with the publicly known facts about this dreadful man – he had assaulted a defenceless 'fallen woman' with a knife in a degrading, potentially homicidal manner – nudging a cautious man into an injudicious act.

Lawende raised his finger and pointed, 'yes,' he affirmed, 'that's the man I saw!' And why not – the police, the press, the public, practically everybody wanted it to be William Grant.

The disgusted suspect smiled sourly, shook his head and spat on the floor. The normally reserved detectives in the room were beaming and smiling at each other. All, that is, except one; Lawende recognised the same tall, posh-accented gentleman from 1891; the senior officer who still looked as if he had wandered in by mistake while on his way to his gentleman's club. Again this amiable big shot strolled over, shook Lawende's hand and thanked him for his help – but could Lawende see there was some kind of strain the other man was valiantly suppressing? This policeman seemed to be not happy that 'The Ripper' had surely been identified at last, and that made no sense. All the evidence against William Grant was overwhelming. The horrific saga even had a somewhat happy ending: the final victim had lived to tell the gruesome tale and to see the monster brought to justice.

Poor Macnaghten – having viewed photos of Montague Druitt the Chief Constable could perfectly see how the generic resemblance to this William Grant could cause this potentially catastrophic error (the single, surviving photos of Grant bears a resemblance to Druitt, but was not reproducible for this book). With all the pressure of his other duties and cases, Macnaghten had to consider, yet again, what the Reverend Charles Druitt would decide to do if he had grounds to fear that this Grant was going to be railroaded for all the other Whitechapel murders (despicable swine that he obviously was for such a cowardly act committed against Alice Graham).

The positive witness identification only leaked to *The Pall Mall Gazette* and yet, as the cogs of justice started to roll, this prize 'Ripper' suspect was not even charged with attempted murder (he would serve several years in prison for felonious wounding – cold comfort for his victim who had suffered a blade thrust into her vagina).

The capture of William Grant in 1895 before he could kill an East End poverty-stricken woman, supported by the extraordinary affirmation by the critical Whitechapel witness, should have been the satisfying if belated climax to the whole 'Jack the Ripper' saga. Instead the affair was almost instantly forgotten (despite a momentary revival of interest fifteen years later). Fortified by Lawende's confirmation, why did Scotland Yard not pursue Grant as the 1888 to 1891 murderer with greater vigour? That same issue of *The Pall Mall Gazette* of 7 May 1895, chock-full of insider morsels as it is, may provide the answer. Although Macnaghten is never mentioned, we believe it has his fingerprints all over it. For example, almost casually the journalist insinuates that the letter that had coined the infamous nickname was a hoax. Much later it raises the eyewitness identification only to quash it under the dubious legal and evidential grounds that it was all, well, a bit too late:

WHITECHAPEL 'RIPPING' CASE
EXHAUSTIVE POLICE ENQUIRIES.
SOME CURIOUS COINCIDENCES.

.. there is one person whom the police believe to have actually seen the Whitechapel murderer with a woman a few minutes before the woman's dissected body was found in the street. That person is stated to have identified Grainger [Grant] as the man he then saw. *But obviously identification after so cursory a glance, and after the lapse of so long an interval, could not be reliable.* (Our italics)

Earlier, the article had named the Chief Inspector who had operational control of the Whitechapel investigation, Donald Swanson. He also worked directly under Dr Robert Anderson though in contrast to

Macnaghten, Swanson both admired and liked his pious superior. Somebody in the know had revealed that Swanson – and by implication Anderson too – knew who the real 'Jack' was, and it was certainly not this ship's stoker, quasi-surgeon from Ireland.

> The theory entitled to most respect, because it was presumably *based on the best knowledge*, was that of Chief Inspector Swanson, the officer who was associated with the investigation of all the murders, and *Mr Swanson believed the crimes to have been the work of a man who is now dead*. (Our italics)

Other contemporaneous sources reveal that Swanson and Anderson believed the murderer had been a young, sexually dysfunctional man who had been a patient in an asylum, and who had subsequently died. In fact, he had been deceased relatively soon after Mary Jane Kelly's murder on 9 November 1888, and thus could not have killed either Alice McKenzie or Frances Coles. The man's family may have known the awful truth and bundled him into a madhouse before the police could bring him before the courts. It was all moot, however, as he expired soon after. Superficially it sounds like this pair of senior policemen had accepted the Druitt solution.

Actually there is no evidence they knew anything about Montague Druitt. Anderson and Swanson believed in the guilt of another Whitechapel suspect entirely: Aaron Kosminski, the Polish immigrant barber who had entered Colney Hatch asylum. Much of what they thought they knew, however, was quite mistaken – he had not been sectioned in early 1889 and had also not died soon afterwards. He was placed in care in early 1891 (a few days before the Coles' murder) and only died the year after the Great War (in fact, he outlived Dr Robert Anderson, who had told his son that the murderer had died long ago in an asylum). Anderson and Swanson did not even know the man's full name, to them he was just 'Kosminski'.[1] In other words the loathed Dr Robert Anderson (with his sidekick Donald Swanson, whom Mac professed to respect) had been comprehensively played by the 'honourable schoolboy'. In order to distract his priggish boss from going anywhere near the red herring of William Grant as 'The Ripper', Macnaghten had introduced Anderson to one of the minor, camouflage suspects from his own 1894 memorandum.

It is unlikely Anderson knew of this document's existence, as the 'draft' version would have informed him that 'Kosminski' was likely to be still alive as late as 1894. In addition, the draft version, composed for the public, contained a deception that even Anderson might spot: the beat cop who perhaps saw this Polish suspect in Mitre Square. This was an inversion of a Polish witness (Lawende) sighting the gentile suspect, almost certainly Montague Druitt, fused with the latter's arrest by PC Spicer.

> No. 2. Kosminski, a Polish Jew, who lived in the very heart of the district where the murders were committed. He had become insane owing to many years indulgence in solitary vices. He had a great hatred of women, with strong homicidal tendencies. He was (and I believe still is) detained in a lunatic asylum, about March 1889. This man in appearance strongly resembled the individual seen by the City P.C. near Mitre Square.

All Macnaghten had to do as the William Grant balloon began to be pumped up by the press was to tell Dr Anderson that he had found out that one of their suspects, from a list of hundreds, had expired in an asylum several years ago. That it in itself counted for little. Rather, it was the *reason* Mac manufactured for this Polish man's premature demise that he knew would be decisive proof *to his superior* that he must have been the foul killer. Anderson, a sexually repressed Victorian *par excellence* was utterly committed to the ludicrous nonsense that so-called 'self-abuse', the Biblical sin of Onan – or 'solitary vices' as Mac endearingly calls them – were so evil that any man capable of such heinous sacrilege against their own body was capable of anything including murder. Macnaghten misinformed Anderson that in the asylum, this 'Kosminski' had masturbated himself into an early grave.

Fifteen years later Anderson would write thunderously, in his insufferably self-serving memoirs, about the Polish lunatic as a 'loathsome creature whose utterly unmentionable vices reduced him to a lower level than that of the brute'.[2] Macnaghten, despite his upper class privilege, had a broader upbringing and was far more liberal minded in the company he kept, for example at the Garrick Club. One can easily imagine Macnaghten and Sims laughing uproariously over Anderson's stiff and humourless memoirs of 1910. He had fallen for Mac's ruse, hook, line and sinker back in 1895.

The filed version of Macnaghten's memo, if Anderson should bother to look it up, need cause no problem for this prankish bit of deflection away from the William Grant red herring. In both, Mac had backdated the Polish patient's incarceration from 1891 to 1889. Only verbally had Druitt's demise been grafted onto a suspect that Macnaghten predicted correctly would fixate his boss (whereas the draft version, safely kept at home, gave the game away – 'Kosminski' was still alive). The Chief Constable could hardly have done better than if he had announced to the fundamentalist stuffed-shirt that Satan himself was stalking the East End on all hooves:

> (2) Kosminski – a Polish Jew – & resident in Whitechapel. This man became insane *owing to many years indulgence in solitary vices.* He had a great hatred of women, specially [sic] of the prostitute class, & had *strong homicidal tendencies*: he was removed to a lunatic asylum about *March 1889*. There were many circumstances connected with this man which made him a strong suspect. (Our italics)

Having successfully misdirected two of his senior colleagues by claiming their favoured suspect was deceased when he patently was not, Macnaghten did it with others too in order to create a buffer between Druitt and the Yard[3] (*see* Chapter XIX).

As the ten-year deadline approached Macnaghten seems to have convinced Charles Druitt that the family surname must not under any circumstances be exposed in the public sphere. The Dorset reverend could reveal what he felt he must of the truth – which Sims had come very close to doing in 1891 – but must deploy a go-between to communicate with the press. This intermediary would need to render the profile of the murderer unrecognisable as a Druitt. Charles must find somebody in whom he had the confidence to do this tricky and risky task; a trusted confidant who, at the very least, must not have the same surname. Reverend Charles had no trouble finding such a person and close by: his brother-in-law, Arthur du Boulay Hill, Isabel Majendie Hill's brother, Colonel Majendie's second cousin and Charles' best friend. Reverend Arthur had known Montague Druitt at Winchester College when he was an assistant master, alongside his uncle, the deputy J. T. H. du Boulay, another cousin of Colonel Majendie. It is highly unlikely Macnaghten would have thought this was the best choice – a man related by marriage to the Druitts who was *also* a clergyman – but there were limits as to how far even he could control this 'sticky wicket'

While Reverend Charles Druitt was the kind of man who tried to do things the right way for the greater good and was frequently overcome with self-doubt, the Reverend Arthur du Boulay Hill believed that he almost always did the right thing for the greater good and did it correctly. Arthur was a man of considerable education and good standing within the community and from an old and very good family. Arthur believed this background equipped him with an ability to know what to do in any difficult situation; he was a problem solver. Yet his self-confidence could be problematic as his zeal meant he never backed down – Arthur could also be a problem starter. When anyone brave enough attempted to inform him that he was perhaps too dogmatic or perhaps lacking empathy and needed to adopt a broader view of things, Arthur ignored the gentle hint, believing that in time, people would come to see that he was proved right again. On the other hand, Arthur was much loved by many of his parishioners and by his sister Isabel and her husband Charles. They saw Arthur as reliable and trustworthy; he was Charles closest confidante, apart from Isabel, during his adult life.

Arthur could display kindness and concern but his actions often painted him more as the dotty vicar rather than the Renaissance man he felt himself to be. Educated at Winchester and Oxford where he had won a scholarship to study Natural Science, Arthur was studious and determined. In 1874 he graduated with a first class degree. Like his best friend Charles, Arthur was politically a Liberal and the two men were regular attendees at party meetings becoming part of a philosophical split within the Liberal Party over Irish Home Rule. Apart from his parish duties, Arthur was closely involved in the establishment of parish schools and was a tireless fundraiser for such causes. He and his sister Isabel Majendie Hill were accomplished musicians; they regularly performed at benefit concerts as vocalists and pianists. At one such event, in Breamore, they performed the genteel piece 'Friendship'. Arthur, the more serious musician of the two, provided a solo performances of 'Storm' on the pianoforte and then a rousing vocal and piano performance of the popular 'Here's A Health Unto His Majesty', a seventeenth-century patriotic song.[4] It was written at the time of Charles II. Arthur's performance was by all reports greatly appreciated by the large audience, who demonstrated their approval with 'repeated applause'.[5]

> Here's a health unto His Majesty,
> With a fa la la la la la la,
> Confusion to his enemies,
> With a fa la la la la la la.
> And he who would not drink his health,
> We wish him neither wit nor wealth,
> Nor yet a rope to hang himself.
> With a fal lal la la la la la la la.

Arthur might well have taken heed of the second to last line of this ditty, for time after time, he metaphorically took (nearly) enough rope to hang himself, and the Druitt family, when doing what he believed to be just the right thing. To understand the character of Reverend Arthur du Boulay Hill is to understand why he undertook a risky mission ten years after the suicide of a man he had known well, Montague John Druitt. From his employment as an assistant schoolmaster at Winchester College in Montie Druitt's final years and marrying in 1888, just one week after the wedding of Reverend Charles and his sister Isabel, he would by 1890 enter into his ninth year as Vicar of Downton with Nunton parish in Wiltshire.

Incidents such as the one reported by *The Salisbury Times* of 22 March 1890 heralded a souring of relations between some parishioners and the Reverend du Boulay Hill. Frank Noble, one of Arthur's parishioners found himself arrested and charged for bad behaviour in church. Before Judge Swayne, Reverend Arthur stated that he had felt that due respect was not being given to him by a group of four or five younger male parishioners who had 'behaved very unbecomingly' by 'sitting down, and talking and laughing' while 'he was conducting divine service in the church'. Arthur it seems was fed up with the frivolity in the pews and forcefully convinced Mr W. C. Street the churchwarden that one of the lads needed to be made an example of and therefore Mr Street must request that the police arrest young Frank Noble.[6] It is clear that the churchwarden was not convinced that Arthur's idea was a good one but Mr Street, as Arthur informed Judge Swayne, 'at last came to the conclusion' that Arthur's idea was in fact the correct one and Noble was duly arrested and charged with 'indecent behaviour in the parish church, Downton'. Once in the dock and having had a stern dressing down by the magistrate that such behaviour would not be tolerated, Reverend Arthur and Mr Street generously requested that Frank Noble be let go. They felt that their aim had been achieved and no other young man would attempt such 'indecent behaviour' in Downton Church again. This event proved to be both a humiliating and expensive one for young Frank. The judge agreed to release him but not before he could find the funds to pay a fine and costs and as a souvenir of the event he was to receive a written caution. There is nothing further written about Frank Noble but one imagines that after this incident there was an abundance of vacant seating available during Arthur's divine services at Downton.

In 1895 Arthur pushed the goodwill of his parishioners beyond the point of no return. On 4 January *The Salisbury Times* sent a reporter to investigate yet another of Reverend Arthur's controversies. Again this took place at Downton but this time the victim of Arthur's 'dottiness' was far worldlier than poor Frank Noble. Mr Mitchell, a local grocer who owned a small plot of land in Gravel Close, had found himself being sent a summons via the County Court from Reverend Arthur du

Boulay Hill, demanding that he pay two years' arrears of a tithe to the church. Mr Mitchell knew that although living close to the Downton Parish boundary he, in fact, did not have to pay that tithe and if he could access the map he could prove it!

Immediately, Mr Mitchell sought out Reverend Arthur 'and pointed out that he was wrongly charged'. According to Mitchell, Arthur 'expressed his regret things had gone so far and promised that the error should be rectified.' Mr Mitchell took Arthur's word as truth until a few days later when another warrant was served on the now seething grocer. This time a repossession cart arrived and the contents of Mr Mitchell's house were seized to cover the cost of the unpaid tithe. It is reported that Mr Mitchell who 'felt very indignant' revisited Arthur. There is no report about what happened at the second meeting of the grocer and the vicar but suffice to say, the reporter discovered that 'the dissenting community and the majority of the church people are much annoyed at these proceedings'.

To add to the hostility expressed towards him by the Downton parishioners, Arthur found himself further humiliated. The accusation that he had acted unjustly and even greedily towards the grocer must have added insult to injury for even the editor of *The Salisbury Times* now commented on the incident. 'We shall be glad to receive and to publish anything which can be said in explanation of this affair, which it is hoped, has arisen through an inadvertence, and not with any desire to make an unfair demand, or to give annoyance'.

Records show that Reverend Arthur du Boulay Hill soldiered on at Downton Parish and by all accounts was a diligent vicar, a champion of religious education and a passionate promoter of bell ringing. It must also be noted however, that over the years similar stories emerged, demonstrating Arthur's propensity to stubbornness and his belief that he 'ought not give way as far as compromise goes'. It seems a fair assumption that because of Arthur's frequent *faux pas*, the parishioners of Downton were somewhat relieved when church officials, who administered the province of York in the Church of England, sought out a new vicar for their Nottinghamshire parish of East Bridgford – and Arthur's name was put forward. It seemed to be a good opportunity for a fresh start all round.

Arthur and Gertrude left the parish with mixed feelings, particularly as they would be moving far away from Charles and Isabel.[7] With a sense of duty, Reverend Arthur du Boulay Hill relocated to Nottinghamshire where by all accounts he became a much-loved conscientious clergyman, local historian and promoter of bell ringing (an impressive two-light memorial stained glass window dedicated to Reverend Arthur du Boulay Hill can be seen in the church of East Bridgford Nottinghamshire to this day). By 1898 – and until his retirement from East Bridgford in 1926 – the Reverend Arthur du Boulay Hill could rightly claim that he was truly 'a north country vicar'.[8]

At the beginning of the year that would see the dreaded truth about Montague J. Druitt resurface in ways that might make the consequences hard to predict, Vicar Arthur du Boulay Hill had a serious accident. According to *The Pall Mall Gazette* of 1 March 1898, the vicar fell off his bike. Arthur broke his nose and dislocated his jaw; he was bedridden for weeks. A surviving letter has Charles writing to his mother, Isabella, on 28 February 1898 reporting that his brother-in-law is 'suffering from all the effects of nervous shock ... I trust the shock of the accident will not have permanently upset his nerve.' Reverend Charles may have just been referring to Arthur's capacity to carry out his clerical duties. Was he also alluding to his coming task of revealing the truth about 'Jack the Ripper' which might be like cycling into a lion's den?

With the troika reduced to a duo after Sir Vivian Majendie's death on 25 March 1898, Macnaghten and Sims seem to have made a decision as to how to 'play this game'; how they would respond to the scheduled debut of Reverend Charles Druitt's attempt to salve his conscience by sharing a truth – a truth that nobody was expecting or was going to welcome. Professionally, Macnaghten knew that he had a solid chance to succeed Dr Robert Anderson as Assistant Commissioner of CID within a few years. The Druitt solution, if it spiralled out of control, however, could still derail his policing career. In terms of public relations a ruthless strategy was adopted by the duo, we think, to undermine Vicar Charles Druitt and his mouthpiece, Vicar Arthur du Boulay Hill.

This discrediting would be done before the latter published as well as in the immediate aftermath. To snuff out the clergymen's intervention as just eccentric clerics getting the wrong end of the stick – a tiresome stereotype even in 1898 but a useful one nonetheless. The police chief and the famous writer would get in ahead, and have the last word. They would reintroduce the unnamed Druitt for the first time since 1891 on their own terms – as a prime suspect of whom police were in hot pursuit. Naturally there would be no mention of an earlier arrest, or the confession to a clergyman or a French asylum, or the drowning taking place at Chiswick, or the family being accessories after the fact – or even the existence of a family at all. Why should Scotland Yard have to look like complete chumps over this intractable case as they were closing on barrister Druitt (albeit, without knowing his name)?

Major Arthur Griffiths was the nation's chief warden of prisons and a popular true crime writer. In 1898 he was preparing his ambitious and comprehensive two-volume work on the history of British crooks, crime and coppers that had taken years to research and compile. In the course of his research he interviewed the Chief Constable, Melville Macnaghten, whom he characterises as a 'man of action': 'It is Mr Macnaghten's duty, no less than his earnest desire, to be first on the scene of any such sinister catastrophe. He is therefore *more intimately acquainted perhaps with the details of the most celebrated crimes than anyone in Scotland Yard.*' (Our italics)[9]

These words conceal from us that Major Griffiths had decidedly mixed feelings about Macnaghten. This was due to the Chief Constable, quite unexpectedly, showing him the 'draft' of his 1894 memorandum on the Whitechapel murders. The final version of this document, wherein Mac flat out lied, was held in the Home Office archive (in fact, it never went further than Scotland Yard's archive). Despite being handed such a remarkable scoop the textual evidence indicates, at least, that Major Griffiths quite simply did not fully believe 'Good Old Mac'. He was sceptical that the clueless constabulary of 1888 to 1891 now, suddenly, had a very promising suspect, in fact they had three of them. Macnaghten assured the major that had the 'mad doctor' not drowned himself they might have gained a conviction.

Yet Griffiths must have responded by asking probing questions – as did a few in the press when his book was published – such as how all this was not better known and how was it that the 'Jack the Ripper' murders, which lasted over a protracted period of several years, now turned out to have been a brief season of slaughter by a singular maniac and that this was apparently known to the police *at the time*. If Griffiths recalled all the agitation over suspect Tom Sadler and victim Frances Coles in 1891 – let alone over William Grant and Alice Graham just three years before – he must have thought this all sounded decidedly fishy. Almost with disdain, he buried the 'Ripper' revelation of the chummy Chief Constable not in a pertinent chapter but in his introduction where he implies that the unnamed M. J. Druitt was a suspect while alive:

> The outside public may think that the identity of that later miscreant, 'Jack the Ripper,' was never revealed. So far as actual knowledge goes, this is undoubtedly true. But the police, after the last murder, had *brought their investigations to the point of strongly suspecting* several persons, all of them known to be homicidal lunatics, and *against three of these held very plausible and reasonable grounds of suspicion.* Concerning two of them the case was weak, although it was based on certain colourable facts. (Our italics)

After disposing of the Polish and Russian suspects, Major Griffiths deals with the 'drowned doctor', allegedly Scotland Yard's super-suspect. Even though propriety prevented their being named to avoid even the possibility of a libel suit by any members of the Druitt family the author discreetly disguised his blood relations as 'friends'. The major probably never realised that Mac in the same document had *already* disguised a young barrister as a middle-aged, fully qualified physician:

> The third person was of the same type, but the suspicion in his case was stronger, and there was every reason to believe that *his own friends* entertained grave doubts about him. He was also *a doctor in the prime of life*, was believed to be insane or on the borderland of insanity, and *he disappeared immediately after the last murder*, that in Miller's Court, on 8th of November, 1888. On the last day of that year, *seven weeks later*, his body was found floating in the Thames, and was said to have been *in the water a month*. The theory in this case was that after his last exploit, which was the most fiendish of all, his brain entirely gave way, and he became furiously insane and committed suicide.... (Our italics)

Not until Macnaghten deployed his version from his 'draft' memo and it was published by such a sober and credible source as Major Arthur Griffiths did Montague Druitt return, after an abortive debut at both ends of 1891, as the solution to five of the Whitechapel murders. This time round, Mac made it quasi-official and chose to reveal the Thames finale. This was because he may have assumed – wrongly as it turned out – that Charles Druitt was going to do so too. Ergo, other details, such as Druitt's true age and profession would have to be altered for public consumption, just as his family had been, by disguising them as 'friends'. This mere cameo in Griffith's non-fiction epic caused a minor sensation in the press – no doubt as Macnaghten hoped it would to counter the vicar.

Charles Druitt felt comfortable entrusting Arthur du Boulay Hill to help him compose a testament outlining just enough of the truth about Montague's double life – without naming him. They agreed that it then would be sent to the *Daily Mail,* a respectable national newspaper (in a letter from 7 September 1897, Charles wrote to his mother mentioning that he was changing his regular newspaper order from *The Standard* to *The Daily Mail*). In early January 1899, ten years since the funeral and burial of Montague Druitt in Wimborne Minster, the sifters of the voluminous correspondence to the London offices of *The Daily Mail* opened a letter which aroused their curiosity. This letter claimed to solve the 'Jack the Ripper' mystery. A middle-ranking cleric of the

Church of England, who headed a parish in the north – and who had candidly provided his own name for verification – claimed to know the identity of the murderer, a man long deceased. This 'north country vicar', somewhat presumptuously had written a short article which he expected the *Daily Mail* to publish without dissent. The gist of the vicar's story was that a pillar of the British bourgeoisie suffered from 'epileptic mania' a Victorianism for a mental affliction in which a person loses all control of themselves during an epileptic-type fit. A sufferer may even lose their memory of what they have done, which may include, murder, theft, riot, arson, assault and suicide. A patient so afflicted can rave and shriek and be gripped by an uncontrollable maniacal fury.[10] The gentleman sufferer of this lethal epilepsy had, the vicar wrote, confessed his crimes to another clergyman while in a lucid state. He then soon after expired (which implied he had committed suicide). Strangely, from the newspaper's point of view, the clergyman had titled his narrative:

THE WHITECHURCH MURDERS – SOLUTION OF A LONDON MYSTERY

Why on earth would the vicar, or anybody for that matter, choose to substitute 'Whitechurch' for Whitechapel? The article the cleric had written seemed to, sort of, explain this pointless change – he asserted that his information was 'substantial truth under fictitious form', whatever that might mean. As best as the intrigued editors could figure out, the vicar was admitting that he was communicating untruths about the killer's identity – again, what a peculiar thing for an Anglican cleric to do and to admit he was doing (but exactly the sort of idiosyncratic act the Reverend Arthur du Boulay Hill would do). To history's loss, the newspaper would ultimately decline to publish *The Whitechurch Murders* ... but did quote from the vicar's letter in a subsequent article published on 18 January 1899 openly musing over such a bizarre communication. Below they quoted the vicar directly:

> I received information in professional confidence, with directions to publish the facts after ten years, and then *with such alterations as might defeat identification*. The murderer was a man of good position and otherwise unblemished reputation who suffered from *epileptic mania* and is long since deceased. (Our italics)

Knowing what we know about the particulars of Montague Druitt, he *was* a man who held the 'good positions' of barrister and schoolmaster – whereas a fully qualified surgeon was and is a great position – and, despite committing suicide, had died with his reputation intact (as he had been officially judged to be only temporarily deranged). Knowing Arthur, the *Mail* may have misunderstood the clergyman's salvo in a vital way. The latter had perhaps only fictionalised the *name* of the murder location. 'Substantial truth' means most but not all of the facts, while 'under' means the title the data dangles beneath is openly fictitious – but nothing else. Frustrated as much as they were excited that they might be on the verge of a worldwide scoop – the genuine solution to this infamous mystery – the newspaper dispatched one of its canniest reporters up north to meet with the vicar. As delicately as possible he was to see if the clergyman would be prepared to go on record and come clean as to exactly what was fiction and what was fact in his narrative. The following is our reconstruction of this encounter based on the subsequent *Daily Mail* article.

Arriving at the vicarage the reporter might have feared he was going to encounter a completely dotty cleric, perhaps in need of urgent medical care for his own wandering wits before he accidentally drowned a baby during a christening. If so, such fears were not realised. To the contrary the journalist found a confident, sharp-witted clergyman who was happy to host his guest for hours, yet whose sympathetic demeanour did not signal any softening in his determination to withhold the whole truth about 'The Ripper' – on this topic the vicar could be characterised as adamantine.

The journalist trotted out the lines that he and his bosses had agreed upon; he pointedly asked why the clergyman could not identify the murderer by name and the exact circumstances of his premature demise. As in: 'we need proof of your claims, reverend, in order to publish with integrity.' *The vicar calmly demurred,* 'Proof is impossible, under seal of the confession.' *He did blithely admit that he personally had known the murderer and, what is more knew with absolute certainty that he was guilty, though he, in mitigation, explained that 'Jack' suffered from a mental illness that was beyond his capacity to control or even, at times, to recall his bestial crimes.*

'Will you,' the journalist entreated, 'share this deceased man's name with us and our readers?'

'No,' replied the vicar, shaking his head, without any rancour. It was the kind of negative response that exhibited the rock-like sanctimony of a Christian Warrior who had just been asked, rather impertinently, if he would mind denying the literal truth of the Virgin Birth, the Trinity and the Resurrection.

As if aware he looked a tad sanctimonious, the vicar assured his guest that there was nothing personal in his refusal, or that he meant to cause any discourtesy towards the readers of The Daily Mail. *He told the journalist he would never be sharing the secret with anybody.*

The journalist perhaps tried to appeal to the cleric's vanity: 'I have been authorised by my chief to inform you, reverend, that if you do not make clear to me, right now in this interview, what parts of your "Whitechurch Murders" are factual, we will not publish it – and you will find no other reputable newspaper will be sympathetic to your cause.'

As he sipped his sixth cup of tea and stroked his white beard, the vicar must have shrugged: 'Then by all means don't publish,' he replied, as he smiled sweetly at the younger man.

Looking over the vicar's article, the persistent if perplexed reporter thought to inquire if he, the vicar, had heard this madman's confession?

Finally the shale of ice between them began to thaw a little.

'Not I,' replied the vicar, 'a "brother clergyman" of mine heard the poor man's confession.'

'Are you going to tell me this other clergyman's name, vicar?' He shook his head with the same amiable refusal. The journalist smiled back at him, leaned forward and asked in a low voice; could you not even give me a 'guarded hint'. After a pregnant pause a little more of the story not contained in the vicar's article peeped out from above the parapet of this one-man Jericho's Wall.

'The murderer died', lamented the vicar as he bit heartily into a scone, 'very shortly after committing the last murder.'

The two men said nothing.

An implication sat heavily in the air, one as thick as the proverbial London fog. After unburdening his tormented conscience to a priest 'Jack' surely must have taken his own life. Reaching the end of his scheduled interview time with the patient clergyman, and needing to catch a train, the journalist tacked again; he tried to arouse the vicar's ire to force him to make a slip. Something like: 'Well, at least we can assure our readers, vicar, that according to the trusty word of a man of the cloth this infernal beast is safely in his grave.'

On cue the vicar bristled at this crude denunciation of a fellow, English gentleman he had once known; the journalist could see the pained cleric obviously recalling the madman with respect and affection. 'Sir, I'll have you know that before he was defeated by illness, he was engaged in rescue work among the depraved women of the East End', before lamenting, 'eventually his victims'.

'He wasn't a clergyman too, was he vicar?'

The sheer effrontery of this query nearly caused the vicar to remonstrate with something like: 'Certainly not, he was a ...' Whatever the clergyman was about to divulge he caught himself in time. He calmly switched gears to share with the wily reporter that the murderer had acquired – somewhere, somehow – the necessary anatomical skills: the assassin was 'at one time a surgeon'.

At the door the clergyman and the journalist shook hands and smiled. The former wished the latter a safe trip and apologised for his wasted journey. The journalist knew he had extracted a few further nuggets of gold about this alleged Whitechapel solution but the motherlode still lay well out of reach.

And then at virtually the last possible moment the 'north country vicar' made a request that nearly broke the whole story wide open. At least, if the newspaper was prepared to pursue a big clue the clergyman had so generously – if unwisely – handed to them like a well-stuffed Christmas stocking.

'I must ask you not to give my name,' the vicar entreated, 'as it might lead to identification.' The journalist remained smooth and agreeable, but at that moment he knew the stubborn yet affable cleric meant that his surname could somehow, posthumously, identify the perpetrator of the crimes.

'Good God – the journalist must have mentally exclaimed; this priest must be related to the deceased killer!'

Going over the journalist's account of his interview with the sphinx-like vicar – a sphinx who may have partly divulged how to solve his riddle – the editors in London would have thought that the latter's surname was unlikely to be the same as 'The Ripper'. Yet he was sufficiently connected to this deceased gentleman that his name could trigger recognition among somebody reading the Daily Mail *which suggested he might be linked by marriage.*

If the 'north country vicar' really was Reverend Arthur du Boulay Hill, the most cursory checking would have shown that he was a cousin of a celebrated Victorian: the late Colonel Sir Vivian Majendie. By marriage, Arthur's family was also attached to the extended clan of another famous Victorian: the late Dr Robert Druitt. One of Arthur's brothers-in-law was Charles Druitt who lived in Dorset; he was one of Dr Druitt's sons and also a Church of England clergyman.

Could he have been the 'brother clergyman' who took the confession of the maniac?

Was there anybody on the newspaper's staff who could recall that strange story from 1891 of a 'West of England' politician who was shooting his mouth off about the fiend being a surgeon's son who had killed himself while in the grip of some kind of violent mental affliction? The west would generally fit the broad location of Reverend Charles Druitt's parish. If the same intrepid journalist who had just returned from the north had now been sent west, he would have quickly discovered that Reverend Charles' parish was interchangeably called Whitchurch Canonicorum or Whitechurch – the name which appears on his parish stationery. Was the enigmatic vicar, therefore, trying to supply a guarded hint as to the identity of the murderer after all? He had volunteered on a silver plate that his own name was recognisably connected to the murderer's and his clerical brother-in-law's parish matched the redundant title of the article. The next line of inquiry would have been to simply find out if some wing of the Druitt clan had a tragic member who had died prematurely in 1888 or, even more incriminatingly, who had committed suicide in that year.

Though Colonel Majendie, their close friend, was safely in the arms of his maker, Macnaghten and Sims, after reading that article about the vicar – especially his claim about his name – must have braced themselves. The vicar's amateurish intervention could have led to days of unwanted publicity. However, so far as we can learn, the *Daily Mail* chose not to pursue any such lines of inquiry. We believe potential libel suits from influential members of society related to the churchman, not to mention the Church of England itself, dissuaded the decision-takers at the newspaper from turning the story into a 'seven-day wonder'. And so the decision, probably reluctantly, was taken not to publish the vicar's name or his article. Instead they published their own candid report on a story they could not publish. Perhaps this was done in the hope that somebody would recognise who these characters might be and hopefully prompt someone to communicate with the newspaper and supply verifiable information – in effect to do their dirty work for them. This was *The Daily Mail's* provocative headline of 18 January 1899 and the stunted scoop still provoked worldwide interest and puzzlement:

WHITECHAPEL MURDERS
DID 'JACK THE RIPPER' MAKE A CONFESSION?

The resulting article also showed that Macnaghten's and Sims' plan – to nullify the vicar by using a major – was working a treat. Major Arthur Griffiths' debut of a disguised Druitt the month before is referred to as the new yardstick against which other spurious claims on this mystery must now be measured, including this meddlesome vicar:

> Certainly Major Arthur Griffiths, in his recent work on 'Mysteries of Police and Crime', suggests that *the police believe the assassin to have been a doctor, bordering on insanity, whose body was found floating in the Thames soon after the last crime* of the series; but as the Major also mentions that this man was one of three known homicidal lunatics against whom the police 'held very plausible and reasonable grounds of suspicion', that conjectural explanation does not appear to count for much by itself. (Our italics)

We believe that Macnaghten and Sims must have read those words with a sigh of relief and satisfaction. Their efforts to muddy the waters, placed on hold in 1894, had now come to fruition four years later. If the Chief Constable had agreed with Reverend Charles Druitt that he, and his brother-in-law, must use a mixture of fact and fiction to protect the family, he might, with his backslapping relations with the press, have anticipated that it would be very unlikely for a national newspaper to publish such an overtly ambiguous account.

Sure enough, the clergymen's balloon was quickly and quietly deflating on schedule. The timing of the vicar's intervention also confirmed another aspect of the case Major Griffiths had revealed on Macnaghten's behalf. The so-called 'Jack the Ripper' had not killed up to a dozen women between 1888 and 1891, but only five 'unfortunates' over a season. As with so many who were perplexed by the new timeline for the sensational crimes, the *Daily Mail* did not grasp that the police must have been humiliatingly chasing a ghost for years as they mistakenly thought subsequent Whitechapel homicides were by the same hand. Macnaghten had obscured this embarrassment via the Major by pretending that the police knew *at the time* that Mary Jane Kelly was the last victim of this assassin whose brain – so it was self-servingly claimed – must have been turned to something like curdled oatmeal by his unspeakable performance in Miller's Court:

> We thought at first the vicar was at fault in believing that ten years had passed since the last murder of the series, for there were other somewhat similar crimes in 1889. But on *referring again to Major Griffiths' book*, we find he states that the last 'Jack the Ripper' murder was that in Miller's Court on November 9 1888 – *a confirmation of the Vicar's sources of information.* (Our italics)

Ironically, the vicar's candid admission of mixing fact and fiction about a deceased Ripper was being unfavourably compared to a reliable authority, Major Griffiths, but readers could not know that his version too was a mix of fact and fiction, albeit covertly (and that both profiles were likely of the same man). We think 'Good Old Mac' used his friendly relations with a journalist to brief him against the vicar, and in so doing he may have blundered by revealing *how* the Vicar's Ripper died, which the latter had refused to divulge. From the *Western Times* of 19 January 1899:[11]

LONDON LETTER – JACK THE RIPPER

In police circles there is the most deep distrust of the new version as to who Jack the Ripper really was. The new version is that he had been a surgeon and engaged in rescue work in the East End, and then, after confessing his crimes to a clergyman who told the story to another clergyman, now the narrator, *committed suicide in the Thames*... Naturally one story is as good as another, and the police offer none of their own, but prudently deny [it].... But the mystery *will be solved some day*. (Our italics)

It would be George Sims who would have to reverse this bungle – with as much bracing hypocrisy as he did against MP Farquharson – by unfairly portraying the vicar as ignorant and naïve. The famous true crime writer would gruffly assert he could prove that the real killer had no time to confess because he killed himself immediately, which meant ignoring that Major Griffiths had admitted there had been three mysterious weeks between the murder of Mary Jane Kelly and the self-murder of the mad, middle-aged physician in the Thames River. Obviously Macnaghten and Sims decided that desperate times called for desperate measures (never was the 'custard and mess' put-down truer than the slop he now peddled as *haute cuisine* to discredit Vicar Arthur du Boulay Hill's stillborn revelations). From *The Referee* of 22 January 1899:

There are bound to be various revelations concerning Jack the Ripper as the years go on. This time it is *a vicar who heard his dying confession*. I have no doubt a great *many lunatics have said they were Jack the Ripper on their death-beds*. It is a great exit, and when the dramatic instinct is strong in a man he always wants to an exit line, especially when he isn't coming on in the little play of life any more. (Our italics)

After that opening salvo of lies and bluster Sims then tries to put a bandage on the raw wound for Macnaghten; the police had narrowly missed the English patient.

> I don't want to interfere with this mild little Jack the Ripper boom *which the newspapers are playing up* ... but I don't quite see how the real Jack could have confessed, seeing that he committed suicide after the horrible mutilation of the woman in the house in Dorset-street, Spitalfields ... . [The Ripper] was in the last stage of *the peculiar mania from which he suffered.* He had become grotesque in his ideas as well as bloodthirsty. *Almost immediately* after this murder he drowned himself in the Thames. *His name is perfectly well known to the police. If he hadn't committed suicide he would have been arrested.* (Our italics)

It seemed to do the trick, along with the reticence of the vicar who seems never have contacted the media again. A Whitechapel murderer who confessed to a clergyman was a one-day wonder in the press and then, with no follow-up or sequel, it was instantly forgotten (and not rediscovered until 2008 by researcher Chris Scott). Interestingly French newspapers were fascinated by the vicar and unlike their English counterparts tried to make sense of the title Whitechurch.

MURDERS OF WHITECHURCH

> [The vicar] presents this twofold peculiarity of having been written by an ecclesiastic and to make known, in a fictitious form, the (truth) on Jack the Ripper, the mysterious murderer whose crimes bloodied, formerly, the district of Whitechapel. It will be remembered that, during several months, it was not long before a week was discovered in the morning, in some deserted street, the mutilated cadaver of a bad girl. The police never managed to discover the culprit; then, these repeated murders stopped suddenly; *it was supposed that the assassin was dead, and it was thought possible to identify him with a dangerous madman, whose body was recovered in the Thames about this time.* (Our italics)

The propaganda efforts involved initially Major Griffiths – a puppet with the strings pulled by Mac – then by the Chief Constable himself anonymously briefing a reliable reporter. Within days it had been followed up by George Sims supplying the *coup de grace* with his literary shiv in the clergyman's back. All this was done to persuade the public that these two deceased 'Ripper' candidates were a pair of entirely separate men.

This ludicrous notion had seemingly gained adherents across the Channel as we see in the *Journal des Débats* 2 February 1899, discovered by the American writer and researcher Mark Kent (PA USA)).

> *This hypothesis is believed by the author of the novel* [sic]. He claims to have received in confession the confessions of the real criminal who authorised him to publish the tale at the end of ten years, with the *necessary alterations to disrupt all research*. The reporters, as we think, hastened to interview for clarifications. The vicar has naturally withdrawn behind the secret of confession. He merely stated that Jack the Ripper was a surgeon, dead today, a man of the best world, of unblemished reputation, and to whom the mania of the crime had come, cruel irony, since he had affiliated with a league for the moralisation of women of bad life! Which proves that when you enter a league, you never know where it leads you. (Our italics)

In a media game of ping pong the French interest in the eccentric vicar was noticed by elements of the English press, for example in the *Evening Express* of 1 June 1899:

> Our neighbours across the Channel sometimes profess to know more about us than we know ourselves., but it is rather startling to read in such a well-informed paper as the *Journal des Débats* that the novel [sic] which is agitating England at this moment is 'The Murders of Whitechurch'. It is said to be the true story of the Whitechapel Murders as confessed to a country vicar. 'Jack the Ripper' was a highly respected doctor, whose mind had been warped by joining a National Protestant League, and he made the confession with the stipulation that it should be made public at the end of ten years. Whitechurch N.P.L. brings the excitements quite close home...

His precarious health finally took its toll on Reverend Charles Druitt; he died on 20 October 1900. Emily Druitt wrote from Whitechurch to her sister, Gertrude, in Strathmore Gardens who was too ill to attend the funeral: 'This morning we went to church at 9:30 following Charley [in the coffin] in due order the church was very full altogether; there were 19 officiating clergy. Arthur [du Boulay] Hill who has made all the arrangements walked with us as mourners.' Charles' widow, Isabel Majendie Druitt, wrote a touching tribute to her husband in a private letter to his sisters, shortly after his death. In the letter dated 20 October 1900, she seems comforted to be able to assure them that he died with a clear conscience, because all that he did in life was done with the best intentions, right and pure, and Charles always walked with Our Lord:

My Dearest and Kindest Sisters

Just now my one thought is the deepest, deepest thankfulness for these 12 years of perfect happiness-and my darling was *so content and untroubled but there is nothing to be troubled at.* He was always standing in the presence of his master every thought and every motive utterly single-hearted in his service-and now he sees his face. (Our italics)

For a woman who had endured so much it was no small mercy that Isabella Druitt passed away in late 1899, ahead of her beloved Charles. She died knowing that, as planned, the 'north country vicar's' revelations had fulfilled Montie's last wish, but for the family the sky had not fallen in. There was no no need for Macnaghten, with Sims as his mouthpiece, to ever mention the 'drowned doctor' solution again. Yet like addicts who claim they just need one more hit, they could not leave it alone. Macnaghten's penchant for public relations meant he could keep propagating a 'shilling shocker' version which improved the Yard's reputation. Mac and 'Tatcho' seem to have felt the coast was clear and, as a consequence, they shaped the public narrative about the escape of 'Jack the Ripper', confident that the press – and anybody who knew the Druitt clan – would remain clueless as to whom they were specifically referring. This would include all other police figures who had been involved in the case – but Macnaghten had taken steps to neutralise the grumbling and scoffing of his colleagues.

The Big Sleep

From 1902, in his 'Mustard and Cress' columns in *The Referee*, in interviews, his large 1907 piece for *Lloyds Weekly* magazine, and in his memoirs ten years later, Sims as Dagonet added details to the profile of the 'mad doctor'. These details were unknown to Major Griffiths because they had not been included in either version of Macnaghten's 1894 memorandum. For example, that the doctor had been twice a voluntary patient in private asylums suffering from a 'peculiar mania', that he had confessed to his physicians treating him that he wanted to savage East End 'harlots', that his close 'friends' suspected he was the killer – though apparently only *after* the murder of Mary Jane Kelly – and when they moved to have him re-sectioned they found he had vanished from his palatial abode. The friends alerted the police chiefs at Scotland Yard, who in turn somehow already knew about him being the likely 'Ripper' and had launched a dragnet to arrest him. A month later he floated to the surface of the Thames (initially Sims dated this correctly as 31 December 1888, but after a few years he had begun backdating the recovery of the corpse to *early* December).

In 1903 a fierce-looking Polish immigrant named Seweryn Antonowicz Klosowski, who went by the name George Chapman, was convicted and executed for poisoning one of his mistresses (though he was suspected of having bumped off two other woman who had also tragically become this violent misogynist's 'other half'). Since in 1888 he had lived in Whitechapel, there was plausible press speculation about whether or not he had been 'Jack the Ripper'. This notion seems to have bothered Macnaghten, who by then was Assistant Commissioner of CID. At the Yard, where he was deliriously happy to be in charge of solving crimes while free of the killjoy Anderson. Mac, alone, had learned how close their search in asylums, at home and abroad, had come to catching the real 'Jack'. His efforts to communicate that truth, albeit veiled and improved for the public, had been in effect since 1898. It had accelerated in the early Edwardian years as Sims' assured his readers 'the police were in search of him alive when they found him dead'.

The media focus on George Chapman threatened to undercut that carefully nurtured revision which had, since 1888, to some extent, restored the Yard's dented reputation for competence and efficiency, at least in regards to 'The Ripper'. We think the police chief briefed a reporter whom he could trust to try and wrench the narrative back to the Druitt solution, as reported in *The Dundee Evening Post* of 25 March 1903:

'The [George Chapman] theory is reasonable enough' said *a gentleman well versed in the annals of crime*, to a press representative on Monday, 'but *I have every proof – of a circumstantial and private character*, of course – *in my possession* that Klosowski and Jack the Ripper are not identical personages. *Some day the truth concerning those murders may be revealed*. Meanwhile it is pretty safe to affirm that a report circulated at the time, that they were committed by *a student of surgery suffering from a peculiar form of murder mania* was the true one. It has even been definitely reported that *the student – long since dead* – has been identified to the *satisfaction of the police* as the guilty man. But all this apart, the series of crimes in the two cases are as distinct that I should scarcely suppose any student of criminology could accept the conclusion that with the capture of Klosowski the mystery of the Whitechapel murders has been solved.' (Our italics)

The smooth operator Macnaghten had nonetheless managed to make another slip-up (he had even used the same sunny phrase about the truth coming out 'someday'). It was a natural mistake: no doubt having not thought about Montie Druitt for some time, years even, the Assistant Commissioner forgot that the cover story was that the gentleman murderer had been a middle-aged, qualified surgeon. Instead the chief's powerfully retentive memory reached back to what he had learned in 1891; Druitt had actually been a young, medical student who had not completed his studies (Montie had only 'dabbled in science', as Sims had put it accurately in 1891).

And yet again it would fall to George Sims, as Dagonet, to clean up this small mess of his pal's making when, the following day, the retired Chief Inspector, Frederick Abberline, began enthusiastically briefing a reporter from *The Pall Mall Gazette* that the poisoner Chapman must also be the Whitechapel killer. Abberline was asked about the suspect who drowned in the Thames and revealed that he must have been told a fraction of the truth by Macnaghten. For example, Abberline knew that Druitt was included in a Home Office Report that did not categorically say he was the solution. This was perfectly true of the filed version. Macnaghten had, however, withheld from the same police sleuth he admired, what he had learned 'several years after' Abberline had retired; this suspect had confessed to a priest and had been the unidentified English patient fleeing from a French asylum. The oblivious Abberline even tells the journalist that he has interrupted him while composing a letter to none other than Macnaghten; he is about to inform the new Assistant Commissioner about the Chapman 'solution'. He dismisses the 'drowned medical student' solution, completely oblivious that it is 'Good Old Mac' who is the secret orchestrator of this propaganda – as recently as just the day before the ex-Inspector was interviewed.

Pushing back against Abberline, without naming him, in his column Sims tartly plays the Home Office report as a trump card: as being definitive and having been seen by Major Arthur Griffiths. What he is not revealing is that this is the 'draft' version of the same document, one that was never sent to that department of State nor filed in Scotland Yard's archive (Sims dealt with Abberline having correctly remembered that Druitt was a 'young doctor' or 'medical student' by ignoring it).

The famous writer is on firmer ground when he debunks George Chapman as the Whitechapel killer due to the method and motive of the homicides being so starkly different:

> I have no time to argue with the gentlemen, some of them ex-officers of the detective force, who want to make out that the report to the Home Office was incorrect. But putting all other matters on one side, it is an absolute absurdity to argue that a cool, calculating poisoner like Klosowski could have lived with half a dozen women and put them quietly out of the way by a slow and calculated process after being in 1888 a man so maniacal in his homicidal fury that he committed the foul and fiendish horror of Miller's-court. A furious madman does not suddenly become a slow poisoner. 'Jack the Ripper' was known, was identified, and is dead. Let him rest.

In the same year Reverend Arthur du Boulay Hill returned briefly to the local media spotlight, this time with an unambiguous triumph as recorded by the *Grantham Journal* of 4 September 1903. It also shows that English class-stratification extended even to horticulture:

> Horticultural Show – The annual show of the East Bridgford Horticultural Society was held on Tuesday last, in a large marquee erected on a piece of ground facing the cricket field. The exhibition was divided into three sections, *the first limiting the competition to gentlemen, professional gardeners, and farmers; the second to tradesmen and gardeners; and the third to labourers,* and there was a stipulation that all the specimens should be grown by the exhibitors. The first-class included some extremely fine flowering plants, collections of fruit, flowers, and vegetables, considering the backward season experienced, and the vegetables were surprisingly good. *The principal prizes were secured by the Rev A Du Boulay Hill, the president of the Society,* and Mr W F Fox, J P and Dr C H Duff, two of the vice presidents. (Our italics)

In the years before the First World War, police detectives and chiefs not privy to the second stream of intelligence about Montague Druitt – which was all of them – voiced their dissent from the 'drowned doctor' so-called definitive solution. A solution they all seem to have wrongly assumed was some kind of empty, media-generated piece of flannel. Relieved of his duties at the accession of Edward VII, Sir Robert Anderson is never known to have commented on the 'mad doctor' controversy. He just repeated his Polish lunatic solution that we argue had originated with a manipulative Mac. The latter's puritanical boss had enthusiastically gripped this Pole with both hands as it reinforced his prejudice about 'unmentionable vices' (his 1910 memoirs caused uproar in the British Jewish community because, by then, Anderson's sincere but crumbling memory had added a Jewish witness who supposedly refused to testify against a fellow Hebrew. The retired chief was aghast at being denounced as both a fool and an anti-Semite – including by a spiteful Sims – but it is likely that he was conflating Jewish witness Joseph Lawende's affirming the 'Ripper' suspect William Grant as the man he had seen with Catherine Eddowes in the same year, 1895, that Macnaghten had first informed his arrogant superior about 'Kosminski').

As Sims was the public face and persistent proponent of the 'drowned doctor' solution he sometimes came under scrutiny from other perplexed journalists as to his source for his insider solution to the Whitechapel mystery. He usually replied with his own version of a jovial 'no comment'. Every now and then, however, he admitted he must be circumspect to prevent the ruination of the killer's ultra-respectable relations. A fellow reporter on *The Gloucester Citizen* of 9 January 1905 extracted such a concession from the celebrity writer with the top-floor contacts:

JACK THE RIPPER

Inspector Robert Sagar, who is just retiring from the City Police, is entirely *at variance with Mr George R. Sims as to the identity of 'Jack the Ripper'*. I see he has just stated, in an interview, that the City Police fully believed this man to be a butcher who worked in Aldgate, and was partly insane. It is believed that *he made his way to Australia and there died*. Mr Sims, from information which came under his notice, has told me on more than one occasion he is convinced that these murders were committed by a medical man who afterwards *committed suicide near the Embankment*. This man was well-known in London as subject of fits of lunacy, and *he belonged to one of the best families in town*. It is *consideration for his relatives which has prevented 'Dagonet' from making a full disclosure of such evidence as he possesses* ... The doctor in the Sims' theory was never in the asylum. (Our italics)

Regarding that last line the unnamed reporter is mistaken as Sims had written that his 'mad doctor' had been in a private asylum – twice. The paradoxical aspect of this 1905 comment by Sims is that he has already revealed so much about the deceased doctor that his prominent family's friends and neighbours would easily be able to recognise him *and them* – except that Sims' 'drowned doctor' solution is, as we know, a deflective mix of fact and fiction. Apart from Frederick Abberline, those who implicitly or explicitly rejected the 'drowned doctor' solution included the retired police figures Sir Robert Anderson, Donald Swanson, Major Henry Smith, Jack Littlechild, Tom Divall, Robert Sagar and Edmund Reid.[1] Even Mac's own protégé: the stalwart Fred Wensley, who would eventually rise to become Chief Constable of CID, and who, in his memoirs, would praise his mentor in gushing terms as a 'very great gentleman' seems to have been kept completely clueless about Druitt. Of these policemen, only Divall let the 'cat of the bag' by actually naming Macnaghten as his source of (dis)information, in his memoirs of 1929, irreverently titled *Scoundrels and Scallywags and Some Honest Men*:

> The much lamented and late Commissioner of the C.I.D. Sir Melville Macnaghten *received some information* that the murderer had gone to America *and died* in a lunatic asylum there. This perhaps may be correct, for after this news nothing was ever heard of any similar crime being committed. (Our italics)

The only truth here is that Mac's suspect was most certainly deceased and he, the police chief, had 'received some information' about him; directly and personally. This need to occasionally lend Druitt an American identity for misdirection purposes can also be seen in George R. Sims' most detailed article about the 'Ripper' murders for *Lloyds Weekly* magazine of 22 September 1907. After providing his usual profile of the best suspect being a middle-aged, English surgeon who drowned himself in the Thames immediately after eviscerating Mary Jane Kelly, we think Sims then does another variation on Montague with this suspect – as this specific person exists in no other data:

> The other theory in support of which I have some curious information, puts the crime down to a *young American medical student* who was in London during the whole time of the murders, and who, according to statements of certain highly-respectable people who knew him, made on two occasions an endeavour to obtain a certain internal organ, which for his purpose had to be removed from, as he put it, 'the almost living body'. Dr Wynne Baxter, the coroner, in his summing up to the jury in the case of Annie Chapman, pointed out the significance of the fact that this internal organ had been removed. But against this theory put forward by those who uphold it with remarkable details and some startling evidence in support of their contention, there is this one great fact. *The American was alive and well* and leading the life of an ordinary citizen long after the Ripper murders came to an end. (Our italics)

We can also add to this line-up of the misled a pushy alienist at the margins of the Whitechapel homicides of 1888, Dr Lyttleton Stewart Forbes Winslow. The flamboyant physician had inserted himself into the police investigation in order to lobby for his 'suspect'; a Canadian lodger and religious fanatic named G. Wentworth Bell Smith with zero evidence against him (he was cleared by the police). This did not stop Dr Forbes Winslow telling anybody who would listen, for year after year, that he had solved the case. On 9 September 1894 a few knife attacks in New York City led to idle speculation that the Whitechapel fiend was in town. Somebody at *The New York Sun* contacted Scotland Yard and received the expected denial, plus something unexpected: 'they have reason to believe that the author of the Jack the Ripper crimes *has been several years in his grave*.' (Our italics) This has to be Macnaghten. The following year the attention-seeking Dr Forbes Winslow began a tour of the States. On 31 August 1895 *The New York Sun* reported that the British celebrity medico had altered his usual account, perhaps to align itself with the paper's earlier scoop. Just this once he revealed: 'Somewhat later the body of the this *medical student was found in the Thames*. He had drowned himself ...' (Our italics)[2] This was a full three years before Major Griffiths would debut a revised version of the Druitt solution.

Also the sometime lawyer for William Grant, George Kebbel, confidently informed the press in 1910 that Grant was believed by police to be the real killer and was long deceased. Neither statement was true.[3] The brilliant painter and Garrick Club member Walter Sickert was fascinated by squalor and true crime. He told an anecdote that the murderer had been a medical student and lodger, whisked away by his widowed mother back to Bournemouth, where he conveniently died.[4] To varying degrees of certainty; Anderson, Swanson, Littlechild, Sagar, Divall, Winslow, Sickert and Kebbel seem to have believed their 'Jack' was deceased due to natural causes or had committed suicide.

In fact, Aaron Kosminski, G. Wentworth Bell Smith, William Grant and American con man Dr Francis Tumblety were still alive, or in Tumblety's case alive long after they were supposed to be dead (and maybe Robert Sagar's deceased Aldgate butcher was really living it up in Melbourne). We think that behind all of these stories is 'Good Old Mac' flattering and playing them all off against each other so that each smugly believed they knew the truth and that Macnaghten agreed with them. Yet only Mac's suspect and solution, Montague John Druitt, was deceased and a suicide (unknowingly Mac's school-boyish prank, over half a century hence, would cause havoc with researchers into this subject, and help besmirch his own reputation for reliability). As explained, this discrepancy between Macnaghten and all of his police contemporaries – which did puzzle a handful of Edwardians – was caused by the former not briefing the latter about what he had learned from the Druitt family in 1891, or even properly showing them either of his 1894 reports. Abberline, for example, could only have known about the official version's contents verbally from Mac, because he appears to be unaware that the 'young medical student's' own family strongly suspected their member's complicity.

The Assistant Commissioner and the popular writer obviously felt that they could not trust anybody with the secret outside of their rarefied circle, and had judged they could live with such a controversy as it was comparatively minor about a case that was by then a generation in the past. Until 1913, Sir Melville Macnaghten had never spoken of the Whitechapel 'Ripper' case in public – at least not for attribution. Whereas George R. Sims and his 'Jack the Gentleman' solution openly dominated the minds of Edwardians across the world to which a legion of illustrators would add the iconic top hat and medical bag. Yet glimpses of the truth are still to be found in Sims' 1907 article; Montie Druitt had likely been 'shrieking' and 'raving' in a French padded cell:

> '[The chief suspect] was a well-dressed ... doctor [who] had been an inmate of a lunatic asylum ... *his disappearance caused inquiries ... by his friends ... made through the proper authorities...* [he] committed suicide ... *a shrieking, raving fiend fit only for the padded cell* ... after the murder he made his way to the river ... and was drowned. (Our italics)

In 1913, however, Sir Melville Macnaghten, with his own mortality staring him in the face, would voluntarily come out from behind the curtain and declare that the identity of 'Jack the Ripper' was known and that he had solved the riddle – though, with much regret, too late to catch him.

'That remarkable man'

In the middle of 1913 the Assistant Commissioner of CID Sir Melville Leslie Macnaghten gave a farewell press conference. Though he was too discreet to admit it, he was retiring due to a serious illness (the sad onset of Parkinson's disease).[1] He was proud of his service, which included catching the wife murderer Dr Crippen and the pioneering of fingerprint identification as both a tool of investigation and for persuading juries it was credible evidence. It did not enter the heads of any of the assembled reporters to ask Sir Melville about 'Jack the Ripper' because he had started on the force in 1889. This was the year after the horrific murders had ended – or such was the revised timeline the popular memory had been manipulated to accept. Ironically the secret architect of this propaganda-driven backdating of the final 'Jack' murder, which was initially believed to be in 1891 to 1888, was, of course, none other than Macnaghten.

It was the retiring police chief who unexpectedly brought up the Whitechapel Murders of 1888. He quite startled the journalists by speaking with a mixture of certainty and opacity about the killer's identity, which he claimed to know without a scintilla of doubt. On this occasion, with his own knighted name on the line and yet under no pressure from the job – as he was unhappily departing it – Sir Melville spoke not only confidently but also quite wistfully of this unnamed maniac, almost as if he had met him.

Perhaps he had *met Montie, maybe at a cricket match at Lords, or of old Etonian Boys versus Old Wykehamist Boys, or, could it have been while visiting Colonel Majendie who had for a time lived almost around the corner from Montague who lodged at the Blackheath School?*[2] *It would have been perfectly natural for the up and coming lawyer to pay a call on the big shot whose relative was marrying Charles, his cousin, who was himself the son of a big shot. It would also have been natural for a handful of the senior, upper-class boys from Valentine's School to be taken with their teacher Mr Druitt, to 'take tea' and learn a thing or two from the highly respected Colonel. If he called on the colonel, was Mac there, still sulking after being blackballed by Warren?*

According to Sir Melville, 'Jack the Ripper' was a 'remarkable man' and a 'fascinating criminal'. What a strange even sickeningly complimentary thing to say about a mass murderer of defenceless women. The press of the UK, and beyond it the world, nevertheless enthusiastically headlined this completely unexpected scoop, as for example *The Evening Telegraph and Post* (UK):

'JACK THE RIPPER'
COMMITTED SUICIDE SAYS
HEAD OF C.I.D.
WHO REVEALS SCOTLAND YARD'S SECRET

The fact that 'Jack the Ripper', the man who terrorised the East End by the murder of seven women during 1888, *committed suicide* is now revealed by Sir Melville Macnaghten, head of the Criminal Investigation Department, who retired after twenty-four years of service.

'Frankly,' he said, 'I am sorry to leave the Force. I love the work and it will be a wrench to give it up,' but he said when one reaches sixty it is time for one to make room for others.

NO REMINISCENCES

There was no case of murder and no important burglary during his time which he did *personally investigate*. Sir Melville confessed that *the greatest regret of his life* was that he joined the Force *six months after* 'Jack the Ripper' committed suicide. 'That remarkable man,' he said, 'was one of the most fascinating of criminals. Of course he was a maniac but I have *a very clear idea of who he was* and how he committed suicide, but that with *other secrets* will never be revealed by me.'

DESTROYED SECRETS

'I have destroyed all my documents and there is now no record of the secret information which *came into my possession* at one time or another.' (Our italics)

Since he started as Assistant Chief Constable on 1 June 1889, and claims this was 'six months after' the murderer was deceased, 'The Ripper' must have taken his own life at the beginning of December 1888. In front of the tabloid throng was this upper-class, still matinee-idol handsome Assistant Commissioner, with a characteristic grin and a twinkle in his eye, claiming he had physically destroyed, for all time, definitive files about the killer's identity. Could he possibly mean it? Had he broken the law? If they were private papers regarding a prime suspect – who could, after all, never be brought to trial – maybe they were his property to burn as he saw fit. But still, the reporters must have pondered, it was a most irregular admission from an establishment figure – practically the establishment personified; Eton College, British India, a knighthood from Edward VII – about what was one of the most infamous cases in all of criminal history.

A satisfied Macnaghten felt he had no doubt achieved his media coup: a relatively minor, respectful article about his retirement as a notable public servant had muscled its way to the front page. No newspaper, however, made the obvious connection; Macnaghten was confirming what his friend George R. Sims had been revealing consistently since 1899 (and just once before in 1891) possibly because the retiring chief never uttered the words 'doctor' or 'Thames'.

That same year, 1913, we think that Macnaghten and Sims attempted to engineer some kind of literary immortality for Montie Druitt and the Whitechapel Murders, and for themselves. They convinced the prominent writer Marie Belloc Lowndes to write the novel *The Lodger* (in addition they persuaded her to provide a fictitious anecdote about her celebrated work's genesis, one that kept them out of it). In this best-selling fictional adaptation of the case the murderer is an English gentleman, an escapee from an asylum and his twisted motive is religious rather than social. He is neither a medical student nor a doctor – and he does not drown himself in the *immediate* wake of his most vile atrocity. George Sims and his 'Tatcho' lotion appear in the novel version, albeit unnamed, and are treated reverentially.[3] In both the novel and the original short story version (1911) Sir Melville is allowed to take an exquisite revenge on Sir Charles Warren by replacing his nemesis. The tall, handsome, charming Police Commissioner is Sir John Burney and is, obviously, a tissue-thin variation on Macnaghten.[4] It is due to the killer wrongly feeling cornered by this idealised Super-Mac in Madam Tussaud's Chamber of Horrors that prompts him to take his own life in Regent's Canal (Sims' home was opposite this waterway). In the short story – but notably not the novel two years later – the dead man's landlord identifies the body but keeps to himself his secret conviction that he is also 'The Avenger' serial murderer, just like William Druitt at Montie's inquest will keep to himself his brother's dual identity. Notably the victims are drunken women rather than street prostitutes (of course the victims of the 'Ripper' were both) which is possibly a nod all the way back to Dr Robert Druitt's advice on the consumption of alcohol in moderation only for young ladies.

Macnaghten in 1914, and Sims 1915, would write that the 'Ripper' was noticed by his 'people' – with whom he now supposedly cohabited – only ever being away from their home the same nights as the murders. This is a direct and shameless lift from the plot of Belloc Lowndes' best-seller, which, with one stroke, allowed Mac and Tatcho to sidestep the clerical confession and the French escapade. (For a fuller treatment of this interpretation of secret facts being hidden by fiction, *see* Appendix I).

Despite what he said at his press conference, and as excerpted in previous chapters, the following year Sir Melville did publish an entertaining book of memoirs, *Days of My Years*, focusing on his school days at Eton, his years in the Raj, and his quarter of a century of distinguished police work (in that book's preface he flatly denied he had ever said at his farewell press conference that 'Jack the Ripper' committed suicide six months before he started on the force, claiming an 'enterprising' journalist made it up.[5] This preposterous bluff must have been due to Mac having second thoughts about having given away the true date of Druitt's suicide, which in his book he would fudge as early November. Macnaghten had made a few small slips over the years – about the killer being a medical student rather than a fully qualified surgeon and about his being the same maniac as the Vicar's Ripper).

In his memoirs, Macnaghten devoted an entire chapter to the Whitechapel Murders titled *Laying the Ghost of Jack the Ripper*. As if chastened by his slip, he did not reveal much more about the deceased killer – not even how he committed suicide. Yet what Mac did add to the historical record was significant for those who noticed, and hardly anybody did – then or since. The retired and seriously ill ex-chief admitted that the 1891 murder after the last and most ghastly one of 1888 was, initially and mistakenly attributed by the police to the same miscreant (he seems to have forgotten there was one in 1889 too, the murder of Alice McKenzie, which *he* had also investigated). He characterises the madman's particular brand of sexual insanity as 'protean'; meaning such a man who could, at will, deploy equally plausible faces depending on the circumstance. He could thus remain just another face in the London crowd. As argued previously Mac also implies that there were facts about the murderer learned in 1888 that were superseded by 'certain facts' provided by 'his own people' some years later and which led to a 'conclusion'. In the final rhetorical flourish of his 'Ripper' chapter, Macnaghten reverts to deflective slyness: as in, no, [the unnamed] Montague had never been 'detained' in an asylum, instead he had been a *voluntary* patient and he had lodged at his secondary workplace and not with the usual landlords of tenements. General Warren, furthermore, had not resigned over the Whitechapel Murders. Macnaghten does refer, however elliptically, to the Druitt family as the locus of the 'certain facts' and to Montie's vanishing act some time after the Kelly murder; the 'protean' madman had managed to extricate himself from Miller's Court in some kind of functional state:

> I do not think that there was anything of religious mania about the real Simon Pure, nor do I believe he had ever been *detained* in an asylum, *nor lived in lodgings*, I incline to the belief that the individual who held up London in terror *resided with his own people*; that he absented himself from home at certain times, and that he committed suicide on or about the 10th of November 1888 after he had knocked out a Commissioner of Police and very nearly settled the hash of Her Majesty's principal Secretary of State.

We think that since Sir Melville did not destroy the official, archived version or the private version of his memorandum mentioning Mr Druitt's name as a Ripper suspect, there can be only one significant document he could have burned – if he really destroyed anything. This would be Montague Druitt's arrest as a Whitechapel suspect at some point in 1888, possibly the true figure behind PC Spicer's embittered and bombastic account of 1931. If Sir Melville did destroy Druitt's arrest record, he was right. Such a putative document or a list of arrests with his name on it – especially if Montie posed as a still active medical student to explain away bloodstains – would be a clincher today. As it was, the version of his 1894 memo he had created for public dissemination did not survive Macnaghten's death. That a reliable copy of it, at least, does exist is due solely to the covert actions of his third and favourite child, Christabel, who became the Lady Aberconway. An aristocrat by marriage (1910) and a kindly, iconoclastic progressive who mixed with famous writers and artists, Christabel Aberconway loved her parents, her husband, her children, her cats, her books and her art, and, according to her sprightly, witty memoir, she coldly detested her much older, conservative siblings.[6]

When Sir Melville passed away on 12 May 1921, his private papers became the property of his widow Dora, who died eight years later. They then fell into the hands of an older sister of Christabel's. At some point after her father's death, Christabel had a typed copy of his 'Ripper' report covertly made for her own archive. She even took the precaution of hand writing the pages mentioning the suspects' names, and details, to make sure the secretary or a servant could not leak Mr Druitt's name (and sure enough, the original memo by her father was neglected and lost by her sister's family). The only question for Lady Aberconway was what to do with the document which proved that the 'drowned doctor' was a real person. In late 1959 two events may have forced her hand. The first book about the Whitechapel murders since the 1930s was being readied by a journalist named Donald McCormick – who never felt hostage to the facts, not if they impeded a good yarn. He was going to accuse a fictitious Russian sabotage agent. At the same time, a relatively hip young television reporter Daniel Farson with his own show that focused on eccentrics and oddballs, *Farson's Guide to the British*, was readying a programme about 'Jack the Ripper' (though popular, Farson's episodes were little more than late night fillers as they were less than 15 minutes long).

By coincidence Christabel had a connection to Farson; her daughter-in-law Rose McLaren was a friend. Lady Aberconway invited the reporter for tea and provided him with a viewing of her copy of her father's memorandum. Farson was so ignorant about the Whitechapel murders – let alone the 'drowned doctor' solution – that he admitted in his 1972 book about the subject that he did not grasp the import of what he held in his hands. Dan Farson was the first person outside a very small and diminishing circle to know the name of the drowned man. The dowager held the young reporter to a condition that explains her long-standing reluctance to ever share the document's contents with established media – she asked for the name 'M. J. Druitt' not to be revealed on air (Farson agreed and simply held up his death certificate with the name blacked out. On air, he referred only to the man's initials: M.J.D.)

Belatedly realising he had a scoop and under the pressure of a broadcast deadline, Farson's research team tried to find further evidence of Mr M. J. Druitt's existence and, initially, drew a blank. Druitt's incorrect age, 41, misled the researcher to look up the wrong year by a decade for the man's birth certificate at Somerset House. At first Farson publicly despaired of ever confirming this man had lived, let alone drowned. By doing a bit of reverse engineering herself his researcher, Jeri Matos, found other Druitts and sources that signposted towards another member of that clan: Montague John who had been 31, not 41, when he killed himself in the river. Incredibly the misdirection of Macnaghten and Sims had come close to defeating the technological age of inter-continental ballistic missiles, plastics and television. Before the programme debuted, McCormick's book was published which had less to do with the historical truth than *The Lodger*. Very much her father's daughter, Christabel took steps to discredit its conclusions.[7] She revealed in a polite but pointed letter to the *New Statesman* that she had documentation by her father, Sir Melville Macnaghten, which named the likely killer. This was five days before Farson's programme aired on 13 November 1959, spoiling his scoop:

> I possess my father's private notes on Jack the Ripper in which he names three individuals 'against whom police held very reasonable suspicion' and states which of these three, *in his judgment, was the killer*. None of these three names is mentioned by Mr McCormick. (Our italics)

A reviewer for the same newspaper, Ralph Partridge, who had met Lady Aberconway and thought this might help with his request, probed to see if she would let him see and publish the alleged murderer's name. He argued that surely it could not harm anybody now with the world on the verge of the 1960s and space travel. Christabel's demurral expressed her concern over the disgrace and hurt that could *still* harm the innocent – and that she also knew, because her father must have told her, that the killer had not produced a family of his own:

> Dear Mr Partridge, Of course I remember you very well and was delighted to receive your letter. At the same time *it shocks me greatly*

when you suggest that the actual name of the suspected 'Jack the Ripper' should be given. *After all he might have a nephew or a niece, born about 1890, who would not yet be 70: they in turn might have a child just about to get married. It would not be very pleasant to know that your uncle or great uncle was suspected of being 'Jack the Ripper', would it!* I would love to show you my Father's notes sometime if they would interest you but only on condition that no names were revealed. (Our italics)

Within six years Montague John Druitt's name was published by another competing journalist and author; an American socialist trapped in London due to the lingering McCarthyite persecution. By hook or by crook, Tom Cullen gained access to a copy of Lady Aberconway's copy of her father's report. With vivid prose that expresses a pungent contempt towards all ruling elites, Cullen wrote what we consider the greatest work on this subject: *Autumn of Terror. Jack the Ripper, his crimes and times* (The Bodley Head, 1965). Cullen's book was the first – and until our two books, the last – to wholeheartedly embrace George Bernard Shaw's satirical notion of the killer as a deranged social reformer. We have argued that Montague Druitt was a mentally and morally deformed criminal motivated by all sorts of bestial urges, which we think he justified to himself by launching a Red reign of terror against the very establishment which had spawned him. Druitt used slaughter to 'heighten the contradictions' to force the ruling classes to confront and then do something about the disgusting slums mere streets away from their mansions and palaces – with demonstrable success. We end with the insightful, mostly ignored, historical recreation by Tom Cullen on Montague Druitt's inner turmoil:

Might not someone of Druitt's education and refinement whose mind was delicately balanced, at best, have been pushed to the edge of insanity by the sights around him in London's East End? The nightly spectacle of women selling their bodies for tuppence or a stale crust of bread ... What might it not have done to Montague John Druitt, whose mind had become unhinged? Such a man overwhelmed by a sense of hopelessness and futility, might he not have conceived it as his mission to call attention to these evils, even to the extent of committing murder? Stranger deeds have been recorded in history as springing from just such motives.[8]

Afterword

If that copy of Sir Melville Macnaghten's memorandum had not been typed up – and hand written – by Lady Christabel Aberconway, and if the archived version of the same document had been lost along with so many other Scotland Yard files over the years, we would not have Montague John Druitt's name on any document naming him as a Whitechapel murder suspect. If that were so, we would have to first identify the man behind the 'drowned doctor'; the Edwardian solution to a Victorian mystery – even prove that there ever was a real person pulled from the Thames at the end of 1888. We would have to reverse engineer from those later sources by learning that 'doctor' and 'surgeon' were used very loosely and interchangeably with 'medical student' without the student graduating (maybe even without registering). We would examine articles about Macnaghten's 1913 press conference; and his vital and candid – up to a point – *Laying the Ghost of Jack the Ripper* chapter from his 1914 memoirs; and the writings of Major Arthur Griffiths and especially of George R. Sims. We would have to locate the 1889 American newspaper article about an English patient in a French asylum; the 1891 articles about Dorset MP Henry Farquharson and his 'son of a surgeon' leak; and the strange intervention of a northern vicar in 1899 whose own name might somehow give away the murderer's identity. Eventually we would have found Mister – not Doctor – M. J. Druitt; a country doctor's son and nephew of a famous physician, a Wykaemist, an Oxonian, a barrister, a teacher, a cricketer and a Thames suicide. Genealogical research would show us that a relation of the Druitt clan was connected by marriage to the clan of a Home Office officer, Colonel Sir Vivian Majendie – a close friend of Macnaghten's and Sims' – had had his clan linked with the Druitts by marriage (a marriage to a Dorset clergyman whose parish's alternate name 'Whitechurch', matches no less, the title of that vicar's unpublished article). This would make it clear why the drowned, young barrister had to evolve into the drowned, middle-aged surgeon – a bit of gentlemanly misdirection to protect a pal's reputation.

Yet the default position of too many writers and researchers on this subject is that it could not be the original solution after all because, by implication, so many years of research and theorising about a mystery – that has not been one since 1898 – would expose too much research as a waste of time (a very debatable proposition). If the alternate scenario outlined above was real, with the two versions of Mac's report missing, these same writers and commentators, the ones who remain rigid and never want it solved, would be fiercely resisting the theory that this drowned lawyer was the 'drowned doctor'. The predictable objections would be that he was not a qualified surgeon, not middle-aged, and not a recluse (as depicted by Griffiths and Sims). We would be assured that it was either someone else entirely or he had never existed; he was just a handy myth no doubt created to improve Scotland Yard's tarnished image regarding the Terror of 1888.

With much handwringing about slandering an entirely innocent and tragic figure, such hypothetical naysayers would demand absolute proof be produced that Mr Druitt was Macnaghten's protean maniac.

Nothing less would do, they'd demand, than a police file – preferably by Sir Melville – that definitely named his fellow gentleman as a 'Ripper' suspect. We would reply: we do not have it, yet counter-argue that the preponderance of the surviving material strongly points to him being the drowned suspect. 'Not nearly good enough' would be the stiflingly doctrinaire reply; 'not without a primary source naming him as the fiend.'

In fact, we live in the universe where those Macnaghten documents do exist and do name M. J. Druitt as the likely 'Ripper'. With this new book, and its new material pointing to why Druitt was believed by a few of his contemporaries to be a serial killer, the goalposts will be, predictably, moved once more. *The demand would be to produce Montague's arrest record, or a transcript of his confession, or hard evidence he was ever in a French asylum under another name.* We counter that the preponderance of the available material – admittedly an incomplete and fragmentary record of the second act of this story – convinces us that these are, 'in all probability', the missing jigsaw pieces of a *solved* multiple-murder mystery. A resolution that has been broadly known since before Queen Victoria died.

Time magazine of 20 May 2008 covered a London exhibition, 'Jack the Ripper and the East End'. Though well-intentioned and well-received, this exhibition nevertheless reinforced the entrenched misconception that all the homicides between 1888 and 1891 were never solved – not even posthumously. There was a suspects' room in which Montague Druitt appeared alongside many others, as if they are all on the same level of historical plausibility. That he was the real person behind what millions of Edwardians believed – the mad gent who killed five of the dozen or so victims and in a tormented state drowned himself in the Thames – was, as usual, unknown. As Sir Melville had written in 1914, Druitt was *still* a face in the crowd; yet another long-shot suspect who had been supposedly shanghaied into the mystery by some Scotland Yard nabob probably motivated by the need to burnish his reputation and hustle his memoirs.

Also mentioned in the *Time* article, almost in passing, is an observation that rarely appears in most books on the subject; the murderer – surely inadvertently – had done some good. That the criminal was, in actuality, a Tory-turned-terrorist as we have tried to argue, lies tantalisingly hidden in plain sight:

Most middle-class and wealthy Londoners were blissfully ignorant of conditions in Whitechapel until the autumn of 1888, when Scotland Yard realized that a serial killer was loose in the area, and Fleet Street helped create the legend — and even the name — of the knife-wielding 'Ripper'. Until the brutal slayings ended some two and a half years later, sensationalistic coverage of the Ripper was relentless, his exploits recounted by reporters and artists in a manner that exposed the squalor of Whitechapel to a fascinated audience — and shaped London's perception of the East End. Playwright George Bernard Shaw once remarked that Jack the Ripper did more than any social reformer to draw attention to the intolerable conditions of Whitechapel's slums.

Did 'Super-Mac' and 'Tatcho' contrive *The Lodger*?

Despite all of Sir Melville Macnaghten's and George R. Sims' precautions to mislead the public and police there is one example of the damaging secret of the Druitts somehow leaking – by name. An Oxonian, a barrister and writer with a corrosive and cynical bent, Frank Richardson, wrote several books, poems and short stories that are not quite serious enough to be called satire and not quite clever enough to be called funny. He committed suicide in 1915 and is completely forgotten. He wrote some pieces for *The Referee*, was a member of the Garrick Club and wrote a brisk tribute to George R. Sims and his 'Tatcho' hair remedy in his book *Shavings* (Eveleigh Nash, 1911). Those connections provide a circumstantial case for Frank Richardson running into Sims – and Macnaghten for that matter – at the club for actors and writers (and a lone police chief who had aspired to go on the stage) and discussing the case. In 1959, Macnaghten's daughter, Lady Christabel Aberconway, would claim that her father complained to her that he was frequently pestered at that club for inside information about the true identity of 'Jack the Ripper'. Was one of his tormentors Frank Richardson?

Assuming the famously close-mouthed Macnaghten did not tell his inquisitor the truth, somehow this literary mediocrity penetrated all of the elaborate layers of disguise and misdirection – and learned the 'mad doctor's' real name. The probable connection is that when Richardson was briefly a young lawyer he practiced in the chambers of Charles Mathews, who had worked alongside and attended social events with Montie Druitt. Both were barristers of the Middle Temple and appeared in trials at the Winchester County assizes and quarter sessions. Later knighted, Sir Charles Mathews was a member of the Garrick Club with Sims, Macnaghten and Frank Richardson.

Richardson as a columnist had shadowed Sims for years and may have realised that the date of the recovery of Montie Druitt's body from the Thames was an exact match for that of the 'mad doctor' believed to be 'Jack the Ripper'. In a typically caustic novel called *The Worst Man in the World* (1908) Richardson revealed not only that he knew Montague's real name, he perhaps had also learned that Druitt was a part-time teacher too:

> Murder is practised solely by the barbarous or the insane. What art could thrive with such exponents? *Doctor Bluitt*, whose fantastic ability was so strikingly exhibited in his admirable series of Whitechapel murders, *flung himself raving into the Thames*. If only he had been sane, he, I fondly fancy, might have *founded a school*. What the art requires is a sane Doctor *Bluitt*. (Our italics)

One possibility is that Richardson, a lawyer with a patchy clientele – and thus time on his hands – was so curious to learn what Macnaghten and Sims knew that he did some research. Ten years later the very first author of a book entirely devoted to the crimes ascribed to 'Jack the Ripper' would be written by our fellow Australian (and Adelaidean) Leonard Matters. He checked which doctor drowned at the end of 1888. He could find no such suicide either in the records at the Royal College of Surgeons nor mentioned in any of the national dailies. As a consequence, Matters prematurely dismissed the 'body in the Thames' solution as nothing more than a myth created to improve the damaged reputation of the force. He was only half-right. By contrast, Richardson may have learned from a slip by Macnaghten or Sims that the murderer was not a fully-fledged surgeon and therefore his full-time profession had to be something else. If so, Richardson could look through the pertinent newspapers from 1888 and 1889, careful to cast his net wider than just the national papers, and in something such as the *Southern Guardian* find 'Sad Death of a Local Barrister' and hit the proverbial jackpot.

Succeeding where others had failed, Richardson found the Thames suicide, Montague J. Druitt; barrister, part-time teacher, sportsman and, he presumed, ex-medical student. Perhaps at the club he caught Macnaghten and Sims off-guard with his discovery. They entreated Richardson to please be mindful of the murderer's relations, as they themselves had been for nearly twenty years – and he agreed. As in, Richardson complied at not revealing the critical details that would

have clinched the suspicions of neighbours, friends or acquaintances:
'Thames suicide' plus 'young barrister'.

With a mixture of vinegar and melodrama that poisons all of Richardson's works, he played with the dead man's name by changing Druitt to Bluitt.

By 1908, the distinguished Reverend William Hough was vicar of St Mary's in Lewisham and Canon of Southwark in Surrey. Hough was married to Georgiana née Druitt. Surely their insular, gossipy community would know that she had a younger brother who in 1888, the year of 'The Ripper', had taken his own life in the Thames. What if one of them happened to read this second-rate novel? 'Doctor Bluitt' would only be a tiny crack, true, but from such modest fissures do boulders and buildings begin their inexorable degeneration into rubble and dust.

Frank Richardson's extraordinary scoop exposed the inherent fragility in disguising Druitt, which arguably Macnaghten and Sims always knew was a calculated risk in their tussle with the northern vicar, yet the ruse still held. It remained in place all the way to their deaths (in the early 1920s). Nobody, in fact, would learn the name of the 'drowned doctor' for another forty-one years (and that was partly due to happenstance).

We think the jolt they received over Richardson's relative ease at identifying Montague, and almost using his actual name in a work for public consumption, profoundly affected Macnaghten and Sims. They knew then that today, or tomorrow, or years in the future, at some point, the truth was going to come out. Consequently we think they decided to leave a legacy about the Druitt solution – yet do it in such a way that they would not be responsible for endangering the reputations of the Druitts and the Majendies. The way to do this was to shepherd the truth into a wholly, not partly, fictional story. Sims had exploited aspects of the truth in short stories such as *The Priest's Secret* and *Dr Swainson's Secret*. He had also created a recurring character, the female detective Dorcas Deane (she took over sleuthing duties due to her husband falling blind). Characters based on both Sims and Macnaghten appear in those stories, as do some elements of the Druitt solution.

In 1905, Sims, we presume, had assisted a hack writer in his orbit, Guy Logan, to create his dreadful serial *The True History of Jack the Ripper* in the tabloid *Illustrated Police News*. Montague Druitt becomes Mortemer Slade, a surgeon from an affluent and noble Yorkshire clan who escapes from an asylum to rampage not only against Whitechapel's poor women but also against his ex-fiancée and her new beau. It is an almost unreadable combination of the

Druitt solution and a Victorian penny dreadful. There are also shameless lifts from Sir Arthur Conan Doyle; the fiend is a criminal mastermind modelled on Professor Moriarty who ends up dead in a river having been struck by a fortuitous bolt of lightning. This happens while he is grappling with his private detective and Sherlockian nemesis (who exhibits a winning, affable personality perhaps inspired by Macnaghten). There are, nevertheless, in Logan's opus some insider facts amidst the 'shilling shocker' detritus. Henry Farquharson, apparently still being punished in death, makes a walk-on appearance as a viper-tongued Tory MP; a Jewish witness sees Mortemer with Catherine Eddowes (which is more accurate than the draft version of Macnaghten's report which has a Jewish suspect seen by a gentile bobby); the villain falsely informs his landlady he is 'going abroad' and muses to himself that he would rather die than live out the rest of his life in an asylum. After slaughtering Mary Jane Kelly and as a police dragnet fast closes, Mortemer Slade experiences chronic depression – even the loss of the will to live.

We believe that Mac and 'Tatcho' then decided that with the porous nature of their facade exposed by Frank Richardson, they would preserve the Druitt solution in a literary work by a more respectable, accomplished and up-market writer, one who would be prepared to let the pair appear as themselves in the narrative. They would generously return the favour by alluding, approvingly, to this definitive fiction-based-on-fact inspired by 'Jack the Ripper' in their own writings. Enter Marie Adelaide Belloc Lowndes. As a writer of sophisticated mystery thrillers, as well as dramas, plays, poems, essays, magazine pieces, reminiscences, royal biographies, and with her acute insight into the psychology of women and the economically pinched, Marie Adelaide Belloc Lowndes (1868–1947) should be better known and appreciated (as she was, by no less than the likes of Ernest Hemingway). Her fame and popularity may have stalled forever due to creating the original Belgian detective template that she felt was stolen by her opportunistic former friend, Agatha Christie.

Lowndes' enduring literary legacy would prove to be her fictionalised version of the 'Jack the Ripper' murders, her best-selling *The Lodger*, which first appeared as a short story in *McClure's* magazine in 1911 and was then expanded by the author into a novel in 1913. It caught the popular imagination and was adapted into plays, movies (one of Alfred Hitchcock's first) radio and television shows. Though several of the historical elements are substantially altered, the novella remains an insightful and chilling tale of some ordinary people's sickening realisation that they are harbouring an insane killer of strangers – but if they simply give him up they will be socially and economically destroyed. In other words, we argue it is the Druitt solution refracted through Lownde's sympathy for the poor and her canniness for an intriguing plot. For the rest of her life, Lowndes claimed that in 1910 she was inspired to write *The Lodger* after being a guest at a fashionable literary dinner in London. This is one of her accounts of what she heard at that dinner party:

> I sat at dinner next to a man who told me that a butler and lady's maid, who had been in his parents' service, had married, and set up a humble lodging house. They were convinced 'Jack the Ripper' had spent the night in their house before and after he had committed the most horrible of his murders. I told him that this might form the core of a striking short story.

She wrote this anecdote almost word-for-word four times in different memoirs across her long life and it never varies. No names were provided by the author of who hosted the party, the man she sat with, nor of the butler and the maid. Nothing is identifiable or individualised. For a famously observant writer it is an anecdote bereft of details, humour or colour. We judge it to be apocryphal. Lowndes associated with other writers and contributed a piece to *Living London* (1902) a socially conscious tome edited by George R. Sims. It is our contention that Sims, and perhaps Macnaghten too, briefed Lowndes on what they knew about the 'drowned doctor' solution.

In 1888 during the Whitechapel murders, as Dagonet, George Sims had humorously disparaged a laundress in Batty Street for causing an unnecessary fuss over a client's bloody shirt (Sims gave her a Cockney accent when she was actually German). In 1911, the author wrote a piece for the *Yarmouth Independent* of 25 February 1911 that may contain the nucleus of what he and Lowndes came up with to 'explain' the origin of her tale. Sims wrote that a few years ago a woman had come to see him who claimed that in 1888 she was an East End landlady and had hosted a suspicious lodger. The night of the double murder this man returned in the early hours, and she and her husband found in his black bag a knife and a shirt with bloodstained cuffs. The foreign lodger, supposedly an American doctor, hastily departed the next day. Now in 1907, this ex-landlady had supposedly recognised her ex-lodger and wanted Sims to inform the constabulary. He claimed he did, and they found nothing amiss. The real murderer,

Sims assured his readers, was the raving lunatic who drowned himself in the Thames. This is the tension that we see in the Edwardian sources about this fictional tale. It is the need of Sims and Macnaghten to simultaneously distance themselves from Lowndes and *The Lodger* while embracing elements of the text for their own purposes.

A major change she made in both short and long versions of the story is that the murderer is not disembowelling prostitutes in a narrow strip of Whitechapel and Spitalfields. Her serial killer is a middle-aged, quietly spoken toff and deranged religious fanatic. He styles himself 'The Avenger' by leaving a calling card at each homicide and is knifing loose women in the foggy streets all over London. He discerns their sinful nature from them being publicly inebriated. It is as if Belloc Lowndes was satirising the social reform theories of Dr Robert Druitt, who had advocated light wines in moderation for working ladies while despairing over how to solve systemic poverty.

Mr and Mrs Bunting are a mature, married couple of servants-turned-landlords who are edging ever closer to destitution due to having no lodgers for their ramshackle but clean and spacious abode in the West End. The arrival of an educated and affluent gentleman seeking rooms is, initially, their deliverance – even though he is quite eccentric; he immediately turns the portraits in his room around to avoid their eyes. But they hardly care when he pays the rent up front for several weeks. The improbable name the new lodger gives his landlords is 'Mr Sleuth' – an uncharacteristically weak choice by Lowndes – which he assures them they will easily remember if they think of hounds.

This may be a subtle joke by Macnaghten. He hated General Sir Charles Warren for terminating his police career before it had even begun. For all their long-lasting enmity, Macnaghten and Warren shared a hands-on approach to their jobs. In October 1888, Warren was much lampooned for running around Regent's Park testing whether two bloodhounds named Barnaby and Burgho could follow the scent of the Police Commissioner (a biased Mac would still denounce this canine-sleuthing effort as worthless in his 1914 memoirs). In *The Lodger* the notion of bloodhounds is also directly mentioned as a potential police tactic to track 'The Avenger' – and similarly disparaged as a waste of time and resources.

This is how Lowndes introduces a figure who is partly based on Montague J. Druitt, whether the author knew, like Frank Richardson did, his real name or not:

On the top of the three steps which led up to the door, there stood the *long, lanky figure* of a man, clad in an Inverness cape and an old-fashioned top hat... *a gentleman*, belonging by birth to the class with whom her former employment had brought her in contact ... . To her surprise, however, her companion's *dark, sensitive, hatchet-shaped face* became irradiated with satisfaction. 'Capital! Capital!' he exclaimed, for the first time putting down the bag he held at his feet, and rubbing his long, thin hands together with a quick, nervous movement...

He threw his head back and passed his hand over his *high, bare forehead*; then, moving towards a chair, he sat down—wearily. 'I'm tired,' he muttered in a low voice, 'tired—tired! I've been walking about all day, Mrs Bunting, and I could find nothing to sit down upon. They do not put benches for tired men in the London streets. They do so on the Continent. In some ways they are *far more humane on the Continent* than they are in England, Mrs Bunting.' (Our italics)

Separately Mr and Mrs Bunting start to notice circumstantial evidence that Mr Sleuth and 'The Avenger' are one and the same individual – an excruciating notion that they both make strenuous attempts to resist in their minds. It becomes increasingly more difficult, as their tenant is a pious Bible-reading recluse but whenever he does go out it is late at night and there is always another stabbing murder of a drunken woman by the time Mr Sleuth returns. He sometimes has what looks like bloodstains on his apparel, which he quickly burns. There are newspapers reports in which police announce what witnesses claim the elusive assassin looks like. Mrs Bunting, her relief only temporary, notices that the descriptions do *not* resemble their lodger.

This 'wrong' description is, nonetheless, a remarkably good fit for Montie Druitt:

WANTED

A man, of age approximately 28, slight in figure, height approximately 5 ft. 8 in. Complexion dark. No beard or whiskers. Wearing a black diagonal coat, hard felt hat, high white collar, and tie. Carried a newspaper parcel. Very respectable appearance.

Another excerpt of this description of the wrong man is also reminiscent of the drowned barrister: 'a good-looking, respectable young fellow of 28, carrying a newspaper parcel.' Here we have Druitt hidden in fiction while also being exonerated as a non-suspect.

Lowndes dips her hat to Robert Louis Stevenson and, we think, at Sims' gentleman maniac that Macnaghten must have assured her was the real solution. She has Mr Bunting's daughter Daisy reading from a newspaper about people's views and theories as to the identity of the murderer:

The AVENGER: A THE-O-RY

DEAR Sir—I have a suggestion to put forward for which I think there is a great deal to be said. It seems to me very probable that 'The Avenger'—to give him the name by which he apparently wishes to be known—comprises in his own *person the peculiarities of Jekyll and Hyde, Mr Louis Stevenson's now famous hero* ...

The culprit, according to my point of view, is a *quiet, pleasant-looking gentleman who lives somewhere in the West End* of London ... On foggy nights, once the quiet household is plunged in sleep, he creeps out of the house, maybe between one and two o'clock, and swiftly makes his way straight to what has become The Avenger's murder area. Picking out a likely victim, *he approaches her with Judas-like gentleness, and having committed his awful crime, goes quietly home again.* After a good bath and breakfast, he turns up happy, once more the quiet individual who is *an excellent son, a kind brother, esteemed and even beloved by a large circle of friends and acquaintances.* Meantime, the police are searching about the scene of the tragedy for what they regard as the usual type of criminal lunatic ... I confess that *I am amazed the police have so wholly confined their inquiries to the part of London where these murders have been actually committed.* I am quite sure from all that has come out—and we must remember that full information is never given to the newspapers—*The Avenger should be sought for in the West and not in the East End of London* ... (Our italics)

There is also a strong echo of Home Secretary Henry Matthews threatening the confederates of the murderer with the full weight of the law, here combined with the reluctant reward offered by the government for conclusive information, in another letter to the paper.

PARDON TO ACCOMPLICES.

DEAR Sir—During the last day or two several of the more Intelligent of my acquaintances have suggested that The Avenger, whoever he may be, *must be known to a certain number of persons*. It is impossible that the perpetrator of such deeds, however nomad he may be in his habits ... must have some habitat where his ways are known to at least one person. *Now the person who knows the terrible secret is evidently withholding information in expectation of a reward, or maybe because, being an accessory after the fact, he or she is now afraid of the consequences.* My suggestion, Sir, is that the Home Secretary promise a free pardon. The more so that only thus can this miscreant be brought to justice. Unless he was caught red-handed in the act, it will be exceedingly difficult to trace the crime committed to any individual, for English law looks very askance at circumstantial evidence. (Our italics)

At one point Mrs Bunting finds herself unexpectedly with a front-row seat at the official inquest into the murders of two of The Avenger's victims. As with William Druitt at his brother's inquest, she keeps mum about what she knows, or believes she knows, about the true identity of the killer. She also recognises George R. Sims, albeit he is not named but that is clearly whom she sees (it is also practically a de-facto advertisement for 'Tatcho'):

Many of the gentlemen — they mostly wore tall hats and good overcoats — standing round and about her looked vaguely familiar. She picked out one at once. *He was a famous journalist, whose shrewd, animated face was familiar to her owing to the fact that it was widely advertised in connection with a preparation for the hair*—the preparation which in happier, more prosperous days Bunting had had great faith in, and used, or so he always said, with great benefit to himself. *This gentleman was the centre of an eager circle; half a dozen men were talking to him, listening deferentially when he spoke*, and each of these men, so Mrs Bunting realised, was a Somebody... Very soon some of the important-looking gentlemen she had seen downstairs came into the court, and were ushered over to her seat while two or three among them, *including the famous writer whose face was so familiar that it almost seemed to Mrs Bunting like that of a kindly acquaintance*, were accommodated at the reporters' table. (Our italics)

The novella climaxes with Mrs Bunting accompanying Mr Sleuth – who is close to a crack-up – and her step-daughter, Daisy, on a visit to Madam Tussaud's. In the Chamber of Horrors they see that some other visitors are the Police Commissioner – the fictional Sir John Burney – who is himself escorting his *French* counterpart accompanied by the latter's daughter. The Commissioner is not a variation on Sir Charles Warren, the controversial police chief during the actual 'Ripper' murders, but in an exquisite bit of private, schoolboy jokey revenge it is instead quite simply Melville Macnaghten in all but name. Lowndes describes Birney as 'a tall, powerful, handsome gentleman, with a military appearance.' In the short story version of 1911 Lowndes introduces the Macnaghten-figure like this:

> *He was a tall, powerful, nice-looking gentleman with a commanding manner.* Just now he was smiling down into the face of a young lady. 'Monsieur Barberoux is quite right,' he was saying; 'the English law is too kind to the criminal, especially to the murderer. If we conducted our trials in the French fashion, the place we have just left would be very much fuller than it is to-day! A man of whose guilt we are absolutely assured is oftener than not acquitted, and then the public taunt us with "another undiscovered crime"!' (Our italics)

The description is lifted almost word-for-word for how Major Arthur Griffiths' described Chief Constable Melville Macnaghten in his 1898 book: 'Mr Macnaghten, the chief constable or second in command of the Investigation Department, is essentially a man of action. A man of presence is Mr Macnaghten – tall, well-built, with a military air ...'

Furthermore Madam Tussaud's was Mac's favourite haunt as a child and, as Assistant Commissioner, he had liaised with the French police over the science of fingerprint identification. In this scene the police chief reveals that while they have not caught the 'The Avenger' he does know his identity. As with the French debacle, the maniac has escaped from an asylum, and the authorities are desperately trying to locate him and have him recommitted. The Macnaghten figure, oblivious that the very same criminal is mere meters away, reveals in the short story version:

> 'Yes'. He spoke very deliberately. 'I think we may say—now, don't give me away to a newspaper fellow, Miss Rose—that we do know perfectly well who the murderer in question is—
>
> Several of those standing nearby uttered expressions of surprise and incredulity.
>
> 'Then why don't you catch him?' cried the girl indignantly.

'I didn't say we know *where* he is; I only said we know *who* he is; or, rather, perhaps I ought to say that we have a very strong suspicion of his identity.'

Sir John's French colleague looked up quickly. 'The Hamburg and Liverpool man?' he said interrogatively.

Here we see a mention of Germany, where Sims had described a violent criminal to pretend to write about a profile of 'Jack' in 1891, a profile that, as argued previously, is obviously Montague Druitt:

'Two murders of the kind were committed eight years ago—one in Hamburg, the other just afterward in Liverpool, and there were certain peculiarities connected with the crimes which made it clear they were committed by the same hand. The perpetrator was caught, fortunately for us red-handed, just as he was leaving the house of his victim, for in Liverpool the murder was committed in a house. I myself saw the unhappy man—I say unhappy, for there is no doubt at all that he was mad,'—he hesitated, and added in a lower tone,—'suffering from an acute form of religious mania. I myself saw him, at some length. But now comes the really interesting point. Just a month ago this criminal lunatic, as we must regard him, made his escape from the asylum where he was confined ...'

The Frenchman again spoke. 'Why have you not circulated a description?' he asked.

'We did that at once,' — Sir John Burney smiled a little grimly, — 'but only among our own people. We dare not circulate the man's description among the general public. You see, we may be mistaken, after all.'

'That is not very probable!' The Frenchman smiled a satirical little smile.

This is the same moment in the novelistic expansion of two years later:

'I myself saw him, as I say, at some length. But now comes the really interesting point. I have just been informed that a month ago this criminal lunatic, as we must of course regard him, *made his escape from the asylum where he was confined.* He arranged the whole thing with *extraordinary cunning and intelligence,* and we should probably have caught him long ago, were it not that he managed, when on his way out of the place, to annex a considerable sum of money in gold, with which the wages of the asylum staff were about to be paid. It is owing to that fact that *his escape was, very wrongly, concealed*—'

He stopped abruptly, as if *sorry he had said so much*, and a moment later the party were walking in *Indian* file through the turnstile, Sir John Burney leading the way.

Mrs Bunting looked straight before her. She felt — so she expressed it to her husband later — as if she had been turned to stone.

Even had she wished to do so, she had neither the time nor the power to warn her lodger of his danger, for Daisy and her companion were now coming down the room, bearing straight for the Commissioner of Police. In another moment Mrs Bunting's lodger and Sir John Burney were face to face.

Mr Sleuth swerved to one side; there came a terrible change over *his pale, narrow face*; it became discomposed, livid with rage and terror.

But, to Mrs Bunting's relief — yes, to her inexpressible relief — Sir John Burney and his friends swept on. They passed Mr Sleuth and the girl by his side, unaware, or so it seemed to her, that there was anyone else in the room but themselves.

Mr Sleuth looked round once more; he really did feel very ill — ill and dazed. How pleasant it would be *to take a flying leap over the balcony railing* and find rest, eternal rest, below.

But no — he thrust the thought, the temptation, from him. Again a convulsive look of rage came over his face. He had remembered his landlady. How could the woman whom he had treated so generously have betrayed him to his arch-enemy? — to the official, that is, who had entered into a conspiracy years ago *to have him confined — him, an absolutely sane man with a great avenging work to do in the world — in a lunatic asylum.*

He stepped out into the open air, and the curtain, falling-to behind him, blotted *out the tall, thin figure* from the little group of people who had watched him disappear ... (Our italics)

It is implied that Mr Sleuth has killed himself, somehow, though his body is never found. It is all kept unsatisfyingly vague. He vanishes and the remaining money he stole from the asylum is sent anonymously by the relieved Buntings to a charity hospital. In the 1911 original, it was clear how the Avenger ended his life – he drowned himself in Regent's Canal (George Sims lived opposite it):

Five days later *Bunting identified the body of a man found drowned in the Regent's Canal as that of his late lodger*; and, the morning following, a gardener working in the Regent's Park, found a newspaper in which were wrapped, together with a half-worn pair of rubber-soled shoes, two surgical knives. This fact was not chronicled in any newspaper; but a very pretty and picturesque paragraph went the round of the press, about the same time, concerning a small box filled with sovereigns which had been forwarded anonymously to the *Governor* of the Foundling Hospital. (Our italics)

We think the above is a fictional version of William Druitt identifying his drowned brother in 1889 and, just like Mr Bunting, keeping to himself the terrible secret of his dual identity. Did Sims, on Macnaghten's behalf, ask Lowndes to remove that line from the expanded rewrite? Was it just too close to the truth for their tastes? William Druitt had also left a sum of money to the Royal Victoria Hospital, Bournemouth, in his will of 1909, and in his case it was a very generous bequest. In his memoirs of 1914 Macnaghten would try to have it both ways: he praises *The Lodger* and its unnamed 'talented authoress' (as if he did not know Lowndes' name) but then adds a bit of literary jiu jitsu to highjack her plot's *deus ex machina*. According to Macnaghten, the reclusive 'Ripper' was out the same nights as the women of Whitechapel who were butchered. He uses a particularly off-sounding word to describe this circumstantial evidence: 'absented'. How can you be *absented* from your own home? You are not a prisoner and surely can come and go as you please. Macnaghten is referring, perhaps unconsciously, to Montie having vanished from the Chiswick asylum:

Only last autumn I was very much interested in a book entitled 'The Lodger', which set forth in vivid colours what the Whitechapel murderer's life might have been while dwelling in London lodgings. The *talented authoress* portrayed him as a religious enthusiast, gone crazy over the belief that he was predestined to slaughter a certain number of *unfortunate women*, and that he had been confined in a criminal lunatic asylum and had escaped therefore. I do not think that there was anything of religious mania about the real Simon Pure, nor do I think that he has even been *detained in an asylum*, nor lived in lodgings. I incline to the *belief* that the individual who held up London in terror *resided with his own people: that he absented himself from home at certain times*, and that he committed suicide *on or about* the 10th of November 1888, *after he had knocked out a Commissioner of Police* and very nearly settled the hash of Her Majesty's principal Secretaries of State. (Our italics)

The Avenger's victims are not 'unfortunate women', but rather homeless alcoholics. Druitt had been a paying lodger at the Blackheath School. Though not a religious enthusiast, Montague did have strong religious influences in his formative years and had confessed his crimes to a clergyman, and had been twice placed in lunatic asylums. Macnaghten gets around this with the word 'detained' meaning; committed by the State rather than as a voluntary, private patient, while the term 'Simon Pure' means a Christian whose piety is only a mask for hypocrisy.

Macnaghten also refuses to use the Thames finale, instead twisting his own metaphorical knife into the unnamed General Warren – who had not resigned over the Whitechapel case – and pointedly distances his account from Sims (and MP Henry Farquharson) for having claimed that Mary Jane Kelly's murder was followed by the killer's immediate suicide the same night. Sims had hyperbolically written in 1907: 'It would be impossible for the author of the Miller's court horror to have lived a life of apparent sanity one single day after that maniacal deed. He was a raving madman then and raving madman when he flung himself in the Thames.' In 1914, Macnaghten decided it was time to extend the gap by at least 'a single day', if not longer. Not a raving madman then and maybe not when he committed suicide either.

The year following those memoirs, and two years following the debut of *The Lodger* as a popular novel, George Sims also exploited the same novel's plot device to explain how the killer's people discovered his guilt. For the first and only time 'Blackheath' was correctly revealed to be the suburb where 'Jack' had resided but Sims must have judged, once more, the coast to be clear (there was, after all, the distraction of a World War underway). From *Pearson's Weekly* of 23 July 1915:

> ... the insanity of revenge upon a certain class of women ... in the case of the *mad doctor who lived with his people at Blackheath*, and who, *during his occasional absences from home committed the crimes* which won him worldwide infamy as Jack the Ripper. (Our italics)

Mac and 'Tatcho' had managed to have their cake and eat it too. They helped, we think, generate Marie Belloc Lowndes' novel that showcased the Druitt solution – on their terms – and enjoyed their flattering cameos in this acclaimed, best-selling work of popular literature. Montague Druitt and his clan remained safely unrecognisable to anybody who still remembered him and the cheeky pair of toffs could then 'borrow' the plot of this novel to avoid having to go anywhere near the clerical confession (and possibly revive the claims of a certain 'north country vicar', who was still alive). Apart from its literary acumen and entertainment value, the genesis and execution of *The Lodger* reveals an incestuous relationship between fact and fiction – and like the shame of incest it was roundly denied by all concerned.

In real life the police were hunting for the fugitive English patient from a French asylum and had missed him. A variation of this bungle is the very climax of Marie Lowndes' short story and her novel; with Macnaghten on the scene causing the demise of the serial killer without even realising it. This narrative arc broke decisively with the paradigm of murder and instant self-murder, relentlessly propagated by George Sims, due to the last and most ghastly murder causing a psychological implosion – confession by suicide. In his 1914 memoir Mac confirmed this gap; the madman must have been compos mentis enough to exit Whitechapel and then – somehow, somewhere – end his miserable existence. Cleaving much closer to the historical reality, Mr Sleuth is lucid if anxious in Madam Tussaud's and only commits suicide because he perceives that the police net is fast closing – and he does not want to return to live in an asylum. Only in the 1911 version, however, does 'The Avenger' clearly drown himself in a tormented state and subsequently have his dual identity posthumously concealed by the person who identifies his waterlogged corpse – like Montie's brother at Chiswick.

The Philadelphia Times
13 January 1889

WHITECHAPEL FIENDS
A Most Remarkable Story That Comes From Paris.
POSSIBLY THIS IS A CLUE
One of the Supposed Murderers, Sent to an Asylum Tells Much
That is Startling

From a Times *correspondent*

Paris, December 24. – About ten days ago the Scotland Yard detectives in London were notified by the chief of the Detective Department, in the Rue Jerusalem, that a clue had turned up here that would probably throw a strong light on the mystery of the Whitechapel murders. Two experienced officers who have worked on the case for months past in London at once came over and were so it is reported at once made acquainted with the following facts:

A few days previously a middle-aged man of respectable attire having the appearance of an Englishman, but speaking French fluently, with but a slight foreign accent, called at the Detective Bureau and expressed a desire to see the chief of the department. He gave an English name and described himself as a British subject, many years resident in France, and added that he was engaged as an attendant at a private retreat for the insane, some 20 miles outside the city, the address of which was also the name of the proprietor he gave.

On being admitted to the presence of the chief he said he believed he could afford some valuable information which might lead to the detection of the perpetrators of the Whitechapel murders. As the Chief was perfectly familiar with the particulars of these unprecedented crimes he was at once all attention and was soon in possession of the following remarkable statement:

THE MAN'S STORY

His informant said that he had been for five years engaged at the asylum as nurse and attendant upon the insane persons there confined. The institution was select, only twenty-five patients being received. The retreat was secluded standing in its own extensive grounds a quarter of a mile from any public road, and the terms being high, only sufferers from among the wealthy classes were confined there. The medical director, who was also the proprietor of the place, enjoyed a high reputation for the treatment of cases of homicidal mania.

Three weeks previously a new patient had been brought to the retreat. As at the time of his admission he was extremely violent, he had been given a private sitting room and bed room, and thus kept entirely apart from the other inmates. The chief's informant had been placed in charge of the new patient and had had the care of him ever since.

THE PATIENT ASKS QUESTIONS

On his admission he was at once placed under the opiate treatment and soon fell into a semi-conscious condition. He remained in this state for about 36 hours, when he rallied and inquired in excellent English of his attendant as to where he was and how he got there. In reply he was informed that he had been ill and was in a hospital. He named in rapid succession three or four London hospitals, asking in each instance if he was in this or that one. The attendant gave evasive replies and summoned the director. When the doctor came into the room he stared blankly at him and then repeated his questions, but this time with some incoherence, and it became evident that the man was relapsing into a condition of lunacy.

More drugs were given him and he again fell asleep. The director then told the attendant that the case was a rather remarkable one and that probably when the patient recovered consciousness he would accuse himself of all sorts of crimes, as the history of the case detailed to him by the medical men who had placed him in the retreat was that of a spasmodically homicidal lunatic who was impressed with the belief that he had already committed a number of atrocious murders. The director had no knowledge himself of English nor had anyone else at the asylum excepting this particular attendant, and the fact that he spoke English was heretofore unknown in the house.

TALKING ABOUT WHITECHAPEL

Twenty-four hours later the patient again recovered consciousness, but this time he was evidently unaware of his surrounding and not in his right senses. He talked incessantly of the Whitechapel murders and spoke as though he himself had perpetrated more than one of them. He fancied that he was conversing with the victims, went through the action of giving them money and then enacted the dreadful details of their slaughter and dismemberment. While this was in progress he broke into a frenzy of rage and fury and the services of two more attendants had to be called in to bind him down in his bed, hand and foot. Finally he became unconscious and relapsed into a heavy slumber.

This, said the chief's informant, had been the patient's condition ever since—long periods of sleep induced by opiates broken by spells of frantic ravings, in which he invariably went through the same pantomime of murder and butchery. The attendant added that he mentioned the names of men, women and places during these periods of frenzy, but whether they were those of persons and localities connected with the crimes in Whitechapel, he could not say, as he had only read the bare outlines of the case as given in the Paris papers. He knew, however, that a large reward was offered for the discovery of the criminal and that, as he informed the chief, coupled with a sense of public duty, had induced him to visit the prefecture.

THE CHIEF INVESTIGATES

The chief was so impressed by the man's story that he at once set off for the asylum, taking the attendant along. He found the facts as stated amply verified by the director, in as far as he was acquainted with them. His story as to the patient's reception only strengthened the police official's opinion that the matter was well worth following up. It was briefly as follows:

About a month previously the director had received a letter from a London physician asking if he could receive as an inmate of his retreat a patient of his suffering from insanity characterized by slight homicidal mania. The sufferer, whose name he gave, was, he said, wealthy and his friends were prepared to pay liberally for his treatment and accommodation. The director replied to this communication, which was couched in excellent French, that if the patient was brought over with the proper certificates furnished by two English physicians and was further submitted to examination by two French doctors, he would be received under the double set of certificates.

In reply came a letter stating that the conditions as far as the English doctors were concerned had been complied with, and adding that the patient, in [the] charge of his friends, would arrive at a certain hotel in Paris early in the morning of a day named. It was further requested that the director would secure the attendance of two Paris physicians at the hotel at ten o'clock on the morning of that day, so that the needful formalities might be completed without delay and the patient conveyed to the retreat. A sight draft on a Paris bank was enclosed in this letter to defray the expense of the physician's fees.

TAKEN TO PARIS

At the day and the hour indicated, the director with two physicians, experts in lunacy, and two attendants went to the hotel as arranged. The party from England had arrived. There were two gentlemen, both men under 40 years of age, one describing himself as a barrister and the other a clergyman. They said they were respectively cousin to and friend of the patient, whom they described as a man of independent means with no nearer relatives. They proffered their address cards both to the director and the medical men. They also brought a letter of introduction from the London doctor, who had been corresponding with the director.

The patient was lying, dozing on a lounge fully dressed. He awoke on the party entering the room and at once began to rave and mumble alternately. The English barrister, who spoke French fluently, explained the case briefly to the doctors, saying the brain had been failing for some six months but the worst symptoms had only developed within the last six weeks. The doctors examined the man, unhesitatingly pronounced him insane and countersigned the English physicians' certificates. The barrister informed the director that his unfortunate friend was an excellent French scholar, so that in his lucid intervals there would be no difficulty in understanding his needs and requirements.

OFF FOR THE ASYLUM

The French doctors then withdrew and the whole party left for the retreat. The two friends stayed only long enough to see the patient settled in his apartment and left, saying they would return to England at once. Three months fees were paid down in advance with an ample sum left to provide for any extras that the patient might require. In case of his death which was not deemed likely, as the doctors took a hopeful view of the case and his physical condition was good, the barrister was to be notified at once, and a weekly letter was to be forwarded to the London physician briefly indicating the patient's condition.

It was at once decided that one of the English detectives should enter the retreat and nominally assist the attendant in charge of the mysterious patient. He at once did so and it is understood that he is convinced from what he has heard of the man's ravings that he has been a participator in the fearful crimes that have for so long terrorized a large section for the inhabitants of the east end of London. The names of at least half a dozen real or fancied confederates, whom he has freely mentioned during his ravings, are also believed to be in the possession of the police.

PROBABLY A CLUE

At the Prefecture the officials, while refusing to confirm or deny the accuracy of the story, admit that they are working in collusion with the London detectives on the Whitechapel mystery. The location of the asylum is refused, as also the name of the suspect inmate. It has been learned, however, from one of the English detectives who came over, that inquiries in London had already resulted in a confirmation of the belief that the lunatic is implicated in the crimes of which he ceaselessly talks.

It has been ascertained that the London doctors who are supposed to have filled up and signed the certificate of lunacy were obscure practitioners who died within the last nine months, and further that the eminent physician who corresponds with the director of the asylum repudiates the letters and points out that they are written in a hand and from an address other than his. The actual address was found to be that of a small newsvendor's shop, where letters are taken in for strangers at a trifling charge. The names and officials given by the supposed barrister and clergyman also turn out to be purely fictitious. Not the slightest clue to the lunatic's identity is said to be forthcoming from his effects. The linen is not even initialled.

The police theory here is that the madman is one of a band of wretches who committed the murders that he became insane and that his companions in crime, fearful that his ravings would, in an English asylum, lead to the arrest of a whole gang, adopted this bold method of disposing of him.

APPENDIX III

Blood Money to Whitechapel
by George Bernard Shaw

The Star, September 24 1888

TO THE EDITOR OF THE STAR

SIR – Will you allow me to make a comment on the success of the Whitechapel murderer in calling attention for a moment to the social question? Less than a year ago the West-end press, headed by the *St James's Gazette,* the *Times,* and the *Saturday Review,* were literally clamouring for the blood of the people – hounding on Sir Charles Warren to thrash and muzzle the scum who dared to complain that they were starving – heaping insult and reckless calumny on those who interceded for the victims – applauding to the skies the open class bias of those magistrates and judges who zealously did their very worst in the criminal proceedings which followed – behaving, in short as the proprietary class always does behave when the workers throw it into a frenzy of terror by venturing to show their teeth.

Quite lost on these journals and their patrons were indignant remonstrances, argument, speeches, and sacrifices, appeals to history, philosophy, biology, economics, and statistics; references to the reports of inspectors, registrar generals, city missionaries, Parliamentary commissions, and newspapers; collections of evidence by the five senses at every turn; and house-to-house investigations into the condition of the unemployed, all unanswered and unanswerable, and all pointing the same way. The *Saturday Review* was still frankly for hanging the appellants; and the *Times* denounced them as 'pests of society'. This was still the tone of the class Press as lately as the strike of the Bryant and May girls.

Now all is changed.

Private enterprise has succeeded where Socialism failed. While we conventional Social Democrats were wasting our time on education, agitation, and organisation, some independent genius has taken the matter in hand, and by simply murdering and disembowelling four women, converted the proprietary press to an inept sort of communism.

The moral is a pretty one, and the Insurrectionists, the Dynamitards, the Invincibles, and the extreme left of the Anarchist party will not be slow to draw it. 'Humanity, political science, economics, and religion,' they will say, 'are all rot; the one argument that touches your lady and gentleman is the knife.' That is so pleasant for the party of Hope and Perseverance in their toughening struggle with the party of Desperation and Death!

However, these things have to be faced. If the line to be taken is that suggested by the converted West-end papers – if the people are still to yield up their wealth to the Clanricarde class, and get what they can back as charity through Lady Bountiful, then the policy for the people is plainly a policy of terror. Every gaol blown up, every window broken, every shop looted, every corpse found disembowelled, means another ten pound note for 'ransom'. The riots of 1886 brought in £78,000 and a People's Palace; it remains to be seen how much these murders may prove worth to the East-end in *panem et circenses*.

Indeed, if the habits of duchesses only admitted of their being decoyed into Whitechapel back-yards, a single experiment in slaughterhouse anatomy on an aristocratic victim might fetch in a round half million and save the necessity of sacrificing four women of the people. Such is the stark-naked reality of these abominable bastard Utopias of genteel charity, in which the poor are first to be robbed and then pauperised by way of compensation, in order that the rich man may combine the idle luxury of the protected thief with the unctuous self-satisfaction of the pious philanthropist.

The proper way to recover the rents of London for the people of London is not by charity, which is one of the worst curses of poverty, but by the municipal rate collector, who will no doubt make it sufficiently clear to the monopolists of ground value that he is not merely taking round the hat, and that the State is ready to enforce his demand, if need be.

And the money thus obtained must be used by the municipality as the capital of productive industries for the better employment of the poor. I submit that this is at least a less disgusting and immoral method of relieving the East-end than the gust of bazaars and blood money which has suggested itself from the West-end point of view.--Yours, &c.

G. BERNARD SHAW

Notes

Introduction
1. *The Mystery of Jack the Ripper*, Leonard Matters, W. H. Allen, 1929; 'Who Was Jack the Ripper?' in *Great Unsolved Crimes*, Dr. Harold Dearden, Hutchinson, 1935; *Jack the Ripper or When London Walked in Terror*, Edwin T. Woodhall, Mellifont Press, 1937
2. *The Gloucester Citizen*, 9 January 1905
3. *The Referee*, 16 February 1902
4. *The Gloucester Citizen*, 9 January 1905.
5. *Jack the Ripper: First American Serial Killer*, Stewart P. Evans & Paul Gainey, Kodansha, 1996
6. *Autumn of Terror. Jack the Ripper, his crimes and times,* Tom Cullen, The Bodley Head, 1965
7. *Jack the Ripper—Case Solved, 1891*, J. J. Hainsworth, McFarland (North Carolina), 2015

Chapter I
1. *Western Chronicle*, 20 May 1887
2. *The Harbour's History*, Poole Harbour Commissioners, 2008
3. The Poor Law Amendment Act 1834
4. *Herts & Cambs Reporter & Royston Crow*, 20 May 1887
5. *Newcastle Courant*, 14 March 1873
6. *The Globe*, 25 September 1880
7. *Hampshire Chronicle,* 30 April 1887
8. ibid
9. *Western Chronicle*, 20 May 1887
10. ibid

11. HO144/196/A46955 Criminal: Young Henry William. Court: Hants Assizes; Offence: Murder; Sentence: Death 1887 Apr, National Archive, Kew
12. *Western Chronicle,* 20 May 1887
13. *Acton Gazette,* 7 May 1887
14. *Sheffield Evening Telegraph,* 29 March 1888
15. *Hampshire Advertiser,* 9 February 1887
16. *Southern Guardian,* 5 January 1889
17. *Amazing Grace: The Man who was W.G.,* Richard Tomlinson, Little Brown, Great Britain, 2015, p x
18. *The Cornish Telegraph,* 27 May 1886
19. *Western Chronicle,* 20 May 1887
20. HO144/196/A46955 Criminal: Young, Henry William. Court: Hants Assizes; Offence: Murder; Sentence: Death 1887 Apr, National Archive, Kew
21. ibid
22. *St James Gazette,* 16 May 1887
23. *The Sporting Life,* 23 May 1887

Chapter II
1. *Western Daily Press,* 23 May 1883
2. *Chatham News,* 31 January 1863
3. *London Evening Standard,* 26 December 1872
4. *Clerkenwell News,* 18 October 1870
5. Druitt Mss 409/19,The Druitt Papers, West Sussex Record Office
6. The Druitt Papers, The National Archives, West Sussex Record Office
7. Druitt Mss 409/18,The Druitt Papers, West Sussex Record Office
8. Druitt Mss N32a,The Druitt Papers, West Sussex Record Office
9. ibid
10. *Hampshire Chronicle,* 22 September 1888
11. *My Life: Sixty Years' Recollections of Bohemian London,* George R. Sims, Eveleigh Nash Company, London 1917, p 175
12. *The Wykehamist,* 1900, Issue 367
13. *Illustrated London News,* 3 March 1900
14. *Hampshire Advertiser,* 13 September 1884
15. *Southern Guardian,* 5 January 1889
16. Queen's Bench Division, Vol 58, Michaelmas 1888 to Michaelmas 1889, p 109. Found by Mark Kent, writer, PA, USA
17. *Dorset Life,* Roger Guttridge, December 2004
18. Druitt Mss 246 LL48,The Druitt Papers, West Sussex Record Office
19. *The Southern Times and Dorset County Herald,* 2 October 1885

20. *Salisbury and Winchester Journal,* 3 October 1885
21. *Autumn of Terror. Jack the Ripper, his crimes and times*, Tom Cullen, The Bodley Head, London, 1965, p 224
22. *The Times,* 7 June 1933
23. Ms5725 Manor House Asylum Casebook and Correspondence, Wellcome Library
24. *Tablet,* 23 February 1889
25. *Western Gazette,* 3 August 1894
26. Ancestry.com.uk
27. *Dundee Courier,* 16 February 1909

Chapter III

1. *The Bristol Times and Mirror,* 11 Feb 1891 (albeit M. J. Druitt is unnamed)
2. *Autumn of Terror. Jack the Ripper, his crimes and times*, Tom Cullen, The Bodley Head, London, 1965, p 224
3. *The Wykehamist,* April 1872, No 47
4. *The Wykehamist,* 17 July 1872, No 99
5. The Bodley Head, London, 1965, p 224
6. *The Wykehamist,* November 1875, No 87
7. *Autumn of Terror. Jack the Ripper, his crimes and times*, Tom Cullen, The Bodley Head, London, 1965, p 25
8. *The Wykehamist,* April 1873, No 56
9. *The Wykehamist,* February 1874, No. 64
10. *The Wykehamist,* 19 December 1876, No 105
11. Druitt Mss 12–13,The Druitt Papers, West Sussex Record Office
12. *Oxford Journal,* 6 July 1878
13. ibid
14. ibid
15. *Hampshire Chronicle,* 18 August 1883
16. *The History of Oxford Canning Club 1861–1911*, Horace Hart, Privately Printed, 1911
17. ibid
18. *Jack the Ripper – Case Solved 1891*, p 98, J. J. Hainsworth, McFarland, North Carolina, 2015
19. *Autumn of Terror. Jack the Ripper, his crimes and times*, Tom Cullen, The Bodley Head, London, 1965, p 227
20. Druitt Mss 11/3,The Druitt Papers, West Sussex Record Office
21. *Punch,* 30 December 1882
22. *The Southern Times and Dorset County Herald,* 2 October 1885

23. *Amazing Grace, The Man who was W.G.*, Richard Tomlinson, Little Brown, Great Britain, 2015, p xi

24. *Montague Druitt: Portrait of a Contender*, D. J. Leighton, Hydrangea Publishing, London, 2004, p 123

25. *Bath Chronicle and Weekly Gazette*, 13 August 1885

26. ibid

27. Druitt Ms239 CC174, The Druitt Papers, West Sussex Record Office

28. Ms5725 Manor House Asylum, Casebook and Correspondence, Letter to Dr Tuke from Dr Gasquet, Wellcome Library

29. Druitt Ms239 CC174 Mss245/4, The Druitt Papers, West Sussex Record Office

Chapter IV

1. *How the Poor Live* and *Horrible London*, George R. Sims, Chatto & Windus, London, 1889, pp 141–42

2. *London Daily News*, 19 October 1887

3. *My Life: Sixty Years' Recollections of Bohemian London*, George R. Sims, Eveleigh Nash Company, London, 1917

4. *The Era*, 27 August 1892

5. *Yorkshire Post and Leeds Intelligencer*, 6 September 1922

6. *The Stage*, 28 November 1895

7. *Days Of My Years*, Sir Melville Macnaghten, Edward Arnold, London, 1914, p 37

8. *Yorkshire Post and Leeds Intelligencer*, 6 September 1922

9. *My Life: Sixty Years' Recollections of Bohemian London*, George R. Sims, Eveleigh Nash Company, London, 1917, p 181

10. *How the Poor Live and Horrible London*, George R. Sims, Chatto and Windus, London, 1889, p 1

11. ibid. p 21

12. *Jack the Ripper: Scotland Yard Investigates*, Stewart P. Evans & Donald Rumbelow, Sutton Publishing, London, 2006, pp 36–37

13. *Pall Mall Gazette*, 17 April 1886

14. *Oxford Times*, 21 May 1887

15. *Sporting Life*, 7 July 1887

Chapter V

1. *Days of My Years*, Sir Melville Macnaghten, Edward Arnold, London, 1914, p 57

2. *East London Advertiser*, 31 March 1888

Notes

3. *Days of My Years*, Sir Melville Macnaghten, Edward Arnold, London, 1914, p 101

Chapter VI

1. https://www.qmgreathall.co.uk/history/
2. *The Complete History of Jack the Ripper*, Philip Sugden, Robinson, London, 2006, pp 42–45
3. *Penny Illustrated Paper,* 8 September 1888
4. *Wilts and Gloucestershire Standard,* 31 October 1857
5. *The Five: The Untold Stories of the Victims of Jack the Ripper,* Hallie Rubenhold, Houghton Mifflin Harcourt, 2019, pp78–84
6. *Autumn of Terror. Jack the Ripper, his crimes and times*, Tom Cullen, The Bodley Head, 1965, pp 26–27
7. *Jack the Ripper: Scotland Yard Investigates Ch. 1: A Gentleman of Angularities*, Stewart P. Evans & Donald Rumbelow, Sutton Publishing, UK, 2006, pp 56–57
8. *The Strange Case of Dr Jekyll and Mr Hyde,* Robert Louis Stevenson, Longman, 1886
9. *Bournemouth Guardian,* 8 September 1888
10. *Jack the Ripper: Scotland Yard Investigates* Stewart P. Evans & Donald Rumbelow, Sutton Publishing, UK, 2006, 'A Gentleman of Angularities', pp 1–9
11. *The Man Who Hunted Jack the Ripper: Edmund Reid – Victorian Detective*, Nicholas Connell & Stewart P. Evans, Amberley, Stroud, 2000, pp 40–44
12. *Days of My Years,* Sir Melville Macnaghten, Edward Arnold, London, 1914, p 273

Chapter VII

1. *The Five: The Untold Stories of the Victims of Jack the Ripper*: Part II Annie, Hallie Rubenhold, Houghton Mifflin Harcourt, London, 2019
2. *Chatham News,* 31 January 1863
3. *How the Poor Live and Horrible London*, George R. Sims, Chatto and Windus, London 1889, p119
4. *The Complete History of Jack the Ripper*, Philip Sugden, Robinson, London, 2006, p79
5. *The Daily Mail,* 18 May 1903
6. *Jack the Ripper: Scotland Yard Investigates*, Stewart P. Evans & Donald Rumbelow, Sutton Publishing, UK, 2006, p66
7. *The Complete History of Jack the Ripper*, Philip Sugden, Robinson, London, 2006, p79
8. *The Mercury,* 22 September 1888

9. *Pall Mall Gazette,* 10 September 1888
10. *Days of My Years,* Sir Melville Macnaghten, Edward Arnold, London, 1914, p 55
11. *Morning Post,* 27 September 1888
12. Coroner's quote about her injuries
13. *The Complete History of Jack the Ripper*, Philip Sugden, Robinson, London, 2006, p 87
14. *Jack the Ripper – The Facts* Paul Begg, Robson Books, UK, 2006, p 80
15. *Woolwich Gazette,* 14 September 1888
16. *The Complete History of Jack the Ripper*, Philip Sugden, Robinson, London, 2006, p 143
17. *Autumn of Terror. Jack the Ripper, his crimes and times*, Tom Cullen, The Bodley Head, 1965, 'Shaw Writes a Letter', pp 208–216
18. ibid

Chapter VIII
1. *A History of Royal Engineers Cricket 1862–1924*, Rowan Scrope Rait Kerr, Chatham, London, 1925
2. *Montague Druitt, Portrait of a Contender*, D. J. Leighton, Hydrangea Publishing, London, 2004
3. *The Times,* September 30 1888
4. *Jack the Ripper – The Facts,* Paul Begg, Robson Books, UK, 2006, pp 136–143
5. ibid
6. *Autumn of Terror. Jack the Ripper, his crimes and times*, Tom Cullen, The Bodley Head, 1965, p 107
7. *The Complete History of Jack the Ripper*, Philip Sugden, Robinson, London, 2006, p 195
8. *Worcestershire Chronicle,* 6 October 1888
9. *Autumn of Terror. Jack the Ripper, his crimes and times*, Tom Cullen, The Bodley Head, 1965, pp 104–105
10. *Jack the Ripper – The Facts,* Paul Begg, Robson Books, UK, 2006, pp 158–159

Chapter IX
1. *The Complete History of Jack the Ripper*, Philip Sugden, Robinson, London, 2006, pp 231–239
2. ibid
3. ibid
4. *Jack the Ripper: Scotland Yard Investigates* Stewart P. Evans & Donald Rumbelow, Sutton, UK, 2006, p 122

5. *The Complete History of Jack the Ripper*, Philip Sugden, Robinson, London, 2006, p 231
6. Deposition of Dr Brown, 4 October 1888 CPL, ff., pp 12–14
7. *The Complete History of Jack the Ripper*, Philip Sugden, Robinson, London, 2006, pp 254–255
8. *Casebook: Dissertations – Montague John Druitt,* Matthew Fletcher, https://www.casebook.org/dissertations/druitt-art.html
9. *Jack the Ripper: Scotland Yard Investigates,* Stewart P. Evans & Donald Rumbelow, Sutton, UK, 2006, p 130
10. *The Complete History of Jack the Ripper*, Philip Sugden, Robinson, 2006, p 263
11. *Jack the Ripper: Scotland Yard Investigates* Stewart P. Evans & Donald Rumbelow, Sutton, UK, 2006, p 140
12. *Days of My Years*, Sir Melville Macnaghten, Edward Arnold, London, 1914, pp 58–59
13. *The Referee,* 7 October 1888
14. *Days of My Years*, Sir Melville Macnaghten, Edward Arnold, London, 1914, pp 58–59
15. *Jack the Ripper: First American Serial Killer*, Stewart P. Evans & Paul Gainey, Kodansha, USA, 1996, p 188
16. *From Constable to Commissioner* ... Sir Henry Smith, Chatto and Windus, London, 1910, 'Of the Ripper and his Deeds – and of the Criminal Investigator, Sir Robert Anderson', pp 149–150
17. Warren, 19 September 1888, to Ruggles-Brise, HO 144/331/A49301C/8
18. *The Complete History of Jack the Ripper*, Philip Sugden, Robinson, London, 2006, pp 153–156
19. Inspector Abberline's Report on John Sanders, 14 September 1888, MEPO 3/140, f. 17
20. *Jack the Ripper – The Facts*, Paul Begg, Robson Books, UK, 2006, p 107

Chapter X
1. *Days of My Years*, Sir Melville Macnaghten, Edward Arnold, London, 1914, 'Laying the Ghost of Jack the Ripper', p 54
2. *Time* Magazine, 'The Thomson Case', 18 January 1926
3. *The Story of Scotland Yard*, Sir Basil Thomson, The Literary Guild, New York, 1936, pp 189–191
4. *Days of My Years*, Sir Melville Macnaghten, Edward Arnold, London, 1914, pp 59–60

5. *The Complete Jack the Ripper A to Z*, Martin Fido, Paul Begg & Keith Skinner, John Blake, UK, 2010 pp 481

Chapter XI

1. *The Pall Mall Gazette,* 9 October 1888
2. *London Daily News,* 10 November 1888
3. *Kilburn Times*, 16 November 1888
4. ibid
5. *Worcestershire Chronicle,* 17 November 1888
6. *I Caught Crippen,* Walter Dew, Blackie & Son, UK, 1938, Ch. 'The Hunt for Jack the Ripper'
7. *Worcestershire Chronicle* 17 November 1888
8. *I Caught Crippen,* Walter Dew, Blackie & Son, UK, 1938, 'The Hunt for Jack the Ripper'
9. *Worcestershire Chronicle,* 17 November 1888
10. *The Five: The Untold Stories of the Victims of Jack the Ripper* Hallie Rubenhold, Houghton Mifflin Harcourt, 2019, p 333
11. *I Caught Crippen*, Walter Dew, Blackie & Son, UK, 1938, 'The Hunt for Jack the Ripper'
12. Statement of George Hutchinson, 12 November 1888, MEPO 3/140, FF. pp 227–229
13. *The Star,* 10 November 1888
14. *I Caught Crippen,,* Walter Dew, Blackie and Son, UK, 1938, 'The Hunt for Jack the Ripper'
15. *The Star,* 10 November 1888
16. *The Strange Case of Dr Jekyll and Mr Hyde,* Robert Louis Stevenson, Longman, 1886

Chapter XII

1. *Eiffel's Tower: The Thrilling Story Behind Paris's Beloved Monument and the Extraordinary World's Fair That Introduced It*, Jill Jones, Penguin Books, 2009
2. *On the Construction of and Management of Hospitals for the Insane*, Dr Carl M. W. Jacobi, London: John Churchill, 1841, pp 42–43
3. *Jack the Ripper: First American Serial Killer*, Stewart P Evans & Paul Gainey, Kodansha, USA, 1996, p 188
4. *The Complete History of Jack the Ripper*, Philip Sugden, Robinson, London, 2006, p. viii

Chapter XIII

1. Druitt Ms 239 Mss 239, The Druitt Papers, West Sussex Record Office

2. *Jack the Ripper – The Facts* Paul Begg, Robson Books, 2006, p 326

Chapter XIV
1. *Acton, Chiswick and Turnham Green Gazette,* 5 January 1889, 'Found Drowned'
2. *St James' Gazette* 18 June 1884

Chapter XV
1. Druitt Mss 234 Mss 228, The Druitt Papers, West Sussex Record Office
2. *The Daily Mail,* 18 January, 1899; *Lloyds Weekly Magazine,* 22 September 1907
3. *Robert Druitt M.D., F.R.C.P., 1814–1883,* William Cholmeley, Pardon & Sons, London, 1883
4. Druitt Mss 409/19,The Druitt Papers, West Sussex Record Office
5. Druitt Mss 239/24,The Druitt Papers, West Sussex Record Office
6. ibid
7. Druitt Mss 409/19,The Druitt Papers, West Sussex Record Office
8. ibid
9. Druitt Mss 239/24,The Druitt Papers, West Sussex Record Office
10. *The Pall Mall Gazette,* 4 November 1889
11. *Newcastle Chronicle,* 11 February 1893
12. Druitt Mss 252,The Druitt Papers, West Sussex Record Office

Chapter XVI
1. *Lloyds Weekly Newspaper,* 2 December 1900
2. *Lost London – The Memoirs of an East End Detective,* Benjamin Leeson, Stanley Pail & Co., London, 1930, 'Jack the Ripper'
3. *Jack the Ripper: Scotland Yard Investigates,* Stewart P. Evans & Donald Rumbelow, Sutton Publishing, UK, 2006, p 250
4. *The Daily Telegraph,* 18 February 1891
5. *Daily Gleaner,* Jamaica, 3 April 1891
6. *Albury Banner and Wodonga Express,* Australia, 25 November 1910
7. *Jack the Ripper: Anatomy of a Myth,* William Beadle, Wat Tyler Books, UK, 1993, pp 121–122
8. *Days of My Years,* Sir Melville Macnaghten, Edward Arnold, London, 1914, p 202
9. *The Honourable Schoolboy,* John Le Carré, Alfred A Knopf, 1977
10. *The Lighter Side of My Official Life,* Sir Robert Anderson, Hodder & Stoughton, UK, 1910, pp 224–225

11. For a fuller treatment of Sir Melville Macnaghten's life and career we recommend our first book *Jack the Ripper–Case Solved 1891*, J. J. Hainsworth, McFarland, North Carolina, 2015

12. *Casebook: Dissertation – Major Arthur Griffiths, Dr Robert Anderson and Jack the Ripper*, Stewart P. Evans, 1998 https://www.casebook.org/dissertations/dst-spe.html

13. *Sutherland Daily Echo and Shipping Gazette*, 13 February 1891

14. *Days of My Years*, Sir Melville Macnaghten, Edward Arnold, London, 1914, pp 56–57

15. ibid. p 80

16. *My Life: Sixty Years' Recollections of Bohemian London*, George R. Sims, Eveleigh Nash Company, London, 1917, p 175

17. *Lloyds Weekly Magazine*, George R. Sims, 'My Criminal Museum – Who was Jack the Ripper?' 22 September 1907

Chapter XVII

1. *Agricultural Express*, 23 April 1892.

2. *Birmingham Daily Post*, 20 June 1892.

3. *H. H. Asquith: Letters to Venetia Stanley*, Michael Brook & Eleanor Brook (eds.) Oxford University Press, 1985

4. *Days of My Years*, Edward Arnold, London, 1914, pp 36–37

5. *The Complete History of Jack the Ripper*, Philip Sugden, Robinson, London, 2006, p 402

6. *Ripperologist: The Journal of Jack the Ripper, East End and Victorian Studies*, Adam Wood, *The Aberconway Version*, online publication, February 2012, No. 124, http://www.mangodesign.biz/rip124.pdf

7. Macnaghten Report, MEPO 3/141 fols. 177–83

Chapter XVIII

1. *Jack the Ripper: Scotland Yard Investigates*, Stewart P Evans & Donald Rumbelow, Sutton Publishing, UK, 2006, pp 243–256

2. *The Crimes, Detection and Death of Jack the Ripper*, Martin Fido, Weidenfeld & Nicholson, London, 1987, p 170

3. *The Complete Jack the Ripper A to Z*, Martin Fido, Paul Begg & Keith Skinner, John Blake, UK, 2010, p 139

4. *The Salisbury And Winchester Journal And General Advertiser*, 12 January 1884

5. *Salisbury and Winchester Journal*, 12 January 1884

6. *The Salisbury Times*, 22 March 1890

7. *Nottingham Journal*, 6 June 1898

8. *Grantham Journal*, 29 October 1938

9. *Jack the Ripper–Case Solved 1891*, J. J. Hainsworth, McFarland, North Carolina, 2015, p 18

10. *Report of the Metropolitan Commissioners in Lunacy*, Lord Chancellor, London: Bradbury and Evans, Printers, Whitefriars, 1844, pp 111–112

11. *A Bridge Too Far: The Curious Case of Mortemer Slade*, David Barret (aka David Orsam) https://www.orsam.co.uk/bridgetoofar.htm The 1899 *Western Times* newspaper source directly links the vicar's 'Ripper' with the drowned 'Ripper'. The writer who found it, however, does not agree with our interpretation of this primary source's content, its significance – nor with the overall thrust of our 'case disguised' thesis.

Chapter XIX

1. *The Man Who Hunted Jack the Ripper: Edmund Reid – Victorian Detective*, Nicholas Connell & Stewart P Evans, Amberley, Stroud, UK, 2000, p. 128

2. *Whitechapel Society Journal*, Issue 75, August 2017, p. 22; *Dr Forbes Winslow and the Drowned Doctor suspect*, Wolf Vanderlinden, online publication: www.whitechapelsociety.com, the writer found the earliest reference to the drowned suspect in the extant record, but – we have good reasons for presuming – will not agree with our interpretation of the source's meaning and implications.

3. *The Ottawa Journal*, 19 April 1910

4. *The Complete Jack the Ripper A to Z*, Martin Fido, Paul Begg & Keith Skinner, John Blake, UK, 2010, pp 470–471

Chapter XX

1. Certified Death Certificate DYD604201– Melville Leslie Macnaghten; St George Hanover Square in the County of London, Cause of Death: Paralysis Agitans (six years) Progressive Asthenia, heart failure.

2. *The Sketch*, 25 April 1894, 'A Chat with the Chief Inspector of Explosives'

3. Marie Belloc Lowndes, *The Lodger*, Pocket, New York, 1940, p 202

4. ibid. p. 291

5. *Days of My Years*, Sir Melville Macnaghten, Edward Arnold, London, 1914, pp. viii–ix

6. *A Wiser Woman? A Book of Memories*, Christabel Aberconway Hutchinson, London 1966, pp 39–40

7. *Ripperologist: The Journal of Jack the Ripper, East End and Victorian Studies*, Adam Wood, 'The Aberconway Version', online publication, February 2012, No. 124, http://www.mangodesign.biz/rip124.pdf

8. *Autumn of Terror. Jack the Ripper, his crimes and times,* Tom Cullen, The Bodley Head, 1965, p. 235

Bibliography

Aberconway, Christabel, Lady Aberconway. *A Wiser Woman? A Book of Memories*, Hutchinson, London, 1966.

Aberconway, Christabel, Lady Aberconway. Letters addressed to Lady Aberconway and to her parents, Sir Melville Leslie Macnaghten and Lady Macnaghten, 1897–1956, British Library.

Amos, Andrew & Hough, William Woodcock (ed.) *The Cambridge Mission to South London: a twenty years' survey*, Macmillan & Bowes, Cambridge, 1904.

Anderson, Sir Robert. *The Lighter Side of My Official Life*, Hodder & Stoughton, UK, 1910.

Beadle, William. *Jack the Ripper: Anatomy of a Myth*, Wat Tyler Books, UK, 1993.

Begg, Paul. *Jack the Ripper – The Facts*, Robson Books, 2006.

British Library, The.

British Newspaper Archives, The.

Brook, Michael & Brook, Eleanor (eds). *H. H. Asquith: Letters to Venetia Stanley*, Oxford University Press, 1985.

Cannadine, David. *The Decline and Fall of the British Aristocracy*, Yale University Press, London, 1990.

Cholmeley, William. *Robert Druitt M.D. F.R.C.P. F.R.C.S.1814–1883*, Pardon & Sons Printers, London, 1883.

Connell, Nicholas & Evans, Stewart P. *The Man Who Hunted Jack the Ripper: Edmund Reid – Victorian Detective*, Amberley, Stroud, UK, 2000.

Cullen, Tom. *Autumn of Terror. Jack the Ripper, his crimes and times*, The Bodley Head, 1965.

Cullingford, Cecil N. *A History of Poole*, Phillimore & Co. 2003.

The Druitt Papers, The National Archives, West Sussex Record Office.

Druitt, Dr Robert. *The principles and practice of modern surgery*, Blanchard & Lea, Philadelphia, 1852.

Druitt, Dr Robert, *Report on the cheap wines from France, Italy, Austria, Greece and Hungary: their quality, wholesomeness and price, and their use in diet and medicine, with short notes of a lecture to ladies on wine, and remarks on acidity*, H. Renshaw, London, 1865.

Druitt, Dr Robert. *Report on the quality of waters used in the in-wards of the parish of St George Hanover Square*, Charles Bevan & Son Printers, London, 1856.

Druitt, Dr Robert. *The Surgeon's Vade Mecum*, Henry Renshaw, Strand, London, 1847.

Du Boulay, Francis Robin Houssemayne. *Servants of Empire*, I.B. Tauris & Co. Ltd, London, 2011.

Evans, Stewart P. & Gainey, Paul. *Jack the Ripper: First American Serial Killer*, Kodansha, USA 1996.

Evans, Stewart P. & Rumbelow, Donald. *Jack the Ripper: Scotland Yard Investigates,* Sutton Publishing, UK, 2006.

Farson, Daniel. *Jack the Ripper,* The History Book Club, UK, 1972.

Fido, Martin. *The Crimes, Detection and Death of Jack the Ripper*, Weidenfeld & Nicholson, London, 1987.

Fido, Martin; Begg, Paul & Skinner, Keith. *The Complete Jack the Ripper A to Z*. John Blake, UK, 2010.

Hainsworth, J. J. *Jack the Ripper – Case Solved 1891*, McFarland, North Carolina, 2015.

Hart, Horace. *The History of Oxford Canning Club 1861–1911*, Privately Printed, London, 1911.

Jacobi, Dr Carl M. W. *On the Construction of and Management of Hospitals for the Insane*, London: John Churchill, 1841.

Jones, Jill. *Eiffel's Tower: The Thrilling Story Behind Paris's Beloved Monument and the Extraordinary World's Fair That Introduced It*, Penguin Books, 2009.

Leeson, Benjamin. *Lost London – The Memoirs of an East End Detective*, Stanley Pail & Co., London, 1930.

Lock, Joan, *The* Princess Alice *Disaster*, Robert Hale, London, 2013.

Lowndes, Marie Belloc *The Lodger*, Pocket, New York, 1940.

Macnaghten, Sir Melville Leslie, *Days of My Years,* Edward Arnold, London, 1914.

Patterson, Michael, *Life in Victorian Britain: A Social History of Queen Victoria's Reign,* Running Press, Philadelphia, 2008.

Report of the Metropolitan Commissioners in Lunacy, Lord Chancellor, London: Bradbury & Evans, Printers, Whitefriars, 1844.

Richardson, Frank. *The Other Man's Wife*, Eveleigh Nash, Fawside House, London, 1908.

Richardson, Frank. *The Worst Man in the World*, Eveleigh Nash, Fawside House, London, 1908.

Rubenhold, Hallie. *The Five: The Untold Stories of the Victims of Jack the Ripper*, Houghton Mifflin Harcourt, 2019.

Patterson, Michael. *Life in Victorian Britain: A Social History of Queen Victoria's Reign,* Running Press, Philadelphia, 2008.

Sims, George R. *Dorcas Dene, Detective,* F.V. White & Co, London, 1897.

Sims, George R. *Detective Inspector Chance,* Ferret Fantasy Ltd, London, 1974.

Sims, George R. (ed.) *Living London*, Cassell & Company, London, 1902.

Sims, George R. *My Life: Sixty Years' Recollections of Bohemian London*, Eveleigh Nash Co., London, 1917.

Stevenson, Robert Louis. *The Strange Case of Dr Jekyll and Mr Hyde*, Longmans Green & Co., 1886.

Thomson, Sir Basil. *Queer People*, Hodder & Stoughton, London, 1922.

Thomson, Sir Basil. *The Story of Scotland Yard*, The Literary Guild, New York, 1936.

Vanderlinden, Wolf. *Whitechapel Society Journal*, Issue 75, August 2017, 'Dr Forbes Winslow and the Drowned Doctor Suspect', online publication: www.whitechapelsociety.com

Wade, Stephen. *Conan Doyle and the Crimes Club*, Fonthill Media, 2013. Wellcome Collection, London.

Wood, Adam. *Ripperologist: The Journal of Jack the Ripper, East End and Victorian Studies*, *The Aberconway Version*, online publication, February 2012, No. 124, http://www.mangodesign.biz/rip124.pdf

Criminal: Young, Henry William; Court: Hants Assizes; Offence: Murder; Sentence: Death, April 1887, National Archives Kew.

Index

About the Authors

Jonathan Hainsworth is an Ancient and Modern History teacher of thirty years' experience, whose research on 'Jack the Ripper' found that a Metropolitan Police Chief had solved the case. Hainsworth wrote a biography of this police chief, *Jack the Ripper: Case Solved, 1891* (2015).

Christine Ward-Agius is a writer, researcher and artist who spent many years working for an Australian Government program to empower sole parents via education, training and employment. For this book she meticulously researched the Druitt family archives, texts, newspaper articles in the British Library and the records of English public schools.